RECORD KEEPING IN PSYCHOTHERAPY AND COUNSELING

Praise for the First Edition

"This book is a lively, reader-friendly compendium of essential knowledge for every clinician that provides specific advice and examples of clinical records while illuminating a wide spectrum of legal, ethical. and complex clinical issues."

–Judith Wallerstein, PhD, author, *The Unexpected Legacy of Divorce*

"Within an ethical and most professional framework ... this book assists therapists in meeting regulations for record keeping while at the same time assuring ways to protect the client. It will become an important resource for psychotherapists."

–Florence Lieberman, DSW, professor emerita,
Hunter College School of Social Work

"Rooted in 30 years of experience with patients, Ellen Luepker provides detailed practical guidelines and especially wonderful examples of how to keep written records that actually improve therapy and meet the requirements of the legal system. Practicing therapists will find [this] detailed guide to be one of the most useful books they read all year."

–Thomas T. Frantz, PhD, professor of counseling psychology,
University at Buffalo

"Ellen Luepker has finally made practical common sense out of the thicket of clinical, ethical, and legal requirements for record-keeping. For HIPAA implementation, this should be on the 'must read' list of every practitioner!"

–Hubert H. Humphrey III, JD, former Minnesota Attorney General

"Luepker's book comprehensively and competently addresses an urgent need in contemporary mental health practice, and deserves a place in the libraries of community mental health practitioners, clinicians in private practice, social work educators and professionals from related fields of practice."

–Lana Sue I. Ka'opua, PhD, associate professor, Cancer Prevention and
Control Program, University of Hawaii Cancer Center

Record Keeping in Psychotherapy and Counseling

Protecting Confidentiality and the Professional Relationship

Second Edition

ELLEN T. LUEPKER

Routledge
Taylor & Francis Group
New York   London

Watercolor illustrations by R. Scott Chase.

Routledge
Taylor & Francis Group
711 Third Avenue
New York, NY 10017

Routledge
Taylor & Francis Group
27 Church Road
Hove, East Sussex BN3 2FA

© 2012 by Taylor & Francis Group, LLC
Routledge is an imprint of Taylor & Francis Group, an Informa business

Printed in the United States of America on acid-free paper
Version Date: 20111220

International Standard Book Number: 978-0-415-89261-2 (Paperback)

Library of Congress Cataloging-in-Publication Data
Luepker, Ellen T.

Luepker, Ellen T.
    Record keeping in psychotherapy and counseling : protecting confidentiality and the professional relationship / authored by Ellen T. Luepker. -- 2nd ed.
        p. cm.
    Includes bibliographical references and index.
    ISBN 978-0-415-89261-2 (pbk.)
    1. Psychiatric records. I. Title.

RC455.2.M38L84 2012
616.89'14--dc23   2011033327

Visit the Taylor & Francis Web site at
http://www.taylorandfrancis.com

and the Routledge Web site at
http://www.routledgementalhealth.com

Contents

Acknowledgments

Many persons contributed generously to the creation of this second edition. I am especially indebted to four colleagues for their help from beginning to end. Gary Schoener, MEq, LP, recommended changes based on his extensive professional experience in ethics and remained available to discuss numerous questions. Kate Cosgriff, LICSW, and Katrin Christensen-Cowan, LGSW, provided insightful suggestions for changes, commented on numerous drafts, and sustained me with their encouragement. I am grateful to Scott Chase for his continuing artistic collaboration and new black-and-white watercolor illustrations. His imagination is invaluable.

Numerous other professionals in education, family therapy, law, nursing, psychology, psychiatry, public health, and social work helped in various ways by recommending changes, reviewing drafts, sharing information, providing support, or allowing me to quote their unpublished materials or personal communications. They include Jon G. Allen, PhD; Judith Aronson, PhD; George Babiola, LICSW; Carole Bender, JD, LICSW; Walter Bera, PhD; Barbara Berger, PhD; Sue Bollinger-Brown, LICSW; Catherine Clancy, PhD; Patricia R. Conrad, MSW; Kate Croskery-Jones, JD, MDiv, MSW; Benita Dieperink, MD; Meg Eastman, PhD; Amy Engel, LCSW; John Finnegan, PhD; Tara Florek; Glen Gabbard, MD; Janet R. Gagerman, PhD; Helen Gilbert, PhD; Stephen Goss, PhD; Laura Groshong, LCSW; Thomas G. Gutheil, MD; Wendy Haskell, PhD; Keith Horton, MD; Ross Janssen, JD; Joel Kanter, LCSW; Helen Kim, MD; Carole Kuechler, PhD; Mike Langlois, LICSW; Carl F. Luepker, MAT; Ian R. Luepker, ND; Russell V. Luepker, MD; Heather McMoore, LICSW; Keith Myers, LICSW; Richelle M. Moen, PhD; Jeannette Hofstee Milgrom, LICSW; Deborah Muenzer-Doy; Kathleen W. Muller, RN, MS, CS; Carolyn Polowy, JD; Lisa M. Richardson, LICSW; Clayton Sankey; S. Charles Schultz, MD; Dan Sheehan; Cathy Siebold, PhD; Cynthia Sturm, PhD; and Kate Thompson, MN, FNP, PMHNP.

I also recognize and thank Lee Norton, PhD, who was instrumental in the first edition.

I am grateful to Routledge Mental Health's publishing staff, especially to George Zimmar, PhD, editor-in-chief, for inviting me to write a second edition. I valued this opportunity to work with him again. External reviewers—Len Sperry, MD, PhD, and Thomas G. Plante, PhD, ABPP—offered wise and immensely helpful recommendations. Marta Moldvai, editorial assistant, efficiently helped manage the project to production, and Amy Rodriguez, project editor, helped carry it to completion.

I could not have met my publisher's deadline without extra help in the final 2 months from Merie Kirby, a talented editor in Grand Forks, North Dakota, whom I appreciate Dr. Young-ok An recommending to me. My thanks also to the University of Minnesota library staff for their able assistance finding references and to Janelle Willard for her competent help creating sample forms and lists.

Last but not least, I thank friends and family members for their encouragement and my husband, Russell, for his continuing patience and support throughout the year I worked on this edition.

The Author

Ellen T. Luepker, MSW, BCD, licensed psychologist and clinical social worker in private practice, is an instructor in the Department of Psychiatry, University of Minnesota, where she teaches psychotherapy. She received her MSW from Smith College and a Bush Leadership Fellowship in Early Childhood Development at the University of Minnesota. Before beginning private practice, she worked in several adult and child settings, including psychiatric inpatient and outpatient services, a child guidance clinic, and Family Service. She has supervised social work students, psychology doctoral students, and psychiatry residents for over 30 years. She conducted the first systematic study of the impact of sexual boundary violations by psychotherapists and clergy (Luepker, 1999). Using this experience, she trained mental health professionals nationally and in Australia, Scotland, Sweden, and New Zealand to treat patients suffering from professional misconduct. In addition, she has published numerous articles and coauthored a book on this ethics topic (Schoener, Milgrom, Gonsiorek, Luepker, & Conroe, 1989). Her first edition of *Record Keeping in Psychotherapy and Counseling: Protecting Confidentiality and the Professional Relationship* was selected by Behavioral Book Club and has been adopted by many graduate training programs. She is a past president of the Minnesota Society for Clinical Social Work and past chair of the Clinical Social Work Federation's committee on law. She has received numerous awards, including the Minnesota Chapter National Association of Social Worker's (NASW) Lifetime Achievement Award, National Academy of Practice's Distinguished Practitioner Award, NASW's Social Work Pioneer Award, and Smith College School for Social Work's Day-Garret Award. A Rotary International Paul Harris Fellow, she serves as Ethics Chair for District 5960. She lives in Minneapolis with her husband, Russell V. Luepker, a cardiologist and epidemiologist, professor of public health, with whom she enjoys their family and shares a passion for sailing.

Introduction

As today's practitioners confront demands to create meaningful and safe electronic record keeping systems, we are challenged more than ever to develop thoughtful ways to describe our patients in human terms and to document our collaborative work with our patients. Many of us are busier than ever and feel we have less time than ever for record keeping, even though we know it is vital to protect ourselves and our patients. We face increasing risks to privacy through thefts of laptops, hard drives, and mobile devices and unauthorized user access. We feel uncertain whether we are keeping up with evolving rules and laws that protect privacy. We struggle over how to navigate electronic communication's impact on the therapeutic relationship.

Whether we keep paper or electronic records, the need for a thoughtful framework to help us remain grounded in our own clinical wisdom has never been more urgent. The purpose of this second edition is to continue to meet the urgent need for knowledge about record keeping in clinical practice, supervision, and training.

EARLY INSPIRATION

The inspiration for this book came from my late father, Prescott Thompson, a psychiatrist and psychoanalyst. He was a faithful and kind teacher who endowed me with a commitment to promoting a high standard of care for patients. My father left his general medical practice in California to become a psychiatrist in Kansas because he wanted to understand what his patients were "really needing." It seemed to him that his patients' physical pain often emerged from emotional suffering. Throughout his career he collaborated with colleagues and worked with countless patients who generously provided him pieces of this psychological puzzle. He discovered it is a meaningful professional relationship that makes sense of suffering.

My father's commitment to developing healing relationships with his patients became an enduring interest of mine. From adolescence on, I watched him and his colleagues earnestly wrestle with issues that lie at the heart of restoring patient health. In a dinner table conversation one evening, he spoke about how he and his colleagues felt confidentiality was the key to protecting the doctor–patient relationship. One of his colleagues noted that psychiatry seemed to be at a crossroads. My father and his colleagues were in the midst of a "historical dilemma" as they attempted to find ways to respectfully respond to a court's need for their patient's information. The group was stalwart: they knew they must protect the patient's confidentiality at all costs. I remember the fear I felt at the thought my father could go to jail for refusing to surrender patient records to a judge.

Little did I know that the golden thread of patient confidentiality would be woven into the fabric of my own work as a psychotherapist and that I would someday play a part in attempting to educate courts about the critical need for confidentiality of psychotherapy records. When I served as chairperson of the Committee on Clinical Social Work and the Law, I had responsibility for developing an amicus brief in the *Jaffe v. Redmond* case, which dealt with the same issue I had learned about over dinner years before. I was thrilled when the U.S. Supreme Court understood our message about the critical need for confidentiality in psychotherapy and when it upheld psychotherapy patients' right to privileged communication in federal courts (*Jaffe v. Redmond*, 1996).

My father helped me in other ways that became some of the most important messages in this book. I learned that the quality of doctor–patient relationships rested not only in patient confidentiality, but in patients' trust in their practitioners, and I saw that the vehicle of trust is reliability. When I was in college and worked at a psychiatric hospital for children, I would sometimes take my guitar to play songs with the patients. One morning, when my father was giving me a ride to the hospital, I realized I had forgotten my guitar. My father gently asked, "Did you promise you would bring it today?" When I nodded, he quietly told me how important it is to follow through on any promises we make to patients. Without complaining about how it might make him late to his office, he slowly turned the car around and returned to the house so I could retrieve the guitar. That incident, and the lesson I learned from it, became etched into the values of my practice. Fidelity to one's promises is the sister of confidentiality. Many years later, after the Walk-In Counseling Center asked me to provide treatment services to clients suffering from practitioners' boundary violations, I learned that broken promises are as harmful as the original injuries with which patients come to practitioners.

As a practicing clinician, I eventually became involved in forensic work. I again turned to my father for guidance. The first time I testified in court he explained the process and taught me skills to remain objective and maintain credibility. Later, Dr. Janet Warren and I developed a national volunteer consultation service for members of the Clinical Social Work Federation. Much of what I offered practitioners was based on my father's wisdom.

THE FIRST EDITION

Let me fast-forward from the personal experiences that contributed to the development of this book to some of the other important factors that complete the circle. In my role as chairperson of the Committee on Clinical Social Work and the Law for the Clinical Social Work Federation and currently for the Minnesota Society for Clinical Social Work, hundreds of psychotherapists have called me with urgent questions and concerns about records. They have asked me such questions as what records should include, how long they should keep records, and how to respond to subpoenas and other third-party requests for records. Many competent practitioners have phoned me anxiously, wondering how to respond to letters from licensure boards informing them of anonymous complaints about their professional conduct. Because regulatory boards' administrative procedures are more ambiguous than court proceedings, clinicians' anxiety when faced with complaints about their practices have reminded me of the excruciating fearfulness about unidentified accusers suffered by the protagonist in Kafka's novel, *The Trial* (Kafka, 2009).

Practitioners were especially concerned about confidentiality. Many believed that documentation of their patients' sensitive disclosures was dangerous to their clients. In their conscientious desire to protect their clients' privacy, many competent, experienced therapists and clinical supervisors continued to dismiss the importance of records as a way to ensure accountability and quality of care.

When faced with complaints to licensure boards about their practices, clinicians questioned whether they could reveal confidential information about their treatment to the licensure boards. Those who did not have contemporaneous documentation were especially frightened. They wondered how they could demonstrate to their regulatory boards their good faith efforts to help their clients.

A majority of the records I have reviewed in malpractice cases have been sparse, illegible, or even nonexistent. Sadly, in some instances, the reputations and careers of competent clinicians and supervisors who provided good care have suffered needlessly, simply because they had not adequately documented their professional services.

All mental health professional organizations now recognize the critical need for records and for protecting the privacy of those records. Many states have made record keeping a statutory requirement for mental health practitioners. But state statutory guidelines vary widely. Unfortunately, none of these sources provides a specific format or discusses a theoretical basis for generating client records.

Practitioners have also called me about responsibilities for records in anticipation of their retirements or in the event they should unexpectedly become incapacitated. Spouses of deceased private practitioners, too, have worried when their spouses left no directions, and they consequently did not know how to respond to ongoing requests for records. Unfortunately, there has been little professional attention to the need to develop plans for records in preparation for interruption or closures of practices.

Furthermore, competent record keeping skills are hard to come by. Graduate school curricula and clinical supervision address the subject sporadically. Practitioners are left to muddle through. They may adopt record keeping systems used by their internships or places of employment (Kagle, 1991) but do not understand the rationale for these procedures. Lack of solid record keeping skills leaves clinicians unable to balance the critical need for accountability and quality of care against the need for confidentiality.

In 1997, after presenting a workshop on record keeping to the Clinical Social Work Federation's board of directors, board members requested I write a text on record keeping. Based upon my knowledge of members' concerns and questions, I agreed there was a compelling need for such a book but did not want to tackle it alone. I therefore asked one of my committee members, Dr. Lee Norton, for assistance. Lee was gifted in sizing up complex concepts and stating them succinctly; in her work helping attorneys to develop mitigating factors to argue against the death penalty, she had reviewed thousands of medical records. She shared my idealism about using records as therapeutic tools. She agreed to provide me with moral support and feedback to drafts of my chapters. Her suggestions for ways

I could present concepts in my book more clearly and her wisdom based on her extensive professional experience in the legal system, where she had trained practitioners to be witnesses and had trained attorneys to work with mental health experts, were invaluable to the success of the first edition.

Over the past decade, the first edition has succeeded in meeting its mission. Since its publication, multidisciplinary associations throughout the country (in Connecticut; Delaware; Georgia; Massachusetts; Minnesota; Oklahoma; Virginia, and Washington, DC) have invited me to present ethics conferences on topics covered in my book. Discussions at these conferences have stimulated opportunities for clinicians to share with colleagues in their own communities complex questions they have about how to handle delicate clinical and ethical issues. I too have felt enriched by these discussions. I have also received enthusiastic and ongoing feedback locally and nationally from professors, students, and trainees, who tell me they find the book accessible and helpful in training programs. "Hold onto the book after you graduate because you will find it even more helpful once you are out in practice," one professor told me he says to his graduate students, who read the book in their supervision and program management course. A chief resident in psychiatry felt it covered essential ethical issues and made it required reading for her residents. A professor in California told me she routinely assigns her MSW (Master of Social Work) students the task of reading the book with their field instructors. A professor in Chicago, who was invited to teach a new graduate-level course on social work and the law, said she had not been able to find a text for her class and was delighted to find my book. A professor who also serves as clinical director of a community mental health center said its contents helped her team members identify what to include in their new electronic records system. New practitioners have said they have used it to establish their practices. Retiring practitioners have told me they have used it as a guide in closing their practices. Clinicians facing court appearances have relied on it as a road map.

WRITING THE SECOND EDITION

Over the course of my career, I have had the opportunity to practice and study in a wide array of settings and capacities, which form the foundation for this second edition. The information and opinions I presented here continue to be based upon my professional experience as a licensed psychologist and licensed independent clinical social worker, in the following areas: clinical practice with children, adults, and families in various professional settings, such as adult and child psychiatric inpatient and outpatient services, family service, schools and a child guidance clinic; private practice; clinical practice and research with patients and families who have suffered from sexual and other professional boundary violations by health care or clergy counseling professionals;

teaching and clinical supervision of new professionals and trainees in psychology, clinical social work, and psychiatry; ethics training of mental health practitioners nationally in the United States and abroad (Australia, Canada, New Zealand, Scotland, and Sweden); consultation on professional standards to regulatory boards and attorneys; expert witness experience in criminal and civil cases; and supervision or consultation to clinicians charged with licensure board complaints.

After agreeing to write this second edition of my book on record keeping, I reviewed the literature to see what other texts on record keeping have been developed over the past decade and found very little (Bond & Mitchell, 2008; Wiger, 2005; Zuckerman, 2008).

The literature I found did not cover many of the clinical issues that I continue to find of central concern to psychotherapists, such as how to use one's self in record keeping to enhance the therapeutic relationship; how to use records as therapeutic and supervisory tools; how to create easy-to-read forms that facilitate understanding; how to handle fears and conduct one's self professionally when attorneys, courts, and licensure boards request clinical records; how to rely on one's own clinical wisdom while ensuring confidentiality of records and implementing the evolving federal privacy and security rules; how to systematically craft supervisory contracts and records together with trainees and supervisees; how to teach record keeping to students, interns, and new professionals; and how to prepare for records in the event of interruptions in or closures of practices. I knew my text would inevitably overlap somewhat with other texts on record keeping and ethics, but I wanted to fill a need by emphasizing these critical clinical concerns.

In the first edition, my purpose in asking Scott Chase to create black and white watercolor illustrations was to help my readers rest while absorbing complex, sometimes tedious, topics in my book. Readers have welcomed his art. I therefore invited Scott to create more illustrations for the second edition that would help me depict new or expanded topics such as retention of electronic records, cultural diversity, teaching methods, and the impact of technology on the therapeutic relationship. The last was particularly important to me; as I wrote the second edition, I came to see this as one of the most challenging areas facing practitioners today.

Readers encouraged me to put my sample forms into a CD format that can be used with the book. I thank my publisher for responding to these thoughtful suggestions.

Two concepts that ran through the recent literature I read are worth noting— the therapeutic relationship and mentalization—both key ingredients promoting successful outcomes in all types of therapy ranging from cognitive behavioral therapy (CBT) to psychodynamic treatment. Data on centrality of the therapeutic relationship (Horvath, 2005) confirmed my intuitive sense that I needed to continue to focus on record keeping as a tool to help develop and support the therapeutic relationship. Descriptions of how mentalization fosters human development, human relationships in general, and in particular therapeutic relationships (Allen, Fonagy, & Bateman, 2008) inspired me to continue considering record keeping as an ongoing, interactive, humble process of mutual learning and discovery between clinician and client.

In order to update this book, I knew I would also need to learn about the new world of electronic record systems. I felt fortunate to have opportunities to consult practitioners from coast to coast on their experiences using electronic record systems; attend a meeting of local community mental health center directors who were discussing their experiences developing electronic medical records systems; and speak with a national trainer who has trained nearly a thousand health care professionals in medical centers ranging from northern California to Virginia. From them I learned that mental health professionals must become team players in developing electronic records systems in order to sensitively address the needs of psychotherapy patients and to provide adequate security. I learned that templates can constrain clinicians who feel they can no longer describe their patients as human beings. ("Five-year-old Johnny arrived for his session today dressed as Darth Vader, breathing threateningly under his black mask.") Yet, as the trainer explained to me, she felt my book can help mental health professionals conceptualize a framework for thinking about records as they take a proactive role in developing electronic record systems that address the needs of their specialized and sensitive work.

As I listened to practitioners and administrators in settings that have used electronic records over many years, I gathered they appreciate their electronic systems' ability to systematically track essential information and allow portability of patient information to other professionals who are serving their patients. They generally felt positive. Yet I wondered what was getting lost. Like the university music professor who observed that composers are now writing in shorter musical phrases because, as he hypothesized, they are composing music on a computer screen which limits their visual ability to take in the larger score, are mental health practitioners doing the same? Are they more constrained today from seeing the full pictures of their patient's stories due to the limitations of having to click on so many different categories and scroll down endlessly to examine longer histories? I concluded I cannot know the answers, but together we need to ask these questions.

I anticipate this book will continue to be a supportive reference, offering a general orientation and practical suggestions for options to consider. However, it is not legal advice or clinical consultation. Practitioners should consult their clinical colleagues, supervisors, and consultants whenever they have questions in specific cases. They should rely on their respective professional associations, regulatory boards, and health care attorneys to keep abreast of their respective jurisdictions' laws and the evolving modifications in state and federal rules that govern record keeping, protect the privacy and security of patient identifiable information, and support appropriate access by patients to their private mental health records. While this book includes examples of forms for illustrative purposes, it does not contain a comprehensive collection of forms. When practitioners require further forms in order to implement evolving laws and rules, they can find them on their respective professional associations' Web sites.

I intend for this second edition to reflect the context of changes over the past decade: demands to develop electronic records; increased risk of loss of privacy due to losses and breaches of electronic records; unprecedented challenges to our ability to portray our patients as human beings, not just as bytes that can be seen rapidly on computer screens; evolving boundary issues related to the impact of electronic communications on the therapeutic relationship; effects of economic recession on patients' ability to find care and on practitioners' ability to make a living and afford costly postgraduate clinical supervision; the influx of immigrants and changing patterns in the family, which are calling us to have even greater clinical sensitivity to diversity; and new state and federal rules to protect privacy. In this era of rapid changes and threats to privacy, I believe there is an even greater need for us to have collegial support in our respective communities, to help us remain grounded and work together to protect our enduring and fundamental professional values.

SUMMARY OF CHAPTERS

I have updated and expanded some of my chapters, and some chapters are entirely new. The book is organized into 13 chapters; most contain clinical vignettes illustrating today's complex challenges, and most contain a summary of relevant ethical and legal issues. Chapter 1 discusses the purposes of clinical records, emphasizing their role in promoting the therapeutic relationship. Chapter 2 identifies reasons and methods for documenting the process of informed consent within the therapeutic relationship at various stages during treatment. Chapter 3 discusses psychotherapists' most frequent questions about characteristics and contents of good records. Chapter 4 summarizes new ethical and legal requirements for protecting confidentiality in an electronic era, as well as new safeguards and laws that assist in protecting records; it also describes the potential for breaches of confidentiality through theft of electronic equipment and unauthorized access to patient-identifiable information. Chapter 5 discusses ethical and legal parameters of exceptions to confidentiality. Chapter 6 follows with practical tips for developing policies and procedures that can protect confidentiality and security of records, whether in verbal, paper, or electronic form, and for handling exceptions to confidentiality. Chapter 7 discusses evolving boundary challenges resulting from the impact of electronic communication on the treatment relationship, such as e-mail, social media, blogs, cell phone devices, and electronic records. Chapter 8 discusses factors to consider in deciding how long to keep records and in creating retention policy and procedure. Chapter 9 discusses ways practitioners can strengthen the therapeutic relationship through using records as therapeutic tools in treatment. Chapter 10 emphasizes the need for supervisory contracts and records to protect one's self, supervisees, patients, and the supervisory relationship and provides new sample forms for the supervision contract and records. Chapter 11 emphasizes the need to generate record keeping skills in students and new clinicians and offers practical tips for teaching record keeping. Chapter 12 presents an orientation to the legal system, including advice for handling subpoenas, using professional judgment to determine whether and how to release records and methods for testifying in depositions and trials. Chapter 13 addresses practitioners' clinical responsibility to respond to patients' attachment needs by proactively crafting plans for records in preparation for temporary interruptions or permanent closures of a psychotherapy practice, and includes new examples of letters that inform patients about therapists' terminal illness or retirement.

Appendices and the CD provide samples of clinical and supervisory practice forms (new forms related to supervision are a major addition to the collection) as well as a list of professional organizations and their Web sites that can aid readers in finding their respective professional organizations' ethical standards.

USES OF THIS TEXT

The primary audience for this second edition continues to include all professionals who practice, supervise, and teach psychotherapy or counseling. The concepts and examples in this book are generic. They are designed to help practitioners in all professions, regardless of clinical orientations, in fields of social work, psychiatry, psychology, marriage and family therapy, nursing, counseling, and pastoral counseling. Due to my broad, multidisciplinary readership, I use the terms "client" and "patient" interchangeably, though each field has its own preferred term.

Both beginning and experienced practitioners can continue to benefit from the content of this book. New psychotherapists can absorb a logical system of thinking about and documenting treatment. More experienced therapists can gather new ideas that easily can be incorporated into their current clinical practices and use it as a desk reference.

The text can be useful in any clinical curriculum that trains psychotherapists. Students will gain a helpful framework for thinking about and generating client records. Similarly, instructors and supervisors can rely upon the text in teaching record keeping and evaluating trainees' performance.

The text can be a resource in clinical supervision of new professionals and in consultation as well. Professionals in other fields will also find it worthwhile. Attorneys, judges, and licensure board administrators can discover how practitioners use principles of ethical decision making when facing complex issues in clinical practice. They can learn about aspects of record keeping in psychotherapy, including mental health professionals' ethical duties to protect patients' confidentiality, and the roles psychotherapists may or may not be able to play in legal settings.

A FINAL COMPASSIONATE WORD FOR MY READERS

I have never met a practitioner who keeps "perfect" psychotherapy records. It is still worthy to strive to do the best we can. I have approached this project with humility, mindful of the draining demands in daily psychotherapy practice. I am also aware that what transpires between words during psychotherapy sessions is often as important, or more important, than the words. It is therefore virtually impossible to document the "truth" of what transpires in psychotherapy sessions. In writing this book, I have looked for ways to provide information that will make record keeping easier, not more of a burden. I would ask my readers to consider not so much what they have done wrong in the past, but what they can take from this book to make record keeping easier and better today and in the future, to benefit themselves as well as their patients.

1

Purposes of Clinical Records

From the very first session, practitioners engage in the process of relationship building. While gathering information from their patients, they seek to develop rapport by listening empathically. They strive to understand the complexities of their patients' diverse contexts. They work to collaboratively construct a hopeful therapeutic relationship, now recognized by researchers to be the key factor in successful outcomes, more significant than type of treatment (Allen, Fonagy, & Bateman, 2008; Gabbard, 2010; Horvath, 2005). Effective record keeping promotes a positive therapeutic alliance and improves treatment outcomes when clinicians' work with their patients reflects respect, concern, and collaboration.

Competent record keeping is not just a boring burden thrust upon practitioners by external forces, and it is not simply good risk management. It becomes a dynamic aide in developing a framework for supporting the therapeutic alliance from the outset and through various stages of our collaborative clinical work with patients.

All mental health organizations have codes of ethics that highlight the paramount importance of protecting patient confidentiality and maintaining the highest professional standards to protect patient welfare. Sadly, few mental health professional organizations or state laws define and describe the characteristics involved in competent clinical record keeping. There is little written about the therapeutic process of record keeping. This leaves practitioners to use what little they can learn in graduate schools or internships, or to devise their own policies and methods in a virtual vacuum. However, several recent developments are challenging graduate schools, clinical supervisors, and therapists to focus on documentation. First, clinical research that highlights the central importance of the therapeutic relationship challenges therapists to document their care and clinical decision-making processes and to use record keeping as a collaborative treatment tool. Second, the Health Insurance Portability and Accountability Act (HIPAA) requires practitioners who generate patient-identifiable health care information electronically to develop written information that explains to their patients how they use treatment records, how they protect the privacy of those records, and how they may have access to their records (U.S. Department of Health and Human Services, 2001c). Third, increasing numbers of malpractice cases and complaints to state licensure boards are forcing clinicians and their supervisors to practice more careful and thoughtful documentation. Fourth, higher rates of litigation in our society mean that more practitioners are receiving subpoenas for patients' records and are struggling to find ways to respond and still protect patients' needs for privacy. Finally, more therapists today are anticipating retirement or leaving their practices for other reasons and must make advance plans for their patients' records.

The need for knowledge and methods in record keeping has never been more urgent. The goal of this second edition is to enhance behavioral and mental health professionals' ability to write, maintain, and use records in order to help develop and preserve the therapeutic alliance, promote healing, and protect patients' privacy.

Systematic clinical records are essential for the following reasons:

1. Records facilitate communication between therapists and clients. Inviting patients to discuss diagnostic impressions and treatment options and to contribute their own perspectives, including on what is helpful and not helpful in their treatment, can help create an atmosphere of safety and mutual respect. Records help patients understand their problems, make meaningful decisions about their treatment, develop insight, and become partners in their own healing. Records help to create trust in professional relationships. The process of informing patients about why and how practitioners maintain and protect their records demonstrates commitment to patient welfare.

2. Records form the basis of sound diagnoses and appropriate treatment plans. Reviewing records over time allows therapists to identify significant patterns and modify diagnostic hypotheses and treatment plans. Keeping records also allows practitioners access to more dates and information than they can reliably maintain in memory.

3. Records provide for continuity of care. Clear, concise records allow other practitioners to follow and understand what has occurred in therapy and the rationale for interventions. New practitioners can pick up where previous therapists left off or explain to patients why they are recommending a different course of action. Without good records, patients' need for continuity of care suffers.

4. Records are necessary for clinical supervision. Records are indispensable tools for evaluating and remediating knowledge and skills. Developing supervision contracts promotes systematic attention to supervisees' learning needs and provides informed consent to supervision. Reviewing records allows supervisors to see how well supervisees or trainees are developing clinical hypotheses and treatment plans and to help them document their findings and interventions appropriately.

Through discussions of records, trainees gain greater objectivity, which ensures better treatment for patients.

5. Records satisfy the requirements of contractual obligations with third-party payers. In many instances, mental health services cannot be reimbursed without documentation of diagnoses, treatment plans, and client progress. A clear record of events also facilitates writing appropriate reports about patients.

6. Records are practitioners' and clinical supervisors' best (and sometimes only) protection against allegations of unethical and harmful treatment. We live in a highly litigious society. Detailed records are the best protection against specious claims. Contemporaneous documentation of events, agreements, and professional decisions can demonstrate the bases for clinical and ethical decision making and provide proof of good-faith efforts.

For these reasons and more, it is essential that practitioners, while developing the therapeutic alliance, become proactive about keeping coherent, concise, accurate, and timely patient records in collaboration with their patients and assiduously protect the confidentiality of those records.

2

Documenting Informed Consent

Imagine Ms. G., a 40-year-old married woman, mother of three young children ages 2 to 6, employed as a high school teacher, who began suffering from flashbacks to childhood sexual trauma soon after learning that her mother was terminally ill with breast cancer. She became unable to sleep, concentrate, or manage her teaching and parenting responsibilities. She was fearful she would kill herself. Her husband and her sister got her to the hospital, where she was admitted to the psychiatric floor. Fortunately, a maternal aunt who lived nearby was able to help with child care and household tasks during the crisis. During her 2-week stay, treatment included psychotropic medications and other supportive services that helped her to soothe herself and protected her from harming herself. Family therapy sessions facilitated her and her husband's ability to communicate their respective needs and to work out how to respond to the needs of their young children. As she approached the day she would be discharged from the hospital, the attending psychiatrist suggested outpatient psychotherapy to treat her posttraumatic stress disorder, major depressive disorder, and the stresses and losses related to her mother's illness. He referred Ms. G. to the psychotherapy clinic at the university hospital, where a third-year female psychiatric resident, Dr. M., was assigned to her for psychotherapy.

Ms. G. felt anxious about the prospect of speaking about her problems to another professional, a total stranger. Even if she mustered the courage to tell her life story, could the new psychotherapist understand her? Had she worked with patients with similar problems? Would the new therapist understand her grief and fear related to her mother's illness; how overwhelming her disturbing memories were; how tense she had been feeling with her husband, who was having problems of his own; how impossible it had felt to juggle the demands of parenting and teaching school? How could she find time for psychotherapy? How long would it take? What would be involved?

Now imagine Dr. M., the psychiatry resident at the university's training program, who was learning to do psychotherapy and having her own worries about the new referral. Faculty in her program had recently identified in professional reports a need for residents to take a more active approach with their patients regarding informed consent to treatment (Hauser, Cording, Hajak, & Spiessl, 2008; Rutherford, Aizaga, Sneed, & Roose, 2007; Rutherford & Roose, 2006). But the challenges of explaining to herself and to her patient what therapy would involve felt daunting. She intuitively understood that her patients were coming to her for comfort, not for informed consent. She therefore consulted her psychotherapy supervisor:

"What do I say when I see her? As I anticipate working with this new patient, I above all want to be able to connect with her. I feel I will have trouble describing exactly what treatment with me will look like. Especially at the very beginning, when I am just getting a feel for what she feels is bringing her in and how I might be helpful. Dr. S. referred her to me because he thinks she will be a suitable teaching case for dynamic psychotherapy. But I feel that the nature of how a dynamic therapist works means I will probably not be able to be as explicit about what treatment with her will look like as I would be able to be if I were doing CBT or DBT [dialectical behavior therapy] with her. How can I still make sure I am going through an ethical process of informed consent?"

Dr. M. found it helpful to hear her supervisor agree with her that empathic and sensitive listening would be her most important task and that informed consent is a process, an integral part of ongoing clinical work (Gabbard, 2010; Pomerantz, 2005). She recognized that the dilemma with a new patient is how to respond to the urgency of what has brought them in while also taking care of the paperwork and other necessary pieces of the frame. Dr. M.'s discussion with her supervisor helped her to relax. She absorbed the concept that her most important task would be to listen compassionately to how her new patient presents herself and to learn from her patient what the patient feels could be helpful. She recognized she could address issues of informed consent naturally, within the context of listening to her patient's history and needs and while collaborating with her patient to coconstruct ideas about what will be helpful. It was also helpful to remember that even before the initial appointment, her new patient could receive anticipatory information regarding the more mechanical aspects of therapy in the mail, and thus keeping some of the nuts and bolts of the informed consent process simpler and minimizing interruption to the natural flow of their conversation in the first session.

Dr. M.'s worries as a trainee illustrate challenges all practitioners face. Patients arrive in therapy feeling anxious. Therapists' ability to engage with patients in a way that helps them to feel safe and helps them prepare for the process of therapy is essential. In the initial session, our primary task is to forge a strong therapeutic alliance, which involves creating the frame for therapy—trust, safety, and confidentiality (Yalom, 2002).

Research demonstrates that a strong therapeutic alliance, which begins as early as in the initial interview, is predictive of future outcome (Gabbard, 2010), and informed consent procedures help to build the therapeutic alliance (Martindale, Chambers, & Thompson, 2009) by demonstrating respect for clients' self-determination and enhancing rapport and collaboration between psychotherapist and patient (Fisher & Oransky, 2008).

How can we listen empathically, build rapport, gradually become acquainted, and collaborate at our patients' own pace, while sharing with them how we understand their conditions and the parameters of the work ahead that we believe may be helpful to them? As an experienced psychotherapy teacher concurred: "In the initial session particularly, the urgency of collecting information, making sure everything is covered, made clear, signed, sealed, and delivered can overshadow the purpose of the context in which this process is happening—establishing the therapeutic relationship" (Barbara Berger, personal communication, January 12, 2011).

This chapter will provide an overview of how practitioners can document the process of informed consent within a natural context of forming and strengthening the therapeutic alliance. It will address the following: (a) how the doctrine of informed consent has changed psychotherapy practice; (b) legal and ethical bases for informed consent; (c) key questions that psychotherapists may wish to answer and document when providing clients with opportunities for informed consent; (d) practical strategies for documenting informed consent in patients' records at each stage of treatment; and (e) a case example that illustrates the process, throughout various stages of therapy, in the documentation of informed consent. This chapter does not offer clinical or legal advice in a given situation. To answer questions about specific case situations, practitioners may obtain information about the laws and ethics codes of their states and professional organizations and obtain clinical or legal consultation.

HOW THE DOCTRINE OF INFORMED CONSENT HAS CHANGED PSYCHOTHERAPY PRACTICE

One of the biggest changes in psychotherapy practice over the past several years has been the evolution of the doctrine of informed consent. This means that competent adult patients (or their legal representatives) have the right to receive information from health care professionals about their conditions, the risks and benefits of proposed treatments and of adjunct treatments, such as medications, or other treatment techniques, and the risks and benefits of no treatment.

The emphasis on patient education in recent decades appears to have positively affected patients' and mental health practitioners' understanding of what patients need to know about psychotherapy. It has helped patients make meaningful decisions about their treatment. While the degree and quality of patient education may vary depending on geographic location, I have observed patients taking a more active role to gather information about their treatment. This has led to a *demystification* of psychotherapy and an evolving collaborative model.

While research literature shows that many different types of psychotherapy are beneficial, in any treatment modality it is critical to establish collaborative rapport with patients and to document that patients have received and understood essential information and have been able to make meaningful decisions about their treatment. Documentation of the process of informed consent demonstrates that therapists are fulfilling their collaborative duties with their patients. Documentation gives greater protection to therapists as well as to patients. Documentation of informed consent adds credibility.

Patients who have described detrimental experiences in a variety of psycho-therapy settings noted that they did not receive sufficient information about their conditions and methods of psychotherapy—including roles of the patient and therapist, options for treatment, and exceptions to confidentiality—and felt as a result they were limited in their ability to make rational, informed decisions about treatment. In an anonymous survey study of patients who had suffered problems related to practitioner sexual misconduct, respondents cited the need for "consumer education" that can help patients to understand what is appropriate and effective treatment (Luepker, 1999).

Concurrent with the need for sufficient information is the need for that information to be easily understood by a range of clients. A recent study surveyed Health Insurance Portability and Accountability Act (HIPAA)–compliant notices of privacy practices used by practitioners throughout the United States. The study's authors found that "almost the entire sample (94%) fell into the difficult range of reading ease" (Walfish & Ducey, 2007). Remembering how very awkward the language in the HIPAA rule is, I am not surprised by these findings. However, given that clients often come to therapists in crisis, materials need to be easy to understand to be effective. They also need to be appropriate for the needs of specific patient groups. For example, a colleague who works with severely mentally ill persons begins his work with this clientele using a family and systemic perspective, not an individual treatment model. Initial contacts occur within family meetings, and his understanding with such patients is that treatment occurs within an "open system," involving concerned relatives, other clinicians, and social agencies. As this sometimes requires home visits, he avoids beginning treatment with an individual therapy model that posits a closed therapeutic dyad that then has to be "opened up" to include others. However, with less disturbed clients, his approach involves a conventional dyadic approach to psychotherapy and confidentiality (Joel Kanter, personal communication, May 16, 2011). In Chapter 6, I also consider differential informed consent approaches in various types of treatment contexts.

SOCIETAL, LEGAL, AND ETHICAL BASES FOR INFORMED CONSENT

Western society has long valued medical patients' right to accurate and thorough information about medical treatment options and the relative risks and benefits of those options. This societal value has led to an increasing emphasis in medicine and social sciences on the importance of the right to self-determination. After World War II, the Nuremberg Codes and Principles prevented experimentation on human subjects without informed consent (Piper, 1994). Later, in 1957, in the Salgo case in the United States, a physician was liable for not giving his patient sufficient information to make it possible for the patient to make an intelligent decision regarding treatment (Sanford, Hartnett, & Jolly, 1999).

State laws vary regarding how much information practitioners must give their patients regarding diagnosis and treatment. Courts have debated this question. They have given psychotherapists some latitude in making decisions regarding how to carry out this doctrine to prevent harm to the individual and to society. Courts have decided that physicians should exercise thoughtful discretion in disclosing potentially disturbing information to the patient (Piper, 1994).

The federal privacy rule (HIPAA), adopted April 14, 2001, and amended August 14, 2002, requires practitioners who generate identifiable information electronically (whether stored on computer, paper, or shared orally) to establish specific written informed consent procedures for patients. Practitioners who are "covered" under the rule were required to implement these informed consent procedures by April 14, 2003. For example, practitioners must inform patients in writing about how their identifiable confidential information may be used, disclosed, and stored. The rule also requires that practitioners inform patients of their rights to have access to their records, including an electronic copy, and to request amendments to their records. Psychotherapists must also inform patients in writing about their options to make a grievance if they are concerned about violations of the rule's provisions (U.S. Department of Health and Human Services, 2001a; Federal Register, 2002). See Chapter 4 for further discussion of HIPAA and Chapter 6 for further discussion of policies and procedures that may assist practitioners to implement this rule.

All mental health organizations include requirements for informed consent in their ethics codes. They uniformly require practitioners to provide sufficient information to patients (or to those who are responsible for patients' treatment) in language that is understandable to them, in order for patients or their representatives to be able to make meaningful decisions regarding treatment. Wellspring Family Services (Wellspring Family Services, 2008) in Seattle, Washington, has an excellent example of a HIPAA compliant "Notice of Privacy Practices" on its Web site (http://family-services.org). The American Counseling Association specifies the obligation to review the rights and responsibilities of both the counselor and the client in writing as well as verbally. See the CD and Appendix J for a list of professional organizations' Web sites; more information regarding respective codes of ethics can be found on these sites.

KEY QUESTIONS TO CONSIDER IN DOCUMENTING INFORMED CONSENT

Psychotherapy patients have taught me they (or their guardians or personal representatives) have several questions that are integral in developing a successful therapeutic working alliance and achieving the best possible therapeutic outcomes. Here are typical questions patients have. Practitioners can document that they have provided answers to these questions and that their patients have understood and been able to meaningfully consent:

- Are the practitioner's credentials, training, and experience relevant to the kinds of problems I need help for? Can he or she help me?
- Does my therapist keep my communications in psychotherapy confidential?
- Does my therapist communicate via e-mail or provide online therapy via Skype? Does my therapist mind if I record our sessions? Can I call my therapist's cell phone? How is confidentiality affected by these forms of communication?
- What are my therapist's policies about becoming "friends" on Facebook?
- What are exceptions to protecting my confidentiality?*
- What procedures do my therapist and office staff follow to protect my confidentiality?
- What are my therapist's fees?
- How and when will my payments be due?
- Does my therapist agree to payment arrangements, such as sliding fee scale or pay-over-time?
- If I fail to make payments, what are the consequences? For example, does my therapist use the services of a collection agency?
- If I am planning to use my insurance coverage or other third-party reimbursement, does my third-party payer require information about me? If so, is this disclosure of information acceptable, and if not, are there alternatives?
- When I signed my insurance contract did I give my insurance company the right to review my entire records? If I did allow for disclosure, am I comfortable with that degree of disclosure? Do I give permission to my therapist to fulfill my third-party payer's demand for information? If not, are there alternatives or remedies?
- What is my diagnosis, and what does it mean?
- How did my therapist come to that conclusion about my diagnosis?
- What does my therapist recommend would be helpful to me? Does my therapist recommend treatment or no treatment? If treatment, what kind of treatment and what will be involved?
- What are the expected outcomes of the recommended treatment?
- What are the risks in the proposed treatment?

---

* Treatment situations and contracts with involuntary patients (e.g., persons referred by forensic treatment units or courts) have built-in disclosure requirements. The need to specify what information must be disclosed and to whom is a necessary part of the informed consent process and treatment contract.

- Are there alternate treatments? If so, what are they, and what are the possible risks and benefits?
- What could happen if I have no treatment?
- What are the recommended frequency and expected duration of the proposed treatment? Why?
- How will I and my therapist know when I am ready to finish therapy?
- When I no longer need therapy, will I have the option to return to my therapist as needed?
- Who will provide care to me in case of emergencies if my therapist is unavailable?
- If I do not like what is happening in treatment, what do I do?

DOCUMENTATION THAT REFLECTS THE PROCESS OF INFORMED CONSENT

Informed consent is a process. It takes place at all stages of the professional relationship: before, during, and at completion of the initial evaluation; and at relevant junctures during treatment (Gabbard, 2010; Pomerantz, 2005). Three types of information that practitioners should document are (a) what information the clinician discussed with the client, (b) whether in the clinician's judgment the patient (or patient's representative) is competent to understand and make a meaningful decision regarding treatment, and (c) the client's decision. What follows is an overview of the informed consent process at various stages of treatment.

Preliminary Verbal and Written Information

It is helpful to answer new patients' preliminary questions on the phone, to send them clearly written information about what they may expect in their initial appointment, and to ask them to read this information prior to their first session. Anticipatory procedures provide patients with an initial overview. They allow them time to formulate questions they can discuss in the initial session. Once they are in the office, patients' signatures acknowledge they have received and read the information.

Preliminary information that documents informed consent needs to include a written description of the therapists' practice protocols, including but not limited to the patient's rights to privacy and confidentiality, exceptions to privacy and confidentiality, security procedures to protect patient identifiable information, where and how to make a complaint about treatment, and a summary of billing procedures. (See CD and Appendix A for a "Sample Client/Patient Information Form.") Being mindful of our treatment contexts is essential as we discern how to proceed with given patients or clients, as noted above. The following primarily illustrates an informed consent process within a more conventional dyadic individual treatment approach, but it can be adapted to meet the needs within modalities such as group or family treatment.

Initial Interview

In order to minimize interruptions to becoming acquainted with the patient, the first session may begin simply by asking if the patient has had a chance to read the "client information" pamphlet or brochure. If the patient did not read it or is illiterate or non-English-speaking and thus cannot read it, the therapist may need to alert the client to essential information without interrupting the primary focus of the interview, which is to learn about the patient and what the patients' problems are. Therapists can be helpful by sharing and eliciting responses regarding the following:

- Relevant information regarding the practitioners' professional training, experience, philosophy of treatment
- Confidentiality parameters and exceptions to confidentiality
- Amount of practitioner's fees
- Who is responsible for payment of psychotherapy services
- Payment policy for missed appointments
- If third-party payer, what disclosure of confidential information will be required for reimbursement
- Consent for disclosure to third-party payer
- Consent for necessary collaboration with other treating professionals and what this might entail
- What types of questions the therapist will be asking in the initial evaluation and why

On Completion of Initial Evaluation

By the completion of the initial evaluation, which may involve one to three sessions, the clinician can be satisfied that the patient (or patient's guardian) fully understands the clinician's opinions and policies regarding diagnosis and treatment recommendations, the risks and benefits of various treatments or no treatment, the limitations of psychotherapy, the frequency and estimated number of sessions required to achieve the client's goals, responsibility for payment and missed sessions, and how available the therapist is to the client, including procedures for "emergency" situations.

Again, practitioners can document whether, in their professional opinion, the client was able to give consent to treatment, and grounds for this judgment and whether the client consented to treatment. Crafting a written treatment plan with their clients, signed by both clients and therapists (see CD and Appendix B for a sample treatment plan form), can be a natural way for practitioners to document mutual agreement on diagnoses and treatment plan while supporting the patient's feeling understood and the patient's role as collaborator. Some therapists have found their patients appreciate their giving them written evaluations, including a summary narrative written directly to the patient (Allen, Fonagy, & Bateman, 2008; Epston, 1994).

During Treatment

Psychotherapy is not a static process—it ebbs and flows depending on a number of variables. As patients and clinicians work together, new information and issues emerge that may alter the clinicians' working hypotheses about diagnoses and treatment. Similarly, patients may come to view their situation in a different light. Changing impressions—on the part of patients and clinicians—can be discussed frequently and treatment goals and interventions altered as necessary, always through a collaborative process. Practitioners may also receive third-party requests for information about clients, or require additional information, such as through psychological testing or medical or other consultations, which they discuss with clients to obtain informed consent. Practitioners should document all such discussions. The sample revised treatment plan (see CD and Appendix C) can be used throughout treatment for documenting progress, new problems, and procedures that practitioners have discussed with their patients.

If a patient makes no progress during treatment, or becomes worse, the situation should be acknowledged and discussed promptly. All available options, including obtaining consultation, terminating therapy, or referring the patient to another practitioner should be explored openly and directly. These discussions, and any resultant decisions, including whether treatment has ended by mutual agreement, should be documented. For an example of a form that can be used collaboratively with patients to demonstrate discussion (or the inability to have discussion) about the ending of treatment, see CD and Appendix D for "Closing Summary."

Methods for Documenting Informed Consent

Methods for documentation of informed consent vary, but a narrative form is clearest. Signed treatment plans (see CD and appendix) are effective strategies to document patients' collaboration and consent to treatment. Some practitioners use "informed consent checklists" that clients can sign and date to help practitioners stay focused on what information they need to discuss and what consent they must obtain. Practitioners can choose a method for documentation of informed consent that works best for them and which clearly (a) conveys whether clients are competent to give consent to treatment and on what grounds clinicians have based this conclusion, and (b) records all discussions with clients about informed consent.

CASE EXAMPLE

The following case example of Dr. M. and Ms. G. illustrates informed consent discussions at different junctures in the evaluation and treatment process and how Dr. M. documented these discussions.

Preliminary Stage

Ms. G., as described earlier, was feeling very anxious about the prospect of beginning outpatient therapy but agreed to Dr. S.'s referral and bravely called the new therapist at the clinic. The therapist was, as often happens, occupied with another patient when she called, so Ms. G. left a message requesting Dr. M. call her back. When Dr. M. returned her call, she listened compassionately for a few moments to Ms. G. and answered her questions. She then said she would like to mail Ms. G. a packet of information about the clinic's practice, plus forms and a questionnaire for her to read, fill out, and bring to the first session to discuss.

Some of Ms. G.'s questions on the phone were about cost of therapy, and Dr. M. asked whether Ms. G. wished to use her health insurance. She explained what information about her condition the insurance company would require in order to pay for the therapist's services. She explained that in the packet of information she was sending, there would be a consent form for her to sign which would allow the clinic to share necessary information with the insurance company. The therapist documented:

> We discussed fee arrangements. Client agreed to make her copayment at the time of each session. She requested that my billing office bill her insurance company for reimbursement of her sessions. She understands the clinic will provide her insurance company with diagnosis, treatment plan, dates of sessions, and understands that if the company requires further information I will first inform her before sending anything more.

Dr. M. was careful to respect Ms. G.'s privacy by asking her whether it was all right for her to mail the clinic's information and forms to her home address and documented the patient's consent: "11/1/01: Patient consented to my mailing intake information to her home address. She stated she will read it and complete the forms and bring them with her to her initial evaluation appointment on 11/11/01 at 1:00 p.m."

Initial Evaluation

At Ms. G.'s initial appointment, Dr. M.'s priority was to help her new patient feel as comfortable as possible as they became acquainted. She observed Ms. G. was physically and mentally shaken, overwhelmed, and sad, but able to speak. "Before we begin discussing the concerns that brought you here, did you receive the information I sent you?" Ms. G. indicated she had and gave Dr. M the signed form. "You noticed our clinic's safeguards to your privacy and confidentiality—that we cannot share your confidential information without your consent unless we are required to do so, for example if you are going to harm yourself or someone else?" "Yes," Ms. G. nodded. As Dr. M. mentioned parameters of confidentiality, including exceptions to confidentiality, she explained what disclosures of Ms. G.'s confidential information would be necessary for providing effective treatment, such as routine communication and collaboration with her psychiatrist who was prescribing medications and with a clinical psychologist who may be providing psychological testing. She obtained the patient's written consent for all routine collaborations with other professionals necessary for her treatment and placed the signed consent in her file. [Later, after the patient left, in order to document informed consent she wrote: "Patient stated she has read the client information I mailed her and signed it; we also discussed parameters of confidentiality, exceptions to confidentiality, and routine disclosures required for treatment. She stated she understood and agreed."]

"Before I ask you about the problems you are having and we begin sorting out together what could be helpful, I want you to have an opportunity to ask me any questions." Ms. G. responded by asking whether Dr. M. had experience with patients with similar problems. Dr. M. replied she is a psychiatry resident in training and briefly summarized her professional experiences in mental health services. She also clarified she would be available for 11 months, until July. [Later, in order to document informed consent, she wrote in the record: "Patient understood reasons for her psychiatrist's referral to me; I answered her questions regarding my professional background and experience with patients who suffer from similar problems; I clarified I would be available until July."]

Dr. M. then gave Ms. G. an overview of the types of questions she would be asking in the initial evaluation, such as what problems she was having, history of problems, what she hoped could be different in her life, her childhood background, and so forth, and obtained her consent to proceed with the evaluation.

As the interview unfolded, the therapist listened, allowing Ms. G. to share her story naturally, with minimum interruptions. She observed Ms. G. was emotionally overwhelmed, anxious, and her mood was depressed. She could discern during the interview however that she was well-oriented to time, person, place, and situation, was coherent, and that her attention and comprehension seemed adequate. She observed (and later documented) that Ms. G. was able to engage in a discussion about her condition and to understand the information Dr. M. provided. At the end of the initial evaluation, the therapist reflected what she had learned from the history the patient described to her. She empathized with Ms. G.'s grief and fears about her mother's terminal illness. She shared with Ms. M. that she thought she was suffering from moderate to severe depression, anxiety, overwhelming intrusive memories of physical and sexual trauma in earlier adulthood that were triggered by the recent crisis of her mother's terminal illness, and noted further she was struggling with suicidal thoughts. The therapist also expressed her concern that while Ms. G. appeared to now have control over her suicidal impulses, had no plan to kill herself, and had no guns in the house, she was indeed still having trouble focusing, concentrating, sleeping, and eating. Dr. M. shared her impressions that Ms. G. seemed to be saying that her most pressing problem was the intrusive flashbacks, and these, Dr. M. believed, were related to posttraumatic stress disorder. She explained that the first step in treating trauma is to reestablish a sense of equilibrium and internal and external safety (Herman, 1992).

Dr. M. shared options for treatment and how these techniques might be helpful to her and how they had been helpful to other clients with similar conditions. The treatment techniques she proposed and documented having discussed with Ms. G. included the following: (a) work together to help her feel more stable (e.g., to clarify strategies to deal with suicidal impulses, to begin to sleep and eat well, to be able to focus, to obtain new and reliable child care services to replace those that her mother had formerly been providing); (b) discuss her relationship with her mother and later, once she was feeling in better equilibrium, learn exercises to help herself: such as "grounding" or "anchoring" herself in the present in order to control her flashbacks; writing a narrative of her traumatic events and how these had affected her; keeping a "flashback journal" to write down and externalize her memories; learning relaxation visualizations to begin teaching herself how to calm herself and focus on the here and now; consider other options such as drawing images of herself in her life before, during, and after her traumatic experiences. (c) Dr. M. also explained the importance of support from others in the successful treatment of posttraumatic stress disorder. She asked Ms. G. to consider whom she could trust to call upon when she needed help.

The therapist ended the initial session by explaining to Ms. G. that a number of treatments for posttraumatic stress disorder were now being used with extremely good results and that she believed her disturbing symptoms were likely to subside over time. She noted that potential risks of treatment for posttraumatic stress disorder can include feeling worse as a result of sharing traumatic events with the therapist. Therefore, the therapist explained, Ms. G. needed to be in charge of what she felt ready to discuss in therapy. The therapist assured Ms. G. she would continually strive to work with Ms. G. on her problems at her own pace and would use all tools available to help her feel better. [Later, Dr. M. documented her clinical impressions, noting she discussed the above recommendations and that she advised Ms. G. that she would be in charge of indicating whether she felt ready or not to begin any particular treatment strategy so that she could go at her own pace.]

Dr. M. noted in the record: "See treatment plan attached that patient and I developed together on completion of her initial evaluation today." (See CD and Appendix B for a sample treatment plan form.)

During Treatment

After the patient had achieved more equilibrium, was able to sleep and eat well, and was no longer suffering from suicide ideation, the therapist and she discussed options for treatment. The patient agreed that she felt safer and could now consider options the therapist had previously discussed. She had found competent day care for her children and other support. She had begun identifying whom she could trust to speak with in order to obtain support in the current crisis. She was ready to write a narrative about her traumatic events. The therapist and patient revised the treatment plan to reflect the improvement the patient had made and her new goals. [Later, the therapist wrote in the progress note: "See revised treatment plan that reflects progress—she is no longer thinking of killing herself, has developed support for herself, has achieved a sense of safety sufficient to begin one of the proposed treatment options—to write a narrative of the traumatic events. Benefits (to integrate trauma) and risks (discomfort from unwelcome memories) discussed with patient."

As therapy developed over time, the therapist was struck by how capable Ms. G. was, but how often she discounted herself and her abilities in their sessions. In the privacy of her supervisor's office, Dr. M. discussed her countertransference feelings of irritation with Ms. G. and gained insights and new options that might be helpful. In her next therapy session with Ms. G., she shared her sense that therapy is a microcosm; by looking at what transpires in their therapy relationship, new insights and possibilities for growth may emerge. With Ms. G.'s consent to proceed, Dr. M. shared her sense of uneasiness and distance when Ms. G. discounted and berated herself. She wondered whether Ms. G. had been aware of treating herself in this way. Had she received feedback from others that she is unkind to herself? Through Dr. M.'s courage to inform Ms. G. about this opportunity to examine the process happening between them in the here and now of their therapeutic relationship, and Ms. G.'s courage to consent to having this discussion, Ms. G. felt freer to explore her fears of competence and ways she sabotages her own success, a final focus in her successful therapy experience with Dr. M. [Later, Dr. M. documented: "informed Ms. G. about and she consented to our reflecting on process in our therapy relationship; this reflective process helped her to clarify obstacles and new options for achieving her goals in her life."]

SUMMARY

This chapter has elaborated the concept of informed consent to include the therapeutic value of demystifying psychotherapy and including the client in the process of decision making in order to develop a strong therapeutic alliance. Effective psychotherapy is a collaborative effort in which therapists listen carefully at all phases in order to become acquainted with their patients and their needs; share relevant clinical information; explain and illustrate possible benefits and risks of therapy; and maintain an atmosphere of joint problem solving and skill building throughout therapeutic relationships. This chapter presented information to be discussed and documented before and during treatment to indicate (a) whether the patient was able to make meaningful decisions regarding the treatment and (b) whether the therapist obtained the patient's informed consent for treatment. Finally, therapists need to be mindful that all information provided to patients (within each therapist's respective practice context), or their guardians or personal representatives, needs to be understandable and appropriate for the nature of the work we are doing.

3

Characteristics and Contents of Good Records

Good record keeping is essential to good psychotherapy. But psychotherapists often lack knowledge about record keeping, and as electronic records become more required this becomes a larger issue. Some practitioners have told me they only write initial evaluations; after that, nothing but a few scribbled notes during sessions. "What else should I be doing?" they ask. Many are so busy keeping up with their appointments that they fall behind in writing their progress notes and cannot catch up. "Is there anything wrong with saving time by typing notes during sessions?" one clinician called to ask me. Because of the paucity of authoritative guidelines and literature on good record keeping, practitioners have trouble finding answers.

The purpose of this chapter is to answer the questions practitioners most frequently have asked me and provide a model of record keeping that promotes the integrity of clinical practice, whether with individuals, families, or groups. Having information and a system for record keeping can make it easier to create more consistent and comprehensive clinical records and prevent pitfalls.

The first section discusses the characteristics of good records. The subsequent section spells out key questions that need to be answered in good records. The third section presents essential contents of good records, and the following section describes what should not be included in records. The final section discusses options for methods of record keeping.

The following concepts are valuable to keep in mind whether records are on paper or electronic. Each clinical practice setting has its own forms or systems for organizing patient information. Ultimately, however, the method of cataloging is less important than the thoughtfulness professionals use in recording the information.

CHARACTERISTICS

Our records must convey, in humane, legible, and plain language, accurate and contemporaneous answers to "who, why, what, when, and how?" A good record is a clear "picture," or "mirror," of a patient. It contains a series of sketches that depict moments in time as well as historical processes: such as patients' history, needs, and the work they engage in during treatment to solve their problems. When we write records, we should be mindful that our clients or patients, their family members, and others could read the records and form impressions about the patient's experiences and about the quality of the therapy. Therefore our "pictures" must contain the hues and shades that define the patient's uniqueness and complexity. Anyone reading our records should be able to accurately identify the tools and techniques we used to evaluate, diagnose, and treat a patient, as well as unmistakable evidence that we made consistent, good-faith efforts to provide the best care possible and avoid causing harm.

Legible (to Self and Others)

Professional written records are legible; one reason why some agencies prefer electronic records is because they are, by nature, always legible. Legible records are essential for continuity of care and for the humane and responsible treatment of clients. Amazingly, this simple concept is lost on a staggering number of practitioners. For example, many talented therapists have conscientiously told me they believe they can best protect their patients by making their records illegible to anyone but themselves. However, even if legal rules or ethics codes did not require that we keep legible records, what would happen if we died tomorrow? How could our colleagues accurately understand our diagnosis and treatment plan and effectively attend to our patients' needs? If a patient's relatives had legitimate access and wanted to see a deceased relative's records after his suicide, would they be able to determine from the therapy records that we had treated their loved one competently and compassionately and took every precaution to prevent the death?

Germane

Good records include only information that is germane to diagnosis, goals, treatment, progress (or lack thereof), and outcomes. One of the most critical areas to include is any risk factor present in the client's condition or environment, for example, suicidal ideation, noncompliance with medication, or risk-taking behavior. Document each of these carefully, followed by recommendations to the client and all preventive actions taken.

Reliable

Notes should be empirical. They should identify the source of the information. If the information is subjective, it should be preceded by "The client stated...," or "The client said his employer stated..." If the information is objective, it should be preceded by "The patient trembled, cried, expressed anger, etc." If the therapist makes an interpretation or conclusion, it should be preceded by, "It appeared that..." or "It seemed that the client...," followed by facts from which those hypotheses developed.

Never include conclusions that cannot be supported theoretically or empirically, or that are prejudicial, such as "client seems to be a victim of sexual abuse," or "the client's mother was unnurturing," or "the client was manipulative."

Logical

Treatment plans follow logically from diagnoses. Progress notes should show treatment geared toward resolving the stated problems and goals. When I reviewed records in malpractice cases, psychotherapists have given the appearance of having acted improperly when their treatment approach did not follow logically from their diagnoses. In one case, for example, a therapist limited her treatment plan for a man who suffered a moderate major depressive disorder and suicidal ideation to "exploration of his early childhood experience." The treatment plan did not mention her attention to his symptoms of depression or the suicide warning signs that were specific to his case (e.g., his rage, reckless behavior, feelings of hopelessness and being trapped, his agitation and dramatic mood changes, his emotional and social withdrawal, and his lack of a sense of purpose in his life). She also did not document his access to guns; his moderate alcohol use; self-care issues such as inability to sleep, eat well, and exercise; or his lack of control over environmental stressors.

In another case involving a patient who was chronically suicidal, the therapist appropriately documented her referral to a dialectical behavior therapy (DBT) group and use of mentalization techniques in individual therapy to help the patient identify triggers for her anxiety and hopelessness, and options to care for herself. The second therapist's documentation showed a logical connection between the patient's chronic problems, need for self-soothing skills, and the treatment plan.

Prompt

Record progress notes promptly, preferably immediately after each session. Practitioners may jot down a few notes during sessions, but these sporadic words are usually too fragmented to convey a comprehensible summary of a session. Note taking during sessions needs to be kept to a minimum in order to attend to the patient. Case examples in Chapters 7 and 9 illustrate how a trainee's being drawn to his screen interrupted his ability to be emotionally responsive to his patient. "You can't tune in to the nuances of the patient if you are staring at your keyboard," as Glen Gabbard put it (personal communication, September 4, 2010).

Writing records during therapy sessions is like writing reviews of movies while watching them; we cannot absorb the full meaning of the movie and how its parts fit together until it is over. It is therefore vital to take a few moments immediately after sessions to summarize the essence, even in only a few sentences. Progress notes that practitioners generate after seeing six clients in a row, or that they write days or even weeks after a session are less reliable and more subject to error by intervening events. The "50-minute hour" emerged from the need to take 10 minutes between each session to record salient information and to care for one's self (e.g., bathroom breaks or other brief tasks).

Chronological

Keeping records chronologically for each session allows others to see that the records are complete and have not been tampered with.

KEY QUESTIONS TO ANSWER IN A GOOD RECORD

Clinical records paint a clear picture of the patient, what the therapist did, and why. In order to do this, the questions below can be addressed in clinical records:

- Who is requesting psychotherapy and for what purpose?
- Who is the client?
- What is my role?
- How would I describe the client? (Use empirical data.)
- What are the client's specific presenting problems? (According to client and collateral sources, if available.)

- What circumstances or events made the patient seek psychotherapy now? What does this patient say, in his or her own words, that he or she wishes could be different in his or her life? What are the patient's goals?
- What is the history of the patient's problems?
- What prior efforts has the patient made—successful and unsuccessful—in trying to solve his or her problems?
- What is the patient's life history, including development, school, family and other relationships, work, financial issues, physical and sexual abuse and neglect issues, alcohol use, nonprescription drug use, and current living arrangements?
- What is the patient's medical and psychiatric history, including any former diagnoses? (One may need to have permission to obtain previous records or speak with professionals who previously treated the client.)
- What further information will I require in order to understand the patient?
- Do I have the necessary consent to provide, receive, or exchange the information needed for treatment planning and clinical care?
- What safety issues, if any, for my client and for others must I consider?
- How can I minimize potential risks to the patient's safety or to the safety of others?
- What treatment plan can I develop collaboratively with the patient that might have the best chance of helping to solve this patient's specific problems and why?
- Do I require consultation or collaboration with others in order to make a diagnosis and treatment plan?
- What procedures would best facilitate the proposed treatment plan and what information makes me think so?
- Have I discussed with my patient information, which he or she can understand, regarding the diagnosis and proposed treatment with me, including possible risks and benefits of various treatments and no treatment?
- Have I discussed with my patient our respective rights and responsibilities?
- Have I informed my client of limitations to privacy and confidentiality?
- Has my patient (parents or legal guardians) consented to treatment?
- When and for how long are my sessions with the client?
- Is my client achieving the goals he or she set forth?
- If progress is unsatisfactory or if my patient is getting worse, have I made appropriate efforts to improve the treatment plan, such as consulting with another professional, referring the client to another professional, or recommending the termination of psychotherapy?
- Have I appropriately utilized resources to rule out the medical causes of my clients' problems, such as psychiatrists, neuropsychologists, neurologists, or others?

- How will I and my patient know when he or she is ready to terminate therapy?
- When termination occurs, have I summarized the problems, treatment intervention, and progress? Is the reason for and nature of termination clear to me and my client?
- What, if any, follow-up procedures do I need to recommend?
- Have I discussed follow-up procedures with my clients at termination?

ESSENTIAL CONTENTS OF GOOD RECORDS

The following outlines the essential contents of good records, which can help practitioners and their supervisees fulfill the various purposes of record keeping. The first part of this section describes the basic structure of the official record, including the phases of evaluation, treatment, and termination. The second part lists other essential contents to remember along the way.

Face Sheet—Demographics

Placing face sheet information at the front of a paper or electronic record allows immediate access to the information we frequently use (see CD and appendix for sample face sheet). It also promotes continuity of care when working with other practitioners. Face sheets may include, at minimum, the following information:

- Date of first appointment
- Client's name
- Date of birth
- Race
- Ethnicity
- English fluency or other language
- Address
- Home and work phone numbers, and which number is permissible to call as needed
- Emergency contacts
- Source of referral
- Legal guardianship information, as appropriate
- Name and address of the person or party responsible for payment of services
- Name and address of third-party payers
- Third-party payer subscriber and group numbers
- Diagnosis
- Name of psychotherapist or counselor
- Name of primary care provider

Evaluation

The evaluation is essential because it provides the basis for provisional diagnoses and decisions regarding services our clients may need. Treatment strategies should continuously refer back to the initial data and be modified later based upon additional assessment information. The initial evaluation also provides data that can be used to assess the client's progress or complete a treatment summary. Topics to include in an initial evaluation include the following:

- Identifying information
- Presenting problems
- History of problems
- Significant childhood and other life history
- Functional status and problems in biopsychosocial functioning
- Health and medical history
- Medications prescribed, if known
- Substance use
- Interview observations and mental status
- Symptoms supporting diagnoses
- Treatment plan
- Plan for collaboration, if any, with other clinicians, with family or caregivers
- Prognosis of treatment

Identifying Information

We start with identifying information that outlines the contour of our clients. As we explore further, we begin to see their complexity, richness, and uniqueness. The identifying information may include name, gender, age, ethnicity, marital status, number of children, occupation or school, living arrangements, reason for referral, and referral source.

The identifying information section can be brief. Here is an example:

Identifying Information: Nancy Jones, 48-year-old divorced African American woman employed as a hospital nurse, has physical and legal custody of her two daughters, ages 14 and 16, with whom she is living in her own home. She was referred by her psychiatrist, Dr. Adams, for psychotherapy to deal with stressors associated with her job.

Presenting Problems

Presenting problems are the problems for which patients seek help. Patients will often naturally share their reasons for seeking help in their own way and time. However, simple inquiries may help them to share what prompted them to seek help, or how they see the problem. The problems they mention, or problems they are reluctant to mention, help to provide focus and direction for the rest of the interview.

Therapist: What problems led you to seek help?
Patient: I'm upset.
I'm having problems with my supervisor.
I cry all the time.
My son and I are fighting all the time.

History of Problems

"There is no meaning without context" (Mishler, 1979). The client's history brings into focus the long journey that brought the client to us. It is one of the most critical aspects of the evaluation. Some of the questions that best elicit the client's history are found below:

- What (perhaps an event or feeling) made the client decide to ask us for help?
- When did the problems start? (onset)
- What was happening in the client's life when the problems began? (context)
- Who did what to whom during the course of the problems?
- What has the client tried in attempting to solve the problems?
- What strategies have been helpful or not helpful?
- What has made certain strategies helpful or not helpful?
- What would the client hope to change in his or her life?
- What type of help does the client want?

Significant Childhood and Other Life History

This section forms the backdrop to our client's picture, informing us about our patient's life experiences and patterns of behavior. It helps us formulate hypotheses about potential transference or other issues that we will experience with our clients and need to address, either within ourselves, in consultation with colleagues or supervisors, or, as appropriate, with our patients. It helps us know what kind of prognosis we might reasonably expect. In this section we include historical information such as the following:

- Birth experience, and circumstances surrounding birth
- Descriptions of parents, siblings, and home conditions
- Family relationships and themes in family life
- School performance and experience with school
- Childhood and adult friendships
- Employment and work functioning

It may be useful in gathering childhood and other life history to use genograms or other visual tools to help us understand the context and meaning to our patients of their childhood and other historical experiences and events.

Medical and Health History

When physical symptoms, such as the inability to sleep or eat properly, impair our patients' ability to function, it may not be possible for them to make use of psychotherapy. Also, what appear to be psychological problems may really be physiological. It is necessary to gather information regarding our client's past and present physical health, including history of illness or disability, eating patterns, physical activity, sleep quality, and tobacco use. This helps us know what medical and health needs they may have, what other professionals may already be involved in their care, what risk factors may apply, and what referrals and multidisciplinary collaboration may be necessary.

Substance Use

When patients are abusing substances such as alcohol or nonprescription drugs, they must first attend to these problems before they can make use of psychotherapy. Evaluation and documentation of substance use is an essential component of a good evaluation.

Interview Observations and Mental Status

In this section of our evaluation summary, we attempt to describe our clients in such a way that they can be readily visualized, either by ourselves or another professional who may need to provide service to them. The information in this section helps us further clarify what clinical intervention is necessary. Descriptions of our clients in this section include but are not limited to the following:

- Physical characteristics: Body build, hair color, type of clothing, grooming, facial expression
- Appropriateness of appearance to the situation
- Mental status: Affect, speech, mood, thought content, judgment, insight, memory, impulse control, attention, focus, concentration, and orientation to person, place, situation, and time; and observations at various junctures of the interview.

Diagnosis and Treatment Plan

Diagnoses should be based on a comprehensive evaluation, including the above information, other diagnostic tools, and collateral consultation if necessary. Treatment plans, in turn, should be based on diagnoses, including, when possible or appropriate, all five axes as described in the American Psychiatric Association's *Diagnostic and Statistical Manual of Mental Disorders,* fourth edition (1994) (*DSM IV*-TR). However, neither diagnoses nor treatment plans are static; they are subject to change based upon new information, the client's response to specific treatments or medications, or external events. Changes in diagnoses or treatment plans need to be documented in detail, with specific contemporaneous reasons for modifications. In this way, the clinician is consistently using a scientific model in which "working hypotheses" are tested and altered according to the client's current status and response to treatment and environmental factors.

See the CD and Appendixes B and C for a sample treatment plan form and sample revised treatment plan form that can be discussed in collaboration with patients as described in Chapter 9.

Ongoing Treatment Progress Notes

Progress notes document what occurs in therapy, especially whether clients are achieving the goals they identified in their treatment plans. Progress notes can be brief, often only a paragraph. But they should allow the reader (who could be anyone, including the patient) to see basic information: the date of the session, names of patient and therapist, therapist's degree, and content or focus of the session. Each progress note should show that what transpired in the session was relevant to the client's problems. Here are examples of progress notes showing a therapist's continuing focus on what the client stated were the problems and the treatment plan the client and she developed together.

> *10/31/11*: After reviewing her goals in the treatment plan we established last week (see individual treatment plan), Jane stated she still feels afraid of telling husband she is upset he continues to do volunteer work instead of getting a job. She stated she continues to feel like a "victim" in her marriage: she pays all the bills while her husband does what he pleases. She spoke about how she feels afraid to tell him she is angry over this unfair situation. To my question whether she has always felt afraid of confrontation, she described memories of her mother's anger at her when she was a young child. She felt afraid of her mother's anger. Her fear of her husband's anger feels reminiscent of what she felt with her mother. We discussed options for recognizing past experiences and anchoring herself in the present in order to clarify her options in the present for taking action to gain more control in her life.

> *11/7/11*: Jane stated she wants to be able to confront her husband about her need for him to contribute money to the family expenses but continues to feel afraid. She said she is having trouble focusing and thinking clearly, and that she "dissolves into tears" when she tries to talk with him. I discussed the possibility of depression and referred her to M. Smith, MD, for a psychiatric evaluation and discussion of whether she may be suffering from depression and whether she could benefit from an antidepressant.

11/14/11: Dr. Smith was able to see Jane immediately. She stated he prescribed Celexa, 20 mg daily. States she is already feeling calmer and feels able to think more clearly.

11/21/11: Jane reported she was able to talk frankly, without fear, with her husband. She told him she had been feeling distressed that he was spending his time volunteering rather than finding another job to reduce the debt he was incurring on her credit cards.

Termination or Closing Summary

The closing summary completes the picture. Gabbard (2009) observes considerable variation in termination and cites a wide range of reasons for termination: mutual agreement between patient and therapist based on achieving goals; preplanned termination based on agreed upon number of sessions; forced termination due to therapist's graduating or changing assignments, patient's relocating, or because the patient's third-party payer discontinues reimbursement; unilateral termination in which the patient feels there is no value in continuing; and unilateral termination due to therapist's belief there is no value in continuing and refers the patient elsewhere. He also describes some patients as "therapeutic lifers," for example, patients who manage as long as they are not expected to terminate (Gabbard, 2010). Whatever circumstance may precipitate the termination, the termination note summarizes the problems, treatment interventions, progress or lack thereof, and how treatment ended. A termination note can be brief; it should include the following:

- Problems for which client requested help
- Treatment given
- Progress, if any
- Reason for termination
- Statement of whether the therapist and client mutually agreed on the termination
- Status of termination: what recommendations have we given to our clients for addressing their ongoing problems? Have we advised our clients they may return as needed? Have we referred our clients elsewhere, and if so, to whom?

The closing summary should be written in narrative form in the patient's record. Practitioners can also document the closing on a form (see CD and Appendix D for sample form). Here is an example of a practitioner's closing or termination summary. Her summary provides an overview of the client's problems, what transpired during treatment, and the client's status at the end of treatment:

Ms. B. ended treatment with me today because her company assigned her to another human resources project in a city on the west coast. A 43 y.o., unmarried, Latina woman, employed as a human resources consultant, she was initially referred to me on 8/18/10 by Dr. Adams, her psychiatrist, who was treating her bipolar mood disorder. Ms. B.'s presenting problems included: history of relationship problems due to her mood swings, distress at not having enough time with significant other, concerns that significant other lacked interest in her, and inability to decide whether to improve the relationship or end it. Her mood instability improved with Lithium and she felt ready to begin psychotherapy. Her goals were to clarify her feelings and to explore what might help in regard to her relationship with her significant other.

Progress: She was seen in weekly individual sessions from 8/18/10 through 10/1/10; weekly joint counseling sessions with her significant other from 10/1/10 to 2/1/11; and monthly joint sessions with her significant other from 2/1/11 to 5/1/11. Initial phase of treatment provided education about the effects of her bipolar mood disorder and the need for a mood stabilizer, helped her to clarify how her condition affected her relationships with family and significant other, and what would be helpful to her in her relationship with her significant other. Joint counseling helped her discuss the strengths and problems in her relationship so she could clarify respective needs and negotiate these. Within 4 months of joint sessions, Ms. B. made progress in learning to speak about her experiences, feelings, and needs, and to articulate these to her partner. She identified appropriate communication tools for "fighting fairly" and practiced these with her significant other with encouraging results. Ms. B. has clarified she wants to remain in the relationship and is feeling more hopeful and stable in her relationship, but still is in the "practicing" phase of trying out the new communication skills she has learned. She feels she will need to continue in treatment in her new city to maintain her progress. I have provided her with names of colleagues in her new city: a psychiatrist who could prescribe medications and a psychotherapist with whom she can work in psychotherapy. With her permission, I have phoned them to discuss my referral. Case closed.

Other Essentials to Include

Now that we have discussed the "skeleton" or outline of our records, there are other essential contents we must keep in mind during documentation of evaluation and treatment.

Client's Name on Each Page

Practitioners can make occasional filing errors and having the client's name on each page prevents mix-ups. In the event that other persons need to access our records, they, too, can avoid confusion when the patient is identified on each page.

Date of Service, Therapist's Signature and Degree on Each Entry

When did the traumatic event happen in my patient's life? When did my patient and I discuss that upsetting event in therapy? When did I make that referral to the psychiatrist? When did I make that report to child protective services? Dates help us keep track. In order for our records to be honest, credible, and appropriate, dates of treatment need to be consistent with, although separate from, dates of service that appear in billing records. Finally, by signing each entry with our name and degree, it is clear to anyone who reads the record who provided the service.

Billing Records with Matching Dates, Type of Service, Length of Sessions, and Type of Payments

Clinical records should include a separate section devoted to billing. This documents when we rendered the sessions, the length and type of service we provided, the cost of services, and in what form the services were paid (e.g., cash, check, or credit card). Clear billing practices protect the practitioner by documenting financial transactions.

All financial arrangements, including flexible or special arrangements, need to be carefully noted. For example, therapists may make arrangements to reduce their fees or, in the case of indigent clients, provide services free of charge.

Consistent, predictable billing procedures help us maintain a structure for our clients and ourselves. When clients can take responsibility for keeping current with their payments, for example, or when they adhere to a consistent payment plan over time, they and therapists can feel more comfortable as participants in the therapeutic relationship. The billing record promotes an atmosphere of partnership in the fiscal domain of therapy.

Informed Consent Forms

Consent forms are the foundation of clinical treatment. They serve several important purposes. First, no clinical work can commence without permission from the client. This implies that the client be informed about all aspects of his or her psychotherapy and, more important, take responsibility for the serious process in which he or she intends to engage. Second, consent forms protect the practitioner by documenting an agreement, or contract, between the client and the practitioner. Third, consent forms enhance the client's emotional and mental motivation for effective treatment.

Consent forms should be thorough but easy to understand and should be discussed with the client before being signed. There are five general types of consent forms.

Consent to Provide Treatment

Unless there are extraordinary circumstances, consent to proceed with an evaluation or with treatment is necessary before practitioners can begin providing services (see Chapter 2). Psychotherapists continue obtaining consent to treatment during evaluations when discussing diagnostic impressions and treatment recommendations, and during treatment when new diagnoses and revised treatment plans emerge. For treatment situations with involuntary patients, which involve built-in disclosure requirements (e.g., with persons referred by forensic units or by courts), practitioners must state the purpose of treatment and identify what information is required to be sent to whom and by when. Clinicians should note in their records when these discussions occurred and the general context of the discussion. In addition to verbal agreement, it is best for the client to sign and date a form consenting to treatment. This form needs to be easy to find in the record. (A time-saving and therapeutically useful method to document informed consent to treatment is to create and cosign the treatment plan with the patient. The CD and Appendix B include a sample treatment plan form that can be developed and signed by both practitioner and patient to demonstrate the patient's understanding and consent to treatment. Trainees or other practitioners in supervision can also use these forms to indicate clients' understanding and consent to supervisors' review of their cases and records.)

Consent for Billing

Patients' consent for billing needs to be documented. Therapists should identify in writing, prior to beginning treatment, who is responsible for payment of services; whether the client requests bills be sent to a third party, and if so, what information will need to be sent for processing claims; and to whom the third-party reimbursement will be made. The CD, as noted in Appendix K, includes examples of statements that clients can sign to indicate their understanding and consent to billing policies and procedures.

Consent for Treatment of a Minor Child

With very few exceptions, therapists cannot treat minors without written consent from the child's parent or legal guardian. Failure to assiduously adhere to this rule can lead to serious legal action against therapists for asking the wrong parent for consent to treat a minor child. For example, a desperate therapist called me to say he had contact only with a child's mother, who was divorced from the child's father. The mother had initiated treatment for her daughter and had been bringing the child to treatment. The therapist had carefully obtained the mother's consent to treat her minor child. Unfortunately, the therapist had failed to ask the mother whether she had legal custody of the child. He discovered she did not have legal physical custody, and therefore had no authority to give the therapist permission to treat her minor child. The therapist did not discover the problem until the child's father, who did have legal custody, learned of his daughter's treatment and became angry at the therapist.

In addition to obtaining consent to treatment from the legally authorized parent, I have found it is also important to discuss the delicate issues of confidentiality when treating minor children. For example, it is critical that parents or legal guardians understand how important it is to balance parents' or guardians' need for essential information against the children's need for confidentiality. Even when such a discussion may not be legally binding, I ask parents or guardians to sign a form indicating that they understand the need for this delicate balance. (See the CD and Appendix E for an example of a statement and consent form for treatment of a minor child.)

In situations when therapists believe minors can receive services under their own authorization, therapists must document what minors have represented to them to lead the therapists to believe this. For example, in a number of states, minors may independently seek assistance around pregnancy or sexual health; in Minnesota, a minor who has been married, who has borne a child, or who is living away from home and managing financial decisions can consent. The National Association of Social Workers (NASW) has published a helpful and detailed review of the legal rights of children in all 50 states (NASW, 2010).

Consent for Disclosures to Third Parties

Practitioners need to obtain valid signed authorization for releases of confidential information to third parties that are outside of the routine provision of a patient's care. (See Chapter 4 for a discussion of ethical requirements and Chapter 6 for a discussion of policies and procedures.) Practitioners can usually obtain guidelines for contents of authorization forms from their own professional regulatory boards or from their professional associations. Practitioners who are covered under the Health Insurance Portability and Accountability Act (HIPAA) can find authorization requirements in the amendments to the rule (Federal Register, 2002). (For sample authorization of release of information forms, see CD and Appendix F.) Information necessary in an authorization form for release of patient-identifiable information generally includes

- Client's full name and address, with an identifier (e.g., birth date or social security number to prevent mistaken identity)
- Name and address of person or organization to receive the information
- Specific information requested

- Purposes for releasing the confidential information (e.g., "to clarify diagnosis and treatment planning")
- Date or event when authorization expires (in some states it is 1 year; others 6 months)
- Client's right to revoke consent at any time, except to the extent action in reliance on the consent has already happened
- Client's or guardian's signature and date
- Witnesses' signature and date
- Any consequences for refusing to sign
- Notarization if necessary

Record of Disclosure

A record of disclosures should be kept in the patient's file and should answer the following questions:

- Date and time of disclosure
- Type of disclosure (e.g., electronic, telephone, fax)
- Purpose of the disclosure
- Organization or individual, including address, to whom the information was disclosed
- Information disclosed
- Copy of signed and dated authorization for release of information

Consent for Audio- or Videotaping Sessions

Therapists also need to obtain patients' signed informed consent for the electronic recording of sessions. Consistent with other consent forms, information includes patient name(s) and birth dates, type of permission granted, specific purpose for which electronic recording will be used (e.g., "for therapist's education, to be discussed with clinical supervisor"), what individual(s) will have access to the recording, duration of consent, and how long recording will be retained in patient's file. Schoener (personal communication, August 10, 2010) notes that when the purpose of the tape is to have a way of reviewing what occurred, as was the case with Martin Orne's treatment of Anne Sexton, normally the therapist tapes over the tape and does not have many on file. Orne, however, for reasons that are unclear, saved them and then later, after Ms. Sexton's suicide, provided her biographer, Diane Middlebrook, with more than 110 tapes of sessions.

Referrals

We have a professional duty to recognize the limitations of our abilities. If we cannot complete a thorough assessment, formulate a diagnosis, or provide the kind of treatment a patient needs, we need to refer the patient to another professional.

The date, reasons for the referral, and to whom the patient was referred should be recorded in the client's file. For example,

> *8/1/11*: I referred Emily to Dr. Smith, psychiatrist at the university student health center, for psychiatric evaluation of her symptoms of depression and whether antidepressant medication would be helpful.

> *12/5/11*: I spoke with Johnny's mother and suggested she take him to his pediatrician, Dr. Jones, for evaluation of the "weird feelings" he reported having in his head.

Preventive Action Taken

If, at any phase of evaluation or treatment, patients become dangerous to themselves or to others, it is essential that practitioners document preventive action. Examples of preventive actions include discussions with patients, use of a structured violence risk assessment instrument, consultations with other professionals, referrals, increased level of clinical care, and legally mandated reporting. Issues for which practitioners may take various kinds of preventive action may include suicide ideation and planning, patients' wish to act upon sexual or violent feelings or intent toward therapists, suspected abuse of children, suspected abuse of vulnerable adults, or foreseeable intent to kill an identified person. In addition to the other preventive measures noted above, in order to meet the standard of care, it is critical to ask patients whether they have a gun or other weapon. Other problems in therapy that may also require some type of preventive action include therapists' strong feelings of attraction, anger, or anxiety, and therapists' physical or mental conditions that impair their ability to practice safely. While it is usually inappropriate for psychotherapists to document their own personal problems in a client's record, it is important to record preventive steps they took to promote patient welfare, such as obtaining professional consultation or terminating treatment due to the therapist's personal incapacitation.

Suicide Warning Signs

The importance of contemporaneously documenting suicide warning signs and our discussions with our clients about their preoccupations such as relationships, work, or self, that cause them to feel suicidal cannot be overstated (Jobes & O'Connor, 2008). It protects patients as well as therapists. Consider the following case example of a competent therapist who became vulnerable to erroneous charges of negligence only because she did not document her conscientious efforts to prevent her patient's suicide.

When patients are suicidal, it is important for practitioners to document the following:

A deceased patient's mother claimed in a legal case that her son's psychotherapist had not taken appropriate action to prevent his suicide. The therapist responded that she had, in fact, taken the following appropriate preventive action. First, she discussed with her patient his despair over his chronic mental illness that made him think of suicide, and she asked him what ideas he had about how he would kill himself. The client stated he was not going to kill himself. She asked him if he had guns in the house or his car or office, and he denied having any guns available to him anywhere. Next, knowing that her client was still at risk given his age (30), gender (male), and history of previous suicide attempts, the therapist repeatedly consulted the client's psychiatrist about his suicide ideation and suicide plan and referred him to the psychiatrist or emergency room (ER) for an immediate reevaluation when he was feeling suicidal.

Unfortunately, the therapist had not documented her discussions with her patient about his symptoms of depression and suicide thoughts and plan, her consultation with his psychiatrist, her specific questions related to suicide warning signs and availability of weapons or other means to kill himself, or her referral of her patient to a psychiatrist for an emergency evaluation. The jury could not tell whether she had done what she claimed. Her failure to record her preventive actions gave the erroneous appearance that she had irresponsibly contributed to her client's death, which undermined her defense in the legal case.

- Current psychosocial variables and stressors, mood disorder, anxiety disorder or personality disorder, substance dependence or abuse, history of emotionally painful family history and abuse, impulsivity
- Recent evidence of passive or active suicide ideation and planning, such as whether client stated he or she was thinking of killing himself or herself and had a plan; whether there were other behaviors suggestive of risk, such as writing a suicide note, recently making a will or funeral arrangements, and so forth
- Assessment of other risk factors including race, gender, age, psychiatric history, alcohol use, history of previous suicide attempts, history of another family member's suicide, social isolation, and accessibility of a gun or other weapon
- Presence of protective factors that limit risk of suicidality, such as a strong support system, ability to problem solve and exercise self-control, strength of therapeutic alliance, ability to establish a therapeutic plan, including goals to increase ability to cope

To protect one's self and one's patient, it is critical to inquire about whether the patient possesses or has access to a gun or other weapon (Jobes, Overholser, Rudd, & Joiner, 2008). When therapists fail to inquire about weapon ownership, they may have no defense when charged with failure to prevent their patient's death. For example, forensic expert Tom Gutheil has expressed to attorneys his reluctance to be retained by the psychiatric malpractice defense side of a suicide case where the clinician has not inquired about weapon ownership (Gutheil, T., personal communication, February 3, 2011).

In ongoing work with suicidal patients, many therapists are now using crisis plans. These are cards on which patients list the things they will do if they feel suicidal. They are designed to help patients prevent suicide. Patients can take the card with them after a session and leave a copy with the therapist for the file. These crisis plans are replacing "no suicide contracts," which experts have now discredited (Jobes et al., 2008).

Here is an example of a psychotherapist's documentation of a patient's suicide risk, the therapist's process of clinical decision making, and the preventive actions he took to prevent suicide:

> Ricardo, 25, who immigrated to the United States 10 years ago, has been suffering from moderate major depressive disorder for 6 months. He has been on an antidepressant for 3 months, under the care of Dr. Moreno, his psychiatrist. While his symptoms of depression improved after taking the antidepressant, he stated he has recently been feeling hopeless, is having difficulty concentrating, focusing, sleeping, and eating. It has been 6 months since his girlfriend died in a tragic car accident. Dr. Moreno and I have been treating his grief and posttraumatic stress. He states now that he is "obsessing" about her death "more than ever." He hates himself, and he blames himself for his girlfriend's death because he was driving the car when the truck skidded over the barrier on the highway and collided with them. Two days ago, he began thinking actively about dying, and, to my question, told me of his specific plan to kill himself: he would drive himself over the bridge near his home. To my question regarding whether he had any guns or other weapons, he denied having any guns or other weapons. I am aware of other potential risk factors for suicide, including that his sister killed herself when she was 15, he is living alone, he recently was laid off from his job, and he recently resumed drinking alcohol after 2 years of sobriety. I asked Ricardo what reasons he might have to live, and he told me of his close relationship with his younger brother and his brother's family. He was aware that his brother would be very hurt if he killed himself and did not want to hurt his brother.

In Ricardo's presence, I called Dr. Moreno's office to request emergency consultation. Dr. Moreno agreed with me that it could be helpful to obtain Ricardo's permission to bring his brother into an extra session that I would schedule so we could further discuss his crisis and enlist his brother's support. After sharing Dr. Moreno's suggestions, Ricardo and I discussed his crisis plan until we could meet tomorrow with his brother. Ricardo created the following plan: (a) he did not feel he could act upon his suicidal thoughts because of his strong Catholic faith and his close relationship with his brother; (b) he felt able to call me or Dr. Moreno's on-call colleague or get himself to the emergency room at the hospital should he feel like he might act on his wish to kill himself; (c) he agreed to stop drinking, contact his Alcoholics Anonymous (AA) sponsor, and attend an AA meeting tonight; (d) he said he would keep his appointment with Dr. Moreno tomorrow morning; (e) he planned to attend his company's human resources meeting next week in order to learn about alternative work options; and (f) he will return with his brother to see me tomorrow at 11:00 a.m. Ricardo and I documented on his crisis card all of the steps that he plans to do to help himself move through his despair and suicidal feelings. He is taking the plan home with him to help him remember to follow through. (See copy of his crisis plan in his file.)

Duty to Warn or Protect

When clients make serious, convincing, and specific threats of harm against a specific, clearly identified victim, practitioners need to make reasonable efforts to assess risk of violence, prevent violence, and document they have done so. Interventions might include using a structured assessment instrument to assess risk of violence, trying to diffuse the anger, trying to dissuade the client from violent solutions, asking the client's permission to discuss the situation with significant others, attempting to help the client to give up weapons or put away weapons, or enlisting family members' help to seek solutions. When clinical interventions fail to prevent risk of harm to an intended victim, practitioners need to communicate the threat to the potential victim or, if unable to make contact with the potential victim, to the law enforcement agency closest to the potential victim or to the patient making the threat. The duty becomes even stronger when practitioners have knowledge of the client's past violent behavior or past careless behaviors (e.g., reckless drunken driving which appeared suicidal or homicidal) and current symptoms of depression. Practitioners must prepare themselves for such contingencies by informing themselves about their own states' legal regulations governing "duty to warn or protect" situations. They can obtain information about their specific duties by asking their regulatory boards for information or by consulting their attorney. Answers to the following questions must be recorded in the record:

- What was the specific threat and toward whom, in the client's own words? For example: "I have a gun and I am so angry at my ex-wife that I am going to kill her when she returns to her home tonight from work." Or, "I have been learning how to build a bomb from instructions on the Internet... I am building the bomb now in my basement...so I can blow up my school and get back at the kids that have been calling me names."
- Was the threat imminent? For example, "I am going to drive over to my ex-wife's house right now and kill her." Or, "I am going to blow up my school tomorrow morning."
- Or not imminent? For example, "One of these days I am going to kill my ex-wife ... mark my words." Or, "If the kids don't stop bullying me, after I finish building the bomb, I will blow up the school."
- What efforts did I make to diffuse the patient's anger, help him give up the weapon, and decrease risk of violence?
- What consultation did I obtain in order to clarify the risk of violence and preventive action I could take (if the threat is not imminent and there is time to get consultation). For example, "I excused myself from the session and placed an emergency call to Dr. Smith, Joe's psychiatrist, to get his consultation in this crisis. He agreed it is necessary to call Joe's ex-wife at her work and warn her of Joe's threat so she can take steps to protect herself. He suggested I give Joe's ex-wife names of resources, such as the name and telephone number of a shelter for battered women."
- Whom did I contact in order to protect the intended victim from specific threat? (Names of intended victim, or law enforcement agency, addresses, and telephone numbers.)
- What did I state to the intended victim or law enforcement agency? For example, "I stated I was calling her because her ex-husband, Joe, just left my office. I informed her he said he was very angry at her and said he was planning to kill her tonight after she arrived home after work. I stated I had tried very hard to diffuse his anger and dissuade him, but he left very angry. I told her I cannot predict dangerousness for certain, but I believe he is capable of carrying out his threat. I stated the reason I am calling is that I have a legal duty to warn her in order to do my best to protect her from harm. Joe's wife sounded scared and appeared to take Joe's threat seriously. I stated further that she may already have an idea how she can protect herself from harm, but gave her the name of a shelter where women can go to be safe when they are in danger...I asked her to write it down."

- What did the intended victim or law enforcement official state in response? For example: "Sergeant Nelson of the third precinct stated he would immediately 'dispatch an officer to the ex-wife's home so that an officer would be there if Joe arrives.'"
- What was the outcome of the threat?

Duty to Report Suspected Child or Vulnerable Adult Abuse or Neglect

As discussed under exceptions to confidentiality (Chapter 5), practitioners need to know their state's legal requirements for reporting suspected abuse or neglect and document all reports they make to protective agencies. They need to inquire how soon their states require that they submit mandated reports of suspected abuse or neglect. Practitioners are not in the role of investigator. When they have reason to suspect abuse or neglect, it is always appropriate to consult with the relevant protective services to determine whether the situation is reportable. Documentation of reports of suspected abuse and neglect follows the same format for documentation in any duty-to-report situation. The following need to be included:

- Client's identifying information (name, address, phone number)
- Practitioner's name and title and address
- What the client stated that led the practitioner to note suspected abuse or neglect
- What preventive action the practitioner took
- What consultation the practitioner obtained
- Name and telephone number of the organization and person the practitioner called to report the suspected abuse
- Response of that person
- Follow-up plans

The following is an example of documentation of suspected child abuse:

3/2/12: In her individual session today Mary stated that she was unable to control her anger with her 5-year-old daughter, Nancy: "I started drinking again because I felt so depressed. This morning I was in a hurry to get to work. I felt furious with Nancy because she could not decide what clothes to wear. I slapped her really hard on the face, leaving welts and bruises." After listening to Mary's account of her behavior with her daughter and wish to be in control of her behavior, I recommended we work together to clarify ways she can control her anger. She agreed. I also explained that I am legally mandated to report suspected child abuse to the child protective agency. Mary chose to make the report with me. I placed the call, spoke with Ms. Anderson, intake worker, of the White County Child Protective Services (CPS) at 9:00 a.m. I reported Mary was in my office, willing to make the report of suspected child abuse herself. Mary took the phone from me and reported all of the above information to Ms. Anderson and answered her questions. Ms. Anderson then told me that the agency would take the report and determine what, if any, action to take. After making the report to CPS, I then helped Mary consider options for controlling her anger with her daughter. Impression: Mary's starting to drink alcohol again reduced her capacity to maintain control over her impulsive behavior and anger. She wants to change and appears motivated and capable of identifying and taking necessary steps to control her behavior. After discussing specific options, Mary agreed to follow this plan: (a) she will stop drinking; (b) she will resume AA meetings near her job each week on Friday at noon; (c) she will apologize to her daughter for slapping her; (d) she will tell her daughter she is getting help to control her behavior in the future; (e) she will talk with her daughter about ways to reduce stress in the morning, such as choosing and setting out school clothes the night before; and (f) she will cooperate with CPS staff if they call and keep her appointment scheduled with me for next week to have my support and monitor her progress.

Duty to Report Mistreatment or Abuse or Neglect of Elder

The following is an example of documentation of suspected financial abuse of an elderly patient and of a report the clinical social worker made to adult protective services:

9/22/11: Ms. G., an 80-year-old woman, was referred to me for supportive psychotherapy 10 months ago after her husband died and she fell on the ice and fractured her leg. After her discharge from the hospital, her 55-year-old unemployed son-in-law, who rents the lower level of her duplex with his wife and teenage children (her daughter and granddaughters), assumed responsibility as her personal health attendant. He also has been assisting her with her tax returns. Her home health aide reported to me that Ms. G. began worrying recently that money appears to be disappearing from her bank account. Ms. G. stated to me that she fears her son-in-law is stealing from her. She is afraid to talk with him about it because she relies on his help and does not want to do anything to harm the relationship. I contacted the adult protection services and spoke with Ms. McClinton, intake worker, who took these alleged facts and stated her department will conduct an investigation. (See CD for "Sample Record of Disclosures" form to document this mandated report.)

Duty to Report Threats Against the President of the United States

Reports of specific threats or plans to kill the president of the United States need to be documented in the record, as well. The format for documentation of such reports to the federal agencies (Federal Bureau of Investigation [FBI] or Secret Service) is similar to documentation of other legally mandated reports: identifying information of client and practitioner, the threat the client stated, date and time of report, to whom the report was made, response of the individual receiving the report, and follow-up actions.

Ethical Dilemmas and Controversial Clinical Decisions

Although ethical dilemmas and the need to make clinical decisions that appear controversial might arise rarely, decision making is necessary to document. This is because one approach does not fit every clinical situation. There are instances when practitioners' rigidity can be detrimental to their patients. While ethics codes explicitly proscribe only a few behaviors (such as sexual contact with clients and treating clients when the practitioner is seriously impaired), in most clinical decisions, therapists must weigh relative benefits and risks to clients (Gartrell, 1992; Schoener, 2010). Examples of ethical dilemmas include whether to disclose personal information about one's self, whether to accept from or give gifts to patients, whether to schedule evening appointments or to make home visits, whether to accept invitations to clients' social events or funerals, whether to acknowledge clients on social media or social networking Web sites, whether to extend a treatment session beyond the scheduled ending time, whether to make home visits, and whether to treat a client's family members, neighbor, or close friend.

What matters most is whether we have conscientiously considered and weighed the various relevant factors in arriving at such clinical decisions. When documenting our decision making, it can be helpful to state in the record how we have considered five key principles:

Beneficence: Is it likely to help the patient?
Nonmaleficence: Is it unlikely to harm the client?
Autonomy: Is it likely to foster the patient's autonomy by respecting client's choices and role in decision making?
Fidelity: Is it consistent with my professional role and the expectations my client has of me?

Justice: Does it balance the needs or rights of one person versus others who may be involved? (Beauchamp & Childress, 2009)

The following discussion shows how a therapist handled complicated decisions regarding management of her client's expression of romantic feelings toward her at the end of his session.

Dr. Melfi, the female psychotherapist in the HBO television series, "The Sopranos," (Renzulli & Taylor, 1999) made a decision to end a treatment session with her male patient at exactly the scheduled time, even though her patient had just professed his interest in how she dressed and had walked across the office to kiss her at the end of the session. As her patient approached her, she appeared motionless but ultimately averted his kiss. She appeared to be keenly aware that patients kissing their therapists was inappropriate in therapy, and understood her professional responsibility to talk with her client about his strong feelings that he had just acted out. But she always adhered impeccably to ending each session promptly after 50 minutes. She stated to her patient that it was important that they speak about the strong feelings he had just expressed for her, but because it was the end of the hour, would he be able to return for another appointment later in the day? Conscientiously sticking to the scheduled time frame of her clinical appointments was normally helpful, but in this instance it was not. Because of his work schedule, the client was unable to return for another appointment. Ending the session exactly on time and not taking a few moments to discuss what had just happened meant the therapist missed the opportunity to bring closure prior to ending the session.

Even when practitioners realize later that a decision was not ideal, they need to document their decision and reasons for it. I do not know how the conscientious therapist in the above example documented her complicated session. In her progress note, it might have been appropriate to document her decision making in this way:

> At the end of the session, Mr. Soprano stated that he wished his wife would dress in a "sexy" way. He stated he was attracted to women who dressed in an "understated way" and who were "gentle and sweet," like me, he said. He then walked over to me and kissed me on the mouth before I could push him away. Because kissing is not therapy, I told him that we needed to discuss what just happened. Because it was the end of the session, however, and it is my usual procedure to maintain consistency of scheduled time for appointments, I stated we needed to end the appointment and offered him an appointment for later in the day. He stated he was unable to return later today. Impression: The important issues he spoke about and acted upon did

not have appropriate closure in this session. Plan: I will raise these issues with him in the next session. Will speak with him about (a) my reflections on how we did not have time to speak about his feelings in this week's session; (b) how his feelings of attraction toward me are a natural response to therapy, but that communication in therapy is limited to words; and (c) in future sessions we need to consider ways he can bring up important feelings earlier in his sessions so we will have sufficient time to discuss them before the end of the session. In addition to talking with him next week, I have requested clinical consultation to discuss the most helpful way to manage these erotic transference feelings.

In another case, involving a similar clinical issue, an adult male client said his former therapist had handled a difficult situation appropriately. He said his previous therapist had reminded him of his mother, whom he regarded as an "angel." She had helped him so much in therapy that he felt indebted to her. Before one of his sessions with his former therapist, he said he felt "impulsive" and "wanted to provoke" his therapist into "becoming angry" with him. He said he therefore walked into his therapy session and, to his therapist's question about what he was feeling, announced: "I am in love with my therapist." His statement seemed to catch her off guard and elicited exactly the response he said he had wanted to provoke: his therapist did become angry with him, and she quickly responded: "Well, if that is how you feel, we need to end therapy." As he recalled, his former therapist then seemed to realize the situation required another response: she switched gears and spoke with him in an accepting and educative way about how feelings toward one's therapist can be discussed and not acted upon in therapy. The client told me how much he appreciated her acceptance of his feelings, her limits for his impulsive behavior, and her not abandoning him.

Interestingly, in her progress note of that session, the therapist documented other issues she and the patient had discussed on that day, but not his erotic provocation or how she had handled it. I cannot know why she did not record this clinically significant incident. However, practitioners often leave out significant events in therapy records when they may feel personally uncomfortable or embarrassed by the situation or when they have not known how to handle it. Had she documented this complex interaction, here is how she might have done it:

Patient began session by abruptly stating: "I am falling in love with my therapist." After I suggested we could end therapy if he felt that way, and he got up from his chair and said "okay" and prepared to leave, I realized it would be more helpful to him for me to allow him to discuss his feelings. I therefore invited him to discuss the feelings he had just shared with me, which he did. I shared it is common for patients to develop strong feelings toward their therapists that can feel like love, that these feelings are useful to discuss in therapy and understand, but are not acted upon. Patient explained he told me he was falling in love with me because he had wanted me to "get angry" at him. He appeared calmer and relieved after our discussion of his feelings and how we would handle his feelings in therapy, and he went on to discuss his efforts in the past week to have better communication with his wife. For example, he stated...

Coordination and Continuity of Care between Professionals Caring for the Client

There are many occasions arising at different junctures during treatment when effective care requires coordination with other professionals. For example, (a) when patients have been treated previously, it may be helpful to speak with their prior practitioners or read their records; (b) when minor children are involved in emotionally or physically unsafe peer relationships in school, it can be helpful to consult with their teachers; (c) when clients are depressed, suicidal, or have somatic complaints, it can be helpful to refer them to psychiatrists or other appropriate professionals for evaluation and medication and to consult with them periodically; and (d) when patients have multiple problems or complex conditions and require multiple health care providers, such as psychotherapist, home health nurse, independent living services worker, primary care provider, and specialists. Names and titles of all persons consulted, whether by phone or in a case conference, need to be documented in the record as well as the content of the consultation or meeting. Unfortunately, increasing pressure on psychotherapists to see more patients in the same amount of time and for less money may deter them from obtaining collateral data. This diminishes continuity of care and increases the risk to patients and others. As a result, psychotherapy training programs may omit the importance of collaborating with appropriate practitioners and otherwise ensuring appropriate care. Nevertheless, this crucial aspect of competent treatment should be observed and documented.

Practitioners may choose to retain copies of other professionals' records in their entirety, extract essential parts relevant to the patient's therapy and discard the rest, or document what they have received and found relevant and then discard it all. In any case, it is useful for therapists to state in the patients' records whatever collateral information they have relied upon to formulate diagnoses and treatment plans. Out of respect for other professionals, I do not forward copies of their records when I receive valid authorizations for release of my patients' records. My own brief documentation in the record regarding what I have relied upon is sufficient and allows other professionals to remain in charge of their own decisions regarding to whom they release their own records.

Communications and Materials from Patients

All electronic and paper correspondence with patients become part of the official record. Mental health professionals providing psychotherapy or counseling need to decide how they can manage and store other written communications or personal materials clients may bring to them, such as poems, journals, original photos, or newspaper articles. I return to my patients their original photos and family documents, which are invaluable to them and future generations. Sometimes patients' requests for therapists to retain personal materials may become a focus of clinical work. For example, a 55-year-old woman in advanced stages of breast cancer was fearful that others could gain access to her prior medical records and requested her therapist store a large box containing copies of her records in the therapist's office. The therapist acknowledged the patient's fears and wish for her therapist to provide a safe container for her sensitive and private information, but respectfully declined the patient's request, realistically noting her file cabinet lacked sufficient space. More important clinically, however, she helped this woman to speak about her feelings and needs: her desire for her therapist to help shoulder her burden, the shame she felt regarding the contents of her records, and possible alternative solutions for storage of the records, including whom she could trust to have access to her private information after her death. The therapist documented the essence of these meaningful existential discussions in her patient's record.

What Not to Include

In the section on characteristics of good records, I stress the importance of including only what is relevant and germane to clients' problems and treatment. It makes common sense therefore that anything irrelevant to the diagnosis and treatment plan should not be included. Other examples of contents that should not be included in records are the following.

Countertransference Fantasies

Common forms of countertransference feelings may include rescue fantasies, boredom or sleepiness, erotic feelings, and feelings of helplessness or incapacitation (Gabbard, 2010). For example, patients with borderline personality disorder and history of victimization frequently elicit strong feelings in therapists, such as rescue fantasies, "splitting" from colleagues, or temptations to bend usual procedures, such as not billing for missed appointments (Gabbard & Wilkerson, 1994; Luepker, 1989). While countertransference feelings are valuable tools that allow practitioners to see patients from a different perspective and help therapists to monitor the meaning of their responses, the patients' records are not the place to document them. Documentation of countertransference impressions in the official record does not contribute to the purpose or quality of the record and may burden the patient if the patient reads the record.

A better strategy is to obtain consultation and to document that we received consultation regarding our questions and hypotheses about the client's diagnosis and treatment. It is appropriate to note whom we consulted and what insights and strategies we developed. In the following example, the therapist was able to document consultation for problems she was having appropriately managing her own feelings in treatment with an impulsive patient, without including her own countertransference reactions in the official record. Even though she discussed her countertransference problems with her consultant, her documentation about the consultation in the patient's record appropriately remained focused on the patient's needs in treatment:

> *11/21/11*: Consulted Dr. Smith regarding Jane Doe's missed appointments and cries for help in her frequent telephone calls to me in between sessions. Dr. Smith confirmed the importance of establishing firm structure. Strategies we discussed: (a) remind patient of policy to give 24-hour notice of missed appointments; (b) remind her of office procedure to charge for missed appointments without 24-hour notification; (c) discuss importance of being able to provide adequate attention to her needs, thus request she bring issues to appointments rather than call in between sessions; and (d) clarify together in writing on individual treatment plan her problems, specific goals, and procedures in treatment.

When practitioners wish to recall their own feelings in order to discuss them with consultants or supervisors, they may choose to write them in "psychotherapy notes." These are meant for their eyes only and are kept separate from the official record.

Sensitive Information

Practitioners understand that explicit documentation of sensitive information such as patients' sexual orientation, details of sexual intimacy, history of sexual abuse, or abortion may be upsetting or detrimental to the patient to read in their records. However, in cases involving certain types of traumatic events, it may ultimately be helpful to have detailed documentation.

Improper Alterations of Records

Information in records needs to be accurate; however, when practitioners delete or change information contained in the narratives of their patients' records, it may give the impression they have done something wrong that they wish to hide.

Occasional errors in our narratives are expected, and we are judged by what we knew or believed at a given point in time. Changes can be potentially confusing. It is better therefore not to change the record. Instead, we can simply add a new note, with updates, corrections, and current date. For example, a therapist documented in an initial evaluation summary that his patient Mary had two sisters and was psychiatrically hospitalized once when she was 25. Months later Mary reviewed her record and discovered a couple of factual errors: she informed the therapist she has three, not two sisters, and had been hospitalized twice, not once. The therapist documented Mary's new information on the date the patient reported it to him. "1/4/11. Mary discovered errors in my intake evaluation summary: she has three sisters, not two, and was previously hospitalized twice for symptoms of mania, not once. The second hospitalization occurred when she was 28, during…"

Details Regarding Clients' Privileged Communications with Attorneys

Clients require support in order to survive severe stresses of litigation and may use their treatment sessions to discuss their lawsuits, including discussions with their attorneys. However, clients' communication with their attorneys is privileged. When therapists document clients' communications with attorneys, other persons who are involved in clients' lawsuits become privy to such information and clients' privilege is lost. When patients' discussions with their attorneys become a relevant focus of treatment, practitioners can document the focus of sessions by citing the material in general ways, without revealing specific data that are privileged. For example, "Client discussed matters related to her upcoming court case. The process of litigation continues to be a serious stressor."

Psychotherapy Notes: Therapists' Notes to Self

"Psychotherapy notes" (HIPAA term) or "psychotherapy process notes" (detailed interactions with patients and therapists' reactions during interviews which trainees document for learning purposes or which experienced practitioners may document when we need to learn from further reflection on interviews) are notes used only for the therapist's own purposes, including for consultation or supervision, and are kept separately from the official medical record.* Examples might include practitioners' notes to themselves regarding counteretransference reactions they wish to remember in discussion with their clinical consultants;

---

* Per HIPAA's definition, a "Medical Record" (in contrast to "Psychotherapy Notes") includes the following: intake information, billing information, formal evaluations, notes of collateral contacts with other clinicians, notes of contact with any members of patient's social/employment network, records obtained from other providers, counseling/psychotherapy sessions start and stop times, the modalities and frequencies of treatment furnished, medication prescribed, all formal diagnoses, functional status and problems in biopsychosocial functioning, description of treatment plan(s), description of observable symptoms supporting diagnoses, description of prognosis of treatment, and description of treatment progress to date (Groshong, Myers, & Schoolcraft, 2010).

or topics they wish to explore further with their clients; or names of significant persons in the clients' lives that they may wish to recall, any of which might be inappropriate to document in the official record. When we take a few moments after each session to summarize in the official record the essence of what transpired during the psychotherapy session in our progress notes, these "psychotherapy notes" may eventually become unnecessary. Shredding them periodically helps to prevent them from accidentally and inappropriately ending up in clients' official records or their being discovered in legal cases or licensure complaints.

METHOD OF RECORD KEEPING: DOES IT MATTER?

In my opinion, it does not matter what methods practitioners choose to use, as long as the records clearly and appropriately portray why the client is seeking help, that the treatment is focused on the clients' presenting problems, whether there is progress, that appropriate professional action is taken, and that they facilitate understanding of the patient and coordination of care among multiple professionals. There are different types of methods that practitioners use, such as the "SOAPIE" problem-oriented record keeping method, which emphasizes the problems and how the treatment addresses the problem, or the "Focus Charting" record keeping method, which emphasizes the focus of treatment (Townsend, 1999). I use the outline of categories I have presented above. It stays consistently focused on clients' problems, states sources of information, and remains focused on the clinical interventions to address the problems. Some practitioners format their records as narratives to patients in order to cover essential information.

Electronic record keeping can present a problem when therapists feel pressed into using templates and condensing their notes in such a way that the individuality of the client is lost. For example, in an evaluation I conducted in a legal case, I reviewed multiple psychiatric hospitalization records of a 17-year-old African American woman, which carefully documented her symptoms of extreme anxiety, self-mutilation, and borderline personality disorder over a period of 1 year. However, her electronic records lacked a narrative regarding her immediate precipitating problems of sexual abuse by her foster care family's 50-year-old friend and inadequate supervision due to her foster mother's illness, which reenacted her earlier history of maternal loss and childhood abuse. Without a narrative to help her piece together the fragments of her history of trauma, she could not get the help she needed to address the unspeakable internal chaos and pain she was experiencing. As this story illustrates, no matter the method of record keeping, the narrative of the patient and the patient's unique human nature needs to be adequately represented.

Regardless of the record keeping methods practitioners may choose, records that describe patients in a narrative form are easier to understand than checklists.

Checklists are an invaluable method for systematically gathering data that is often overlooked in semistructured, open-ended interviews. However, checklists are rarely sufficient unto themselves. They are most useful when they are combined with a narrative format.

SUMMARY

We can fulfill the purposes of records when we describe our patients clearly and succinctly, along with the nature and history of their problems, the treatment interventions we employed, the extent and quality of their progress, the status of termination, and our further recommendations. It is essential that records reflect practitioners' integrity, knowledge, and good-faith efforts to assist patients in achieving their goals. To this end, practitioners must systematically document informed consent, difficult ethical questions, preventive action, and consultation; answer evaluation questions; develop diagnoses and working hypotheses; generate treatment plans and maintain consistent progress notes; document a closing summary; and keep an accurate billing history.

4

Confidentiality in an Electronic Age

Imagine the young woman who grew up in your neighborhood, whose mother is a prominent politician in the midst of a highly publicized race for Congress. She is depressed and has trouble sleeping. Her rapid mood swings make it hard for her to control her thinking. She spends too much money and is anxious about her credit card debt. She knows she needs help but is afraid to get it. She recalls a story her parents told her about a Democratic senator from Missouri, Thomas Eagleton, who had to withdraw as George McGovern's vice-presidential running mate when people discovered he was being treated for manic-depressive illness (Associated Press, 1997; *Time*, 1996). She also hears frequent press reports about hospital staff reading patient records, for example, pop star Britney Spears' confidential psychiatric records (Ornstein, 2008). What if she gets therapy for her problems and someone with a political grudge finds out and uses it against her mother? She wants nothing to stand in the way of her mother's chances. She decides to suffer alone, even it means fighting off those disturbing thoughts of suicide.

Or, imagine a 31-year-old man who was in the middle of therapy when his wife left him. She filed for divorce and attempted to sabotage his chances of visitation with their preschool children because he had a mental illness. Even though he was stable and his mental health problems were not affecting his ability to care for his children, he was afraid. Because his wife was making his mental problems an issue in court, he worried her attorney could get access to his mental health records. He therefore felt he could not tell his therapist everything for fear his wife could use what he said to his therapist to keep him away from his children.

Confidentiality is the cornerstone of effective psychotherapy. Patients must have implicit trust that therapists will respect and protect exquisitely intimate information, as the U.S. Supreme Court noted in its decision to legally protect privilege of client information in federal courts (*Jaffe v. Redmond*, 1996). As these examples show, when patients lack trust that their information will be held in confidence, they avoid seeking treatment or they withhold important information.

Clinicians know that compromising client confidentiality undermines therapy and can cause harm to patients. One of the most frequent consultation requests I have received relates to demands therapists receive from insurance companies and attorneys for confidential patient information that therapists feel may be unwarranted or unnecessary. Many practitioners who are required to send diagnoses and treatment plans electronically to insurance companies worry about unauthorized or unintended access to their patients' private health care information; practitioners are pressed to keep electronic medical records but are unsure how to continue to uphold privacy (Foreman, 2006). Therapists have also described the disruption and anxiety they have felt when process servers have entered their waiting rooms to serve subpoenas or court orders. Many therapists told me they became so alarmed and confused by these unexpected events that they felt paralyzed or temporarily lost their clinical judgment. They struggle with how to respond in the best interest of their patients and themselves. They worry about being pulled into litigation that could have enduring personal and professional repercussions. (See Chapter 12 for further discussion of clinicians and the legal system.) Other therapists have described anxiety over thefts of computers from their consulting offices.

Practitioners used to rely only upon their professional associations' codes of ethics and a patchwork of state privacy laws for protection and guidance regarding confidentiality. However, three events changed the political chessboard of confidentiality issues. In 1994, Karen Beyer, a Chicago clinical social worker, refused to release her psychotherapy patient's records to a federal court without her patient's consent. Her refusal became the focus of the U.S. Supreme Court's landmark decision (*Jaffe v. Redmond*, 1996) to uphold psychotherapy clients' right to decide whether they will release their records in federal court. The court's decision in favor of patients' right to confidentiality in federal courts greatly empowered clients as well as clinicians, and established case law regarding confidentiality in the field of psychotherapy.

Four years after the *Jaffe v. Redmond* decision, the Health and Human Services Department (HHS) published the regulations governing the implementation of the Health Insurance Portability and Accountability Act (HIPAA) to clarify uses and disclosures of patient-identifiable health care information. On February 20, 2008, HHS issued a separate HIPAA Security Rule that established the physical and technical security standards required to guard the integrity, confidentiality, and availability of protected health information that is electronically stored, maintained, or transmitted.

While many mental health organizations believed HIPAA rules did not go far enough to adequately protect confidential patient information, they supported the passage of HIPAA as a step in the right direction (American Psychiatric Association, 2001b). At minimum, when a state's privacy regulations are less stringent or nonexistent, HIPAA offered a uniform national standard for accessing and handling medical information. Patient privacy advocates continued to vigorously lobby Congress to restore patient trust through enacting more stringent protection of mental health care records and restoration of patients' consent for specific uses, disclosures, and redisclosures of their patient identifying information (Peel, 2009, 2010). As a result of these efforts, the Health Information Technology for Economic and Clinical Health (HITECH) provision (2009) of the American Recovery and Reinvestment Act (ARRA) created further rule changes that privacy advocates had been seeking for years. It allows patients to request an electronic copy of their records, the opportunity to see all electronic disclosures of their health information, and also to be notified of any unauthorized breaches. It also extended protections to patients by regulating organizations that store protected health information (PHI) (e.g., health information exchange organizations, regional health information organizations, and vendors that contract with covered entities to provide personal health records). It stipulated that when PHI is transmitted or physically transported, such as on a laptop computer, outside a health care entity, it must be encrypted or otherwise rendered indecipherable to unauthorized individuals (ARRA, 2009; Steinbrook, 2009).

Previously under HIPAA, every patient had the right to access, inspect, and obtain a copy of their PHI, with certain exceptions, such as psychotherapy notes. Typically, however, the electronic records were printed out and patients received a paper copy. With passage of ARRA, now patients have the right to obtain an electronic copy of their electronic records and to have it transmitted directly to a physician or hospital or other entity they designate. Simultaneously, the government also offered incentives to health care professionals to develop electronic records systems.

Yet national debates before Congress continue over whether the evolving electronic records systems will have the technological ability to protect patient privacy. Computer scientists have shown that anonymous data can be reidentified easily (Barber, 2009). Even financial information from personal bank or credit card accounts and computer networks on a major stock exchange, once thought to be secure, have been stolen, increasing mental health practitioners' and patients' concerns (Hotze, 2011).

The purpose of this chapter is to provide an overview of ethical and legal requirements that practitioners need to know in order to develop their own policies and procedures for safeguarding their patients' privacy and confidential information. (See Chapter 6 on developing policies and procedures for protecting confidentiality. Exceptions to confidentiality are discussed separately in Chapter 5.)

This chapter is not legal advice or an exhaustive discussion of each ethical and legal guideline. The legal language of HIPAA and HITECH can be intimidating and difficult to understand. Practitioners need to consult their colleagues, professional associations, and health care attorneys for more detailed information regarding how to understand and apply different ethical requirements or laws to given case situations. It can also help to find clear and concise examinations of the law. The Web sites for respective professional organizations, as well as the Department of Health and Human Service's own Web site, offer useful descriptions of the law and practical guidance on implementation for practices of various sizes, from independent therapists to large clinics and hospitals. (A list of professional organizations' URLs can be found on the CD and in Appendix J.)

DEFINITION OF TERMS

It is important for clinicians to know the differences between the terms privacy, confidentiality, and privileged communication, which are defined below.

Right to Privacy

Privacy is the ability of an individual (or group) to seclude himself or herself or information about the individual and thereby reveal himself or herself selectively. In psychotherapy, privacy is the limitation of awareness of personal information to the patient and to those whom the patient selects. Patients' right to privacy means that patients have the right to keep personal information secluded or concealed from others.

Right to Confidentiality

The words *confidential* and *confidentiality* derive from the same root but are distinct from one another. For example, *confidential* is an adjective. It means "secret" or "of or showing trust." Confidentiality is a noun. It means "entrusted with private matters." Applied to psychotherapy, *confidential* describes information to which no one is privy except the patient, therapist, and those who must have the information in order to provide the services the patient requires. *Confidentiality* refers to the trust the patient places in the therapist to protect against the unauthorized or unlawful disclosure of the patient's confidential information.

Right to Privileged Communication (or Testimonial Privilege)

Privileged communication (or *testimonial privilege*) is a legal term that applies only in legal proceedings and pertains to the right to decide whether confidential information will be revealed in court testimony. The privilege belongs to the person who provided the information. The listener cannot disclose the information unless the speaker gives permission. Privilege protects the privacy of communications from being revealed in court, for example, communication between husband and wife, attorney and client, clergy and church member, physician and patient, and psychotherapist and patient.

PARAMETERS OF CONFIDENTIALITY AND PRIVACY

While mental health professionals are obligated to stringently protect patient confidentiality and privacy, there are exceptions to the patients' rights. Exceptions to the rule often relate to continuity of care, such as the need to routinely provide or discuss patient information with consultants, supervisors, or other professionals who are treating the patient. Similarly, it may be necessary to disclose patient records to health care administrators, regulatory agencies, or accreditation organizations. In addition, practitioners must balance the need for confidentiality and privacy against the need for safety; for example, when patients' lives are in imminent danger or patients are at risk of harming others. In these cases, therapists may have a legal and ethical duty to disclose information even without patient authorization in order to keep patients and others safe. (Chapter 5 discusses exceptions.)

THREATS TO CONFIDENTIALITY AND PRIVACY

External Threats

Changes in Health Care Management Systems

Patterns inherent in health care management have been eroding patient confidentiality and privacy. For decades, all forms of patient information were considered private and unavailable to anyone except the therapist and a handful of persons who were working with the therapist. Even patients rarely saw their own files. But Appelbaum (2000) found that because various sources, such as pharmacies and insurance companies, had free rein to conduct marketing and other studies that readily revealed confidential patient information, patient confidentiality became virtually nonexistent. Chief among practitioners' needs have been strategies for preventing unauthorized and unnecessary access to patients' records by insurance companies. Psychotherapists today remain concerned about how to protect their clients' confidentiality in response to insurance companies' apparently unwarranted case reviews that appear designed to decrease use of mental health services.

Technological Developments

Technological developments have also posed a threat to patient confidentiality. Previously, psychotherapists felt safer because communication was slower and usually required personal contact. Therapists conferred with one another in person or via the telephone. They requested or conveyed information through letters or reports when they believed the exchange of detailed information was necessary. The use of electronic records systems has increased the transmission of information to other professionals at the cost of depersonalizing communication with patients and compromising patient confidentiality. The historical concept of practitioners treating patients in relative isolation and only storing paper records in locked files is disappearing.

Computerization of records complicates efforts to ensure security of patients' information. The ease and speed of access to computerized information carries the risk that clinical information entered by psychotherapists can be obtained by persons who are not authorized to receive it. Consumers and clinicians are concerned with the need to develop safe strategies to prevent unauthorized or unnecessary access to patient records. The February 10, 1999, issue of the *Ann Arbor News* reported that a Michigan-based health care system accidentally posted the medical records of thousands of patients over the Internet (Wahlberg, 1999). On

November 8, 2001, the *Star Tribune* reported that 20 Minnesota children's names and their psychological evaluations were posted on the Internet when a psychology graduate student thought she was sending her files to a secure computer at the University of Montana (Lerner, 2001). More recently, a New York hospital found that portions of records for 6,800 patients had somehow accidentally found their way online; a breach brought to the hospital's attention by one of the patients (Hartocollis, 2010).

As the government encourages practices to implement electronic records, it simultaneously passes stricter provisions to prevent security problems and to assist aggrieved patients after privacy breaches; however, problems persist. Additional threats are associated with the use of cell phones, social media and networking sites, and other electronic media that are subject to data mining, hacking, or inadvertent sharing of content.

E-mail as a method of communication has become second nature for many people but is not without drawbacks. Unencrypted e-mail between patients and their therapists, or between therapists and other professionals, is no more secure than e-mail between any two people. There are several hazards to maintaining confidentiality of patient-identifiable health care information when communicating through e-mail:

- Messages can easily be sent to the wrong person by accident.
- Messages can be read by unauthorized persons off unattended computer screens.
- Messages can easily be printed, forwarded, and stored in an unlimited number of paper and computer files.
- Messages may be discoverable information in legal contexts.
- Messages may be used or disclosed for unauthorized purposes.
- Confidential health care information may be accessed in discarded media.
- Messages may be exposed by computer hackers.
- Messages can be intercepted and altered without detection.
- One party to the communication may falsely claim that the exchange of messages never took place.
- Senders may assume that messages were delivered when they were not.
- Recipients may not pick up their messages within the time frame assumed by senders.
- Messages may contain attachments that the recipient's software cannot read.
- Messages in written form are always subject to misinterpretation.
- Employers may screen messages sent to employee accounts.
- A patient's health information in an e-mail message could be stored unencrypted on a server on the other side of the world (e.g., in the case of Gmail).

Increasing Litigation

Many psychotherapists who have spent their entire careers without coming into contact with an attorney are for the first time finding themselves embroiled in litigation ranging from personal injury suits to fierce custody battles. In most instances, practitioners are understandably worried about the implications of litigation on the efficacy of therapy. In most cases, the legal system only serves to retraumatize or exacerbate the symptoms for which the patient sought treatment. Increasing litigation has forced therapists to learn an entirely new facet of practice—forensics—and to adequately advise their patients about the potential harm of releasing confidential records to the legal system. Moreover, psychotherapists who have never before faced a complaint about their practices have called me in crisis requesting consultation after receiving a notice from their licensure board that an anonymous complaint has been filed. They are mortified to discover they will be forced, under these circumstances, to expose their patients' confidential treatment records in order to explain their treatment to the licensure boards. (Chapter 12's section on "Handling Attorneys' Requests, Subpoenas, Court Orders, and Search Warrants" contains information and strategies psychotherapists can use to handle interactions with the legal system.)

Internal Threats

Threats to patients' confidentiality arise not only from external circumstances but also from simple human negligence. A patient who was waiting for her psychologist to reenter the consulting room after he was called out for an emergency phone call, told me she noticed that her psychologist's computer screen revealed his notes on his previous patient. He apparently had forgotten to log-off before bringing her into his office. She felt sorely tempted to read his other patient's information while waiting for him to return to the office. Danish authors (Hasman, Hanson, Lassen, Rabol, & Holm, 1997) observed that health care professionals commonly discussed patients by name in hospital elevators and other open areas. My colleagues continue expressing concerns about overhearing professionals discussing patients or speaking with patients on cell phones in public places.

There are also published examples of health care employees inappropriately logging on to hospital computers in order to read famous patients' records (Ornstein, 2008). In Minneapolis, a physician who was estranged from his wife obtained unauthorized access to her and their teenage daughter's medical record simply because he worked in the hospital where his child was receiving medical care (Pabst, 2010). There have also been cases where employees who had legitimate access to electronic medical records in general accessed records of patients hospitalized following public tragedies (Lerner, 2011). Schoener noted there are currently no alarm systems to alert administrators to unauthorized access; tracking breaches of confidentiality is at the discretion of administrators and is subject to the limitations of the technology, as auditing capabilities vary greatly among software (personal communication, January 29, 2011).

Common threats to patients' confidentiality and privacy include the following: visible appointment calendars left on desks in unlocked offices; thefts of computers from practitioners' vehicles, consulting and billing offices, or practitioners' homes; visible stacks of paper files in unlocked waiting room closets, reception areas, or closets in practitioners' homes. In 2011, for example, a practitioner employed by a medical center to work with home-bound patients told me his laptop computer was stolen from his car while he was paying for gas en route to his next home visit. He was horrified he had left the hospital passwords taped to his computer. His computer had access to thousands of patients' health care records. He realized their privacy could be compromised and immediately reported the theft to his employer. Even though the employer was able to quickly disconnect access from his computer to patient records and there was no evidence of patients' privacy having been breached, the employer felt compelled under HIPAA rules to sanction him and terminate his job. Shabbir and Jian (2011) reported increasing numbers of thefts of laptop computers and USB flash drives containing thousands of patients' records in the United States and United Kingdom and incidents of WikiLeaks publishing health care information.

PROFESSIONAL ETHICS CODES' REQUIREMENTS FOR PROTECTING CONFIDENTIALITY

All mental health organizations' ethical codes unanimously emphasize the necessity of protecting patients' confidential disclosures and obtaining written consent from patients or legally authorized persons before confidential communication can be disclosed. Exceptions to confidentiality involve emergencies and instances where there is a legal compulsion to breach confidentiality (see the discussion on exceptions in Chapter 5). Professional ethics codes also apply these requirements to practitioners who are engaged in clinical research, supervision, and teaching. Further, many mental health organizations have updated their codes of ethics to include security standards for electronically generated and copied confidential patient information. Professions' ethical standards are more stringent than HIPAA in requiring patient authorization for disclosures of confidential communications. Ken Pope maintains an excellent resource of links to all mental health professions' codes of ethics on his Web site (http://kspope.com/ethcodes/index.php).

FEDERAL LAWS

The Constitution

Privacy has been an enduring fundamental right throughout the history of the United States, but it has never been an absolute right. "Many of the most basic protections in the Constitution of the United States are imbued with an attempt to protect individual privacy while balancing it against the larger social purposes of the nation" (U.S. Department of Health and Human Services, 2000). Many scholars believe that the spirit of the Fourth Amendment to the U.S. Constitution ("the right of the people to be secure in their persons, houses, papers and effects, against unreasonable searches and seizures, shall not be violated") extends logically to the right to privacy of health care information (Carter, 1999).

The Privacy Act of 1974

In 1965, the House of Representatives established a Special Subcommittee on the Invasion of Privacy; and in 1973, the Department of Health, Education, and Welfare (now the Department of Health and Human Services) issued the Code of Fair Information Practice Principles, which formed the basis for the Privacy Act of 1974 that regulates information maintained by governmental agencies. According to the Privacy Act of 1974, the "right to privacy is a personal and fundamental right protected by the Constitution of the United States." This Act regulates the government's use of personal information by limiting the disclosures of personally identifiable information, allowing consumers access to information about themselves, requiring federal agencies to specify the purpose for collecting personal information, and providing civil and criminal penalties for misuse of information (Privacy Act, 1974).

The Social Security Act

The Advisory Committee on Consumer Protection and Quality in the Health Care Industry, a Presidential advisory commission, acknowledged the lack of patient privacy and, in November 1997, recommended a Consumer Bill of Rights and Responsibilities. That same year, Congress required Medicare+Choice organizations to establish safeguards for individually identifiable patient information (Social Security Act, 1997).

European Union Data Privacy Directive

Meanwhile, in 1995, the European Union (EU) adopted a Data Privacy Directive, requiring its member states to have consistent privacy laws by October 1998. The EU urged countries in the rest of the world to adopt similar privacy laws (Stanberry, 1998).

Family Educational Rights and Privacy Act

The Family Educational Rights and Privacy Act (FERPA) (20 U.S.C. § 1232g; 34 CFR Part 99) is a federal law that protects the privacy of student education records. It applies to all schools that receive funds under an applicable program of the U.S. Department of Education.

The Health Insurance Portability and Accountability Act of 1996 (HIPAA)

Escalating concerns in the United States over the need for continuation and portability of health insurance coverage in order to permit employees to continue health care benefits when they are no longer employed, led to passage of Title I of the Health Insurance Portability and Accountability Act of 1996 (HIPAA), and increasing concerns about the privacy, security, and electronic transfer of health care information, both in the United States as well as in the European Union directive, led to the need for privacy legislation covering electronically generated medical information through Title II of HIPAA. HIPAA mandated that if Congress failed to enact legislation to protect privacy of medical records by August 1999, the secretary of Health and Human Services (HHS) must promulgate regulations. Debates focused on the inherent conflict between the individual's right to privacy and the need for access to patients' health information for reasons of public health, research, and health care management. Congress was unable to resolve questions over how to protect the security and privacy of electronically generated medical records. Therefore, Secretary of HHS Donna Shalala assumed responsibility for promulgating new rules. The new Privacy Rule took effect April 14, 2001 (U.S. Office for Civil Rights, 2001), and was amended in August 2002. HIPAA's Security Rule, passed in February 2003, mandated that the same level of safeguards used to protect paper-based records must be applied for electronic health information.

In February 2009, to the relief of privacy advocates, the Health Information Technology for Economic and Clinical Health Act (HITECH Act), part of the American Recovery and Reinvestment Act's economic stimulus law, added critical changes to strengthen HIPAA's security regulations for electronic records. Detailed information regarding security requirements and their implementation are available via the U.S. Department of Health and Human Services Web site (www.hhs.gov).

Before examining HIPAA's provisions, it can be useful to note mental health practitioners' different perspectives on HIPAA. The first is that HIPAA adequately protects privacy. Yet the "P" in HIPAA is for "Portability," not privacy. A second assumption is that it is the final word on privacy of patient-identifiable information and on patient access to his or her own records. It is not. HIPAA permits practitioners to rely upon their own more stringent professional standards and upon their own more stringent state laws for protection of patient privacy and for patient access to their own records. Nevertheless, in my own experiences speaking with mental health professionals around the country, many practitioners appear to be automatically deferring to HIPAA, apparently out of lack of understanding or fear of potentially stiff penalties for violations, rather than relying upon their professional wisdom, professional experience, and standards in their respective professions and communities. Practitioners must develop forms, policies, and procedures to comply with HIPAA's rules, but practitioners also need to consider HIPAA with a more balanced eye.

HIPAA's Benefits

One of HIPAA's purposes is to ensure consistent levels of protection for confidentiality of patient-identifiable health care information (PHI) across the United States. Its intent is to protect health care information that is generated electronically, whether stored electronically, orally, or on paper (U.S. Department of Health and Human Services, 2001b, 2001c). HIPAA, strengthened by HITECH (Federal Register, 2009), emphasizes that health care practitioners and organizations ("covered entities") provide the following:

- Patients' right to receive written notice of privacy practices at their first session about how medical information is used and disclosed
- Patients' right to have access to or copies of their medical records, including to be sent their records electronically
- Patients' right to request an amendment of their medical records
- Patients' right to receive an accounting of disclosures of their health information
- Patients' right to have an option to file a complaint with either health care provider or the Department of Health and Human Services (HHS) if patients believe a health care provider or health plan has violated their privacy
- Patients' right to choose whether to have one's name included in a hospital directory
- Patients' right to choose whether to have medical information discussed with designated immediate family members, close friends, or relatives
- Patients' right to receive notice if a breach of their protected health information has occurred
- Covered entities' requirement to do staff training, to designate a privacy officer and a security officer who will have responsibility for the development, implementation, and enforcement of the organization's formal privacy policies and procedures
- Covered entities' requirement to establish technological safeguards, including mandated data encryption

- Covered entities' responsibility to share only the "minimum necessary" in response to third-party requests for patient-identifiable health care information
- Covered entities' right to afford "psychotherapy notes" greater protection than general medical information (e.g., psychotherapy notes are defined by the rule as "notes that are primarily of use to the mental health professional who wrote them, maintained separately from the medical record, and not involved in the documentation necessary to carry out treatment, payment or health care operations," which must be maintained separately from the medical record. See Chapter 3 for discussion of contents of medical record.)
- Authorized penalties, both civil and criminal, for covered entities' violations of HIPAA
- Covered entities' responsibility to establish written business associates contracts that require business associates to directly comply with HIPAA and be subject to HIPAA's enforcement of rules
- Business associates' responsibility to notify covered entity when a breach is discovered
- Responsibilities of companies that maintain personal health records electronically, but are not covered entities under HIPAA, to comply with HIPAA

HIPAA's Weaknesses

Although critics have agreed HIPAA was strengthened by HITECH, its remaining weaknesses include

- Patients' authorization is not required when their PHI is used and disclosed for treatment, payment, or health care operations, a practice that is contrary to mental health professions' ethics standards that require patients have the opportunity to be aware of and to consent to specific disclosures of their private information.
- Private health care information can be used for marketing unless patients opt-out or object.
- Covered entities' business associates who have access to patient identifiable information may include a long list of persons, such as employees of billing services, attorneys, accountants, data processors, software vendors, and so on.
- HIPAA permits law enforcement access to protected health information, which practitioners may erroneously interpret literally, without thinking through their professional obligations to obtain, where ethically necessary, their patients' authorization.

HIPAA does not preempt state laws that are more stringent in protecting patients' privacy and providing patients with the right of access to their records. It does not supersede local courts' decisions, such as parents' rights to child custody or visitation. It also does not conflict with other federal laws, such as the Privacy Act, which govern health care information that governmental agencies maintain. Therefore, psychotherapists must learn whether privacy provisions in their state statutes are more stringent than the federal rule. They must also be aware of other federal privacy guidelines that apply to their practices (U.S. Department of Health and Human Services, 2001c). Practitioners can mitigate HIPAA's weaknesses by exercising their professional responsibility to adhere to more stringent professional ethical standards and state laws that afford greater protection of confidentiality and greater access to patients of their own records.

According to the U.S. Department of Civil Rights, charged with enforcing HIPAA, "covered entities" are required to comply with the HIPAA rules; however, the regulations state that covered entities may implement a particular standard in a way that is "reasonable" considering the size and complexity of the entity so long as the requirement is addressed. Practitioners covered by the rules need to inform themselves about the rule's provisions by reading the U.S. Department of Health and Human Services Web site or by consulting their professional associations' information materials or by consulting their own health care attorneys.

In Chapter 6, I present suggestions for policies and procedures that are consistent with ethical guidelines as well as with provisions of HIPAA and HITECH.

Drug and Alcohol Abuse Treatment Confidentiality Requirements

Patient information related to substance abuse and chemical dependency treatment is protected by Title 42, Part 2: Confidentiality of Alcohol and Drug Abuse Patient Records (42 CFR Part 2). It applies to practitioners who work in a program covered by 42 CFR Part 2, including any program that receives any Medicare, Medicaid, Social Security, local or state government money, or which is a nonprofit. These regulations are more restrictive than HIPAA's regulations. Regulations under 42 CFR Part 2 prohibit unauthorized disclosure of addiction patients' health records to law enforcement or other officials, even with a subpoena, and require a statement prohibiting redisclosure of records (Electronic Code of Federal Regulations, current as of 10/26/11; Brooks, 2004).

STATE LAWS

Health Privacy Laws

As noted above, HIPAA defers to state health privacy laws that provide greater protection to patients' privacy and confidentiality and greater access by patients to their records. According to the Georgetown University Health Care Privacy Project (2002), however, which conducted an extensive survey of states' privacy regulations, states remained diverse in the rights and protections that they afford. Practitioners were therefore urged to educate themselves about their own state privacy regulations and how they compare to the HIPAA Rule. Georgetown University's Center on Medical Record Rights and Privacy provides summaries of states' respective privacy provisions and is an excellent resource for practitioners. Practitioners may also contact their respective professional organizations for further guidance regarding state provisions and how they compare with HIPAA rules.

Regulatory Boards

Regulatory boards are composed of publicly appointed individuals that guide and oversee various professions. Regulatory boards enforce legislative statutes and promulgate rules regarding professional standards of practice. For instance, in Florida, the *491 Board* governs the conduct of clinical social workers, marriage and family therapists, and licensed mental health counselors, and the *490 Board* governs psychologists. Some of the routine tasks that regulatory boards typically perform include the following:

- Ensuring that requirements for licensure are met by each applicant
- Disseminating information to professionals about statutes and rules
- Enforcing legislative statutes that define standards of the appropriate professional conduct
- Hearing and making decisions regarding complaints about professional misconduct

Regulatory boards hold confidentiality as a supreme element of professional conduct. Nevertheless, boards recognize the inevitable need for exceptions to confidentiality. (Exceptions to confidentiality are discussed in Chapter 5.)

Privileged Communication Laws

All 50 states have privileged communication statutes. The Illinois statute that grants privileged communication to psychotherapy clients of clinical social workers was tested in the U.S. Supreme Court after an Illinois federal appeals court disagreed with a lower court's ruling that Marylu Redmond, a psychotherapy patient of Karen Beyer, a Chicago clinical social worker, could withhold her psychotherapy records from federal court. In an unprecedented display of multidisciplinary solidarity, the major mental health professional associations cooperated and communicated as they developed their respective *amicus* briefs for the U.S. Supreme Court *Jaffe v. Redmond* case and succeeded. In its landmark

1995 decision, the U.S. Supreme Court upheld the principle of privileged communication for psychotherapy patients in federal courts.

SUMMARY

It is undisputed within the field of mental health that confidentiality is the foundation of effective psychotherapy. As our government began seeking to improve ease of communication between health care providers and payers through electronic record systems, unprecedented threats to patients' privacy emerged. Simultaneously, increases in litigation began eroding patients' rights to confidentiality and privacy. But the pendulum began to swing toward addressing the formidable health care crisis. The U.S. Supreme court ruled that clients of clinical social workers had privilege in federal court, which reassured all of the mental health professions whose health care records intersected with those of clinical social workers. Congress enacted HIPAA's privacy and security rules that were aimed at controlling and protecting mental health information that is generated and transmitted electronically and promised means of enforcement for misuse of protected health information. Moreover, these federal rules defer to stricter state rules that may apply in any given case, do not conflict with psychotherapists' legally mandated duty to breach confidentiality when there is a reasonable risk of harm to self or others, and acknowledge the need for practitioners to exercise their professional judgment in determining whether disclosures of confidential information can be harmful to their clients. Further, they granted greater protection to "psychotherapy notes" more than other types of health care records.

In response to continuing consumer and health care professional concerns over the inadequacy of privacy protections and eroding patients' trust in health care services, professions and other privacy rights advocates continued to lobby vigorously (Peel, 2011). As a result of their efforts, the HITECH provisions in the American Recovery and Reinvestment Act of 2009 strengthened HIPAA's security provisions in electronic records that protect patients' privacy and give patients access and control over their own protected health care information. Still, confidentiality and privacy provisions of mental health professions' codes of ethics remain more protective of patients' rights to informed consent and rights to privacy and confidentiality than do the federal rules. Practitioners therefore have a responsibility to remain aware of their codes of ethics. As they engage in clinical decision making to determine what actions may be in their patients' best interest, they can thoughtfully weigh their professions' confidentiality and privacy standards against laws and rules that may "permit" disclosures that could be harmful to their patients. Professions generally agree that state and federal rules need to go further to protect patient confidentiality. Still, they acknowledge that HIPAA's evolving rules have offered a uniform national standard that can be fortified by continued research and empirical data regarding threats to patient confidentiality.

In the next chapters, I discuss exceptions to confidentiality and methods for developing policies and procedures to protect confidentiality and to handle its exceptions.

5

Exceptions to Confidentiality

A 14-year-old girl entered her therapist's office for her weekly therapy appointment looking anxious. A pretty girl with big brown eyes, she was dressed modestly in her usual garb, which covered most of her body. She immigrated to our country a year ago with her parents and three younger brothers, and 6 months ago, her school social worker referred her to the community mental health center. She seemed depressed and was struggling to adjust to her new school. Her parents were unfamiliar with therapy, but agreed. Their only request was that she be assigned to a female therapist. The girl had not been allowed to attend school before, even though her younger brothers had attended school in their former village. Nevertheless, with support from school staff and a kindly Rotary club volunteer who was tutoring her in reading, she was learning English quickly and making progress in her classes. She was also making friends and her depressed mood had been lifting.

Today, however, she was uncharacteristically distant and distraught. After hesitating to speak for several minutes, she reluctantly revealed she had attended a party in a relative's home over the weekend. A 21-year-old friend of her relative took her to a back room in the house, lay down on her, and ejaculated. Her family's cultural traditions proscribed any physical contact with men until after marriage. She was terrified her father would become enraged at her if he discovered this event. She had heard of young girls being murdered by their fathers in "honor killings" in her former country to preserve the father's honor and integrity.[*] Furthermore, she was aware of her parents' right to have access to her treatment records, a law she felt would be detrimental to her survival if the therapist were to document the traumatic event she reported happened over the weekend.

The therapist felt stunned. She was reeling from the emotional impact of hearing of her client's sexual trauma and her intense fear anticipating

---

[*] See the UN Population Fund report *State of the World 2000*, "Chapter 3: Ending Violence against Women and Girls" (www.unfpa.org).

her father's rage. Looking back to her initial session with this girl and her parents, she recalled she had informed her parents about the need for teenagers to have confidentiality in therapy. She had explained to them that even though they did have the legal right to see their daughter's therapy records, it would be most helpful if they could respect her need for privacy. The therapist also recalled she told them she would inform them if there was anything they could do to help. Further, she had explained limitations of confidentiality to her young client, such as therapists' legal duty to report suspected childhood abuse or neglect. Her patient had understood.

Now the therapist felt torn. What the patient had just reported met the definition of suspected child abuse, which she was legally obligated to report to the child protection agency. While child abuse and neglect reporting duties were created to protect children from harm, if she followed her responsibility to make a report to the county child protection agency, her client believed she might die. Would it even be safe to document in the treatment record what the patient reported happened to her, as the therapist would normally do in similar cases? What about the desperate need for a sexually traumatized child to receive support from family and community? Where to begin? The therapist checked with the clinic's cultural liaison who confirmed that in a situation like this, a father from this cultural tradition could indeed commit an "honor killing."[*]

The therapist was scheduled to meet with her clinical supervisor the following morning. After listening compassionately and assessing her client's safety from further contact with the 21-year-old man, the therapist felt assured her patient was not in immediate danger. Fortunately, she had time to weigh her clinical and legal options in consultation with her supervisor and to develop a plan of action that would reduce the risk of harm to her patient and balance her needs for safety and protection.

---

[*] Reports submitted to the UN Commission on Human Rights show that honor killings have occurred in many countries (Mayell, 2002).

As the above case vignette illustrates, while confidentiality is critical in therapy, it is not absolute, and the surrounding concerns can be quite complex. To protect children, practitioners are required to report suspected child abuse. Yet extraordinary variables, such as entrenched ethnic and cultural traditions as described above, can complicate the professional obligation to protect patients from harm.

This chapter focuses on the laws and ethics pertaining to exceptions to confidentiality, focusing on practitioners' duties to prevent harm to patients and others. It discusses the various sources practitioners rely upon in order to determine exceptions to their patients' confidentiality and privacy, their responsibilities to take action, and the importance of exercising sound professional judgment in order to protect one's self and one's patients. Whenever we deal with exceptions or are faced with decisions regarding confidentiality, it is good practice to document in the record our decision-making process, actions taken, and outcomes. The development of policies and procedures for handling exceptions is further explored in Chapter 6.

Examples of exceptions to confidentiality that appear in professional ethics codes, as well as in state and federal legal guidelines, include the following:

- Suspected abuse and neglect of children and of the elderly
- Suspected abuse and neglect of vulnerable adults
- Sexual misconduct involving a mental health professional (e.g., by a psychotherapist with a patient or by a clinical supervisor with a supervisee, trainee, or other employee)

- Threat of violence to patient's self or identifiable victim, including therapist
- Situations in which review of records is necessary to determine the presence or extent of professional misconduct, such as in regulatory board disciplinary actions and civil or criminal cases arising from allegations of misconduct
- Parents' and guardians' right to access minor children's treatment records

Psychotherapists must learn about their own state's laws and rules regarding exceptions to confidentiality and privacy and their duties to report, warn, and protect. Discussing these topics with colleagues, supervisors, and consultants, attending continuing education offerings, reading professional codes of ethics, and local and federal laws, rules, and guidelines are all essential.

This chapter includes a review of possible exceptions to confidentiality. Communication with patients about limitations to confidentiality is critical as part of the initial and ongoing informed consent process, as noted in Chapter 2. It is also critical to document decision making and actions taken related to exceptions in given cases, as discussed in Chapter 6, where I present strategies for developing policies and procedures for handling exceptions to confidentiality.

The following is a brief summary of what professional codes of ethics and state and federal laws state regarding exceptions to confidentiality.

PROFESSIONAL CODES OF ETHICS

Even though specific wording in ethics codes varies, most health care professions note that requirements to protect confidentiality do not apply when disclosure is necessary to prevent serious, foreseeable, and imminent harm to a patient or other identifiable person (American Counseling Association [ACA], 2005; American Medical Association [AMA], 2010b; American Psychological Association [APA], 2010; Clinical Social Work Association [CSWA], 2006; National Association of Social Workers [NASW], 2008). The marriage and family therapy profession's code of ethics (AAMFT, 2001), however, is unclear on this topic. The AAMFT code permits disclosures that are "mandated or permitted by law" but does not mention protecting third parties from harm. However, AAMFT's Web site lists an article by family therapist Ellen Berkemper (2002) which discusses family therapists being confronted with the need for ethical decision making in regard to reporting of child abuse and HIV infection and recommends a method that practitioners can use to guide them in their ethical decision-making process.

STATE LAWS

Child Abuse or Neglect

Dating back to the 1960s and 1970s there has been widespread concern about the need to protect children from physical and mental abuse and neglect. All states have reporting laws for suspected child abuse and neglect. Because language varies, practitioners must know and follow their own states' requirements for reporting suspected child abuse and neglect.

For example, child sexual abuse is defined differently across states. Also, states have different rules about what kinds of conditions must be reported and when and how reports must be made. Most require an immediate oral report, and many require both oral and written reports. All states grant immunity from prosecution to persons reporting child abuse and neglect and most have penalties for failure to report. Due to variations in state laws, practitioners need to learn what their reporting duties are to report suspected child abuse and neglect in their own states, including requirements for timing of reports, and consequences for failure to report. The National Association of Social Workers has published a useful, detailed review of all 50 states' mandatory child abuse reporting requirements (NASW, 2004). However, it is always wise to telephone the relevant agency, such as child protective services, to inquire about one's reporting duty in a given case. Many states have toll-free numbers to facilitate inquiries and reporting.

Elder Adult Abuse

The National Center on Elder Abuse (NCEA), U.S. Department of Aging, cites seven categories of elder abuse: physical, emotional, or psychological, financial or material exploitation, neglect, sexual abuse, self-neglect, and abandonment. States have enacted laws to protect elders from mistreatment, abuse, and neglect. When practitioners treating elders become aware of elder abuse or neglect, they are expected to report it to their state's adult protection agency. NCEA's list of resources in each state is available online (www.ncea.aoa.gov).

Vulnerable Adult Abuse or Neglect

Reporting of maltreatment of vulnerable adults pertains to residents in facilities who are unable to protect themselves from abuse or neglect, usually not outpatients. A facility is generally able to make a report on behalf of any worker who knows of the event involving abuse or neglect.

Sexual Misconduct by Health Care Professionals

Other types of reporting duties for suspected abuse and neglect also vary among the states. For example, only 17 states have statutes that compel psychotherapists to report allegations or suspected sexual maltreatment of patients by health care professionals. That is, if therapists learn other health care practitioners are having sexual relations, or are engaging in inappropriate sexual behavior, with patients, in only 17 states are they required to report this to the regulatory board.

Duty to Warn or Protect Intended Victims of Violence

Other examples of exceptions include states' "duty to warn or protect" laws, such as in California or in Illinois, that provide the grounds for reporting threats of violence. When a client makes a serious and specific threat of harm against a specific, clearly identified victim, many state laws require practitioners to make efforts to prevent harm. Practitioners must prepare themselves for such contingencies by informing themselves about their own states' regulations governing duty to warn or protect situations.

Tarasoff v. Regents of the University of California (1974), known as *Tarasoff I*, dealt with the question of whether a therapist had taken sufficient action by reporting to the police his psychotherapy patient's threat to kill a female university student, Tatiana Tarasoff. Even after the therapist reported the patient's specific threat to the local police, the patient did end up killing Tarasoff, and her family sued the therapist and his clinic, claiming the therapist had not taken sufficient action to protect their daughter. The decision in this case created the legal precedence for states to enact their own statutes mandating psychotherapists to warn third parties that they are in danger of violence by a patient. The California Supreme Court modified this decision in *Tarasoff II* to a duty to protect potential victims which is predicated on the special relationship of therapist to patient. As one Justice wrote, "the protective privilege ends where the public peril begins" (*Tarasoff v. Regents of the University of California*, 1976).

Nationally, however, decisions related to "duty to warn or protect" range widely. Some courts have found such a duty; some have extended it beyond Tarasoff; some have not found such a duty or have limited it to certain circumstances. The Texas Supreme Court, for example, in *Thapar v. Zezulka* (1999) determined that a psychotherapist may breach confidentiality in order to warn, but does not have a common law duty (a duty to adhere to a standard of reasonable care) to do so. However, the Delaware Supreme Court ruled that in Delaware there was a common law duty to persons other than the patient when psychotherapists know the patient is a danger to others. In another case, the California Court of Appeals (*Ewing v. Goldstein*, 2004 and *Ewing v. Northridge Hospital Medical Center*, 2004) extended the responsibility to warn and protect: it ruled that Dr. Goldstein, a psychiatrist, had a duty to contact the police even though it was the patient's father who communicated the patient's plan to murder his former girlfriend to Dr. Goldstein, not the patient himself.

There is also considerable variation among professions *within* the same state regarding definitions of what constitutes a duty to warn or protect and how this duty is to be implemented. In Minnesota only two boards—psychology and social work—enforce a Tarasoff-like rule regarding the "duty to warn or protect" an identified potential victim from harm. This means that if a client tells a marriage and family therapist he intends to kill his wife, that therapist may not be required by law to breach confidentiality in order to report the threat to the potential victim or law enforcement officials.

Some mental health experts, however, believe that a civil duty to warn and protect probably exists everywhere. The duty to protect is a "well-known fact of professional life" (Monahan, 1993). Absent a statute or local case law, standards of professional care may compel a practitioner to breach privacy in order to prevent harm to an identifiable victim. Practitioners can obtain information about their specific duties by consulting clinical colleagues who are experienced in ethics, by asking their professional associations or regulatory boards for information, or by consulting their own attorneys.

FEDERAL LAWS

The Health Insurance Portability and Accountability Act (HIPAA) permits uses and disclosure of protected health information (PHI) without patient authorization in a limited number of situations when required by state law, such as when the practitioner believes the patient may be a victim of abuse, neglect, or domestic violence, or when there is a need to avert or lessen a serious and imminent threat to patients' health or safety or the health or safety of others. The disclosure must be made to a person reasonably able to prevent or lessen the threat. Other disclosures permitted under the HIPAA rule include the following: disclosures for public health activities; health oversight activities, including disclosures to state or federal agencies authorized to access PHI; disclosures to judicial and law enforcement officials in response to a court order or other lawful process; disclosures for research, when approved by an institutional review board; and disclosures to military or national security agencies, coroners, medical examiners, and correctional institutions or otherwise as authorized by law. However, HIPAA allows practitioners to exercise their professional discretion in regard to whether a disclosure is likely to be harmful to the patient. It explicitly requires practitioners to follow their own state statutes when they are more stringent than HIPAA in protecting privacy.

The code that regulates government-funded substance abuse programs, 42 CFR, has far fewer exceptions permitting disclosure of information without the patient's consent, in contrast to HIPAA (Lowinson, Ruiz, Millman, & Langrod, 2005). While HIPAA allows health care providers to disclose information to other health care providers without patients' written consent as part of the treatment, payment, and health care operations, 42 CFR requires patients to consent in most circumstances, even when information is being disclosed to another treating program or physician. Its confidentiality regulations have far fewer exceptions permitting disclosure of information without the patient's consent. It specifies under what circumstances a program would disclose confidential information in response to court orders and to whom. Medical emergency, suspected child abuse or neglect, and crimes on program premises or against program personnel are among the exceptions cited in 42 CFR.

Both HIPAA and 42 CFR override any less restrictive state law that conflicts with them, and both require compliance with any state law that is more restrictive (Brooks, 2005).

CLINICAL ISSUES IN HANDLING DANGEROUSNESS

Because many instances of young people's violence stem from their being bullied, ridiculed, teased, or isolated by their peers or adults, schools are becoming aware of the need to take preventive action. Practitioners may also consider how they may contribute to preventing violence and document their efforts to do so. Because many young people, from middle school to college-age, who have ultimately exploded in violence have given prior warning of their distress through their writings, Internet postings, or in statements to others, practitioners need to take such warnings seriously. Also, the degree to which clients believe they need treatment, receive treatment, and their degree of engagement in treatment are factors that appear to correlate with less violence (Elbogen, Van Dorn, Swanson, Swartz, & Monahan, 2006).

Monahan (2006–2007) notes that since the original Tarasoff case, new developments in science and clinical care have strengthened clinicians' ability to more accurately assess and reduce the risk of violence. Recent research, for example, shows that structured violent risk assessment is superior to unstructured violence risk assessment. A variety of structured risk assessment instruments improve clinicians' ability to forecast the likelihood that an individual will behave violently.* When mental health practitioners determine a patient is at risk for violence, a recourse mental health professionals can consider now, in addition to inpatient commitment, is the option of outpatient treatment commitment, which can help decrease risk of violence by providing ongoing support, assisting patients to comply with medication, and decreasing substance abuse (Monahan, 2006–2007; Skeem & Monahan, 2011).

Monahan (2006–2007), however, notes that despite evidence showing that structured risk assessment is superior to unstructured risk assessment, only a minority of mental health professionals routinely use structured risk assessment. He recommends that mental health professionals "become educated in structured risk assessment, stay current with developments in the field and be

---

* Three examples of structured violence risk assessment tools include the Historical, Clinical, and Risk Management factors ("HCR-20"), the Violence Risk Appraisal Guide (VRAG), and the Classification of Violence Risk (COVR) (Monahan, 2006–2007).

conversant with the law of the jurisdiction." He believes that all patients should be screened for violence risk and for those who score positively on the screen, therapists should proceed to a formal structure violence risk assessment. Monahan provides the following brief illustrative screening questions:

1. Did a violent act or the threat of a violent act precipitate or recently precede the patient's current treatment?
2. Did the patient act violently or threaten to act violently during the current treatment?
3. [If no to both of the above] Does the patient have a documented history of violent acts or threats of violent acts, even though neither has occurred recently?

For cases that raise particular concerns about violence, he recommends mental health professionals "consider intensified voluntary treatment, outpatient commitment, inpatient commitment, or warning the potential victim" (Monahan, 2006–2007).

Schoener (2010) advises practitioners who are treating violent patients to first use their clinical skills before rushing to follow mandated reporting duties. He suggests clinical interventions include determining how urgent the situation is and, if a serious threat is not imminent and there is time, obtaining consultation and documenting the plan of action; trying to diffuse the patient's anger by helping the patient to ventilate feelings; trying to dissuade the client from violent solutions; asking permission to discuss the situation with significant others; attempting to get the client to give up weapons or put away weapons; and, if in a family session, helping the family seek solutions.

When efforts to exercise clinical skills within the therapeutic relationship fail to prevent risk of harm to the client's self or an intended victim, practitioners will need to contact police for an emergency hold and communicate the imminent threat to the potential victim. In the case of minors, the parent, guardian, or school has authority to intervene. If the parents or the school are the intended victims, it is even more critical to notify them of the threat. The duty becomes even stronger when practitioners have knowledge of the client's past violent behavior or past careless behaviors (e.g., reckless drunken driving that appeared suicidal or homicidal) and current symptoms of depression. The critical need for documentation of such reports is discussed in Chapter 3.

Patients' Violence against Practitioners

Research has reported high numbers of counseling staff who have experienced harassment from a current or former client (Romans, Hays, & White, 1996) and many mental health professionals who have been threatened or attacked, with physical assaults more likely in hospitals and clinics than in private practices

(Moran, 2009; Sandberg, McNeil, & Binder, 1998). Moran (2009) further reported many psychiatry residents were reluctant to report patient violence. The study by Gentile, Asamen, Harmell, and Weathers (2002) of patients stalking their psychologists showed that all practitioners are at risk for being stalked.

The American Psychology Association revised its Code of Ethics to give psychologists permission to reveal confidential information without the consent of the individual for a "valid purpose," including protecting the psychologist from harm. Recent court decisions have also upheld practitioners' right to breach confidentiality in order to protect themselves from patients' violence or threats of violence against them by making reports to or seeking assistance from law enforcement (American Psychological Association, 2010).

Federal rules also cite similar exceptions to patients' confidentiality: For example, 42 CFR's restrictive rules governing confidentiality in federally funded substance abuse programs [Title 42 Code of Federal Regulations, Part 2 (2.12(c) (5))] allow practitioners to report crimes patients committed or threatened to commit against the therapy or counseling services' premises or against their personnel by reporting to a law enforcement agency or by seeking its assistance. In such situations, practitioners may disclose the circumstances of the incident, including the suspect's name, address, last known whereabouts, and status as a patient (Brooks, 2005), and practitioners should be certain to document the report, as discussed in Chapter 3.

Threats against the President of the United States

In 1917, Congress enacted a statute that defined threats of various kinds against the president and his successors as a felony (U.S. Code, 1917). In 1971, the purview of this statute was narrowed to three main issues: to protect the president from possible future attacks, to prevent the incitement of others to attack the president, and to prevent disruption of presidential activity (*United States v. Patillo*, 1971).

Because the existence of a threat, even without further action, may lead to restrictions of the president's movements and requires that the Secret Service take protective action, the statute reflected the opinion that the mere verbalizing of a threat against the president remains criminal because of its potential for disrupting the daily life of the president (Griffith, Zonana, Pinsince, & Adams, 1988).

Thus, if a patient threatens the life of the president, psychotherapists have a special duty to report the threat to the Secret Service (W. Menninger, personal communication, 1992). The Secret Service investigates threats and assesses their risk potential to the persons under protection (M. Coggins, personal communication, 1992).

Contagious, Life-Threatening Diseases

Consistent with most professional ethics codes that include exceptions to confidentiality in situations when there is clear, imminent, foreseeable harm to patients and others, American Counseling Association's code of ethics, Section B.2.b., specifically notes, "when clients disclose that they have a disease commonly known to be both communicable and life-threatening, counselors may be justified in disclosing information to identifiable third parties, if they are known to be at demonstrable and high risk of contracting the disease."

In most states, health care professionals are required to report cases of infectious disease and sexually transmitted disease to their state health departments. Every state now has laws requiring health care practitioners to report cases of acquired immunodeficiency syndrome (AIDS), and most states also require the reporting of information related to infection with the human immunodeficiency virus (HIV). State health departments, in turn, are required to report information on the incidence of AIDS to the federal Centers for Disease Control and Prevention (CDC) in Atlanta, Georgia.

In order to prevent discrimination of AIDS- and HIV-infected patients, such as in housing and employment, states have strictly limited practitioners' disclosure of these conditions to state health departments unless patients have given authorization for release of this information. However, many state laws have provisions that allow health care providers to protect other identifiable parties from infection. In these states, practitioners may report instances of HIV or AIDS to spouses, sexual partners, emergency personnel, funeral directors, blood banks, and others who could be harmed unless they had knowledge of these conditions. Psychotherapists therefore may need to consult their attorneys in order to understand and be able to appropriately implement their state requirements relevant to reporting infectious and potentially harmful conditions without patients' authorization.

Pregnant Women Who Have Used Nonprescription Controlled Substances

There is a duty in many states to report habitual or excessive alcohol use or nonprescription controlled substances (cocaine, heroin, phencyclidine, methamphetamine, amphetamine, or their derivatives; tetrahydrocannabinol) during pregnancy. Currently, however, neither law nor accepted medical practice defines what would be "excessive" or "habitual" alcohol use during pregnancy (Schoener, 2010).

Reporting in "Good Faith"

When practitioners determine they have a duty to report, reports must be in "good faith." When a practitioner is unsure about the identity of the person to be reported, for example, the practitioner may not have a duty to report. Never guess about the identity of the person. In one distressing situation, after learning from a patient that she had sexual intercourse with her former therapist, her current practitioner erroneously believed he knew the identity of the previous therapist. He reported alleged conduct by the wrong licensed professional to the licensure board. This confusing and disturbing situation could have been prevented had he waited until his patient was ready to reveal the identity of her former therapist.

OTHER CONSIDERATIONS

Exceptions to Reporting Duties

Some states have exceptions to reporting duties. In Wisconsin, for example, suspected elder abuse does not require a report if the therapist believes that a report might be harmful to the elder. In Minnesota, if a psychologist reports to his own treating psychologist that he had sex with one or more of his patients, the treating psychologist is not obligated to report the sexual misconduct to the licensure board.

HIPAA allows practitioners to exercise professional judgment in allowing access to patients' records when there is potential for physical harm to the patient in doing so.

Consultations

Psychotherapists have an ethical duty to seek appropriate consultations (such as with clinical supervisors, consultants, or government agencies) when they have questions about whether it may be necessary to disclose confidential patient-identifiable information without consent from their patients. When practitioners wonder, for example, whether or not certain types of behaviors trigger a legal duty to report suspected child abuse, they may phone a child protection agency to consult intake workers or supervisors. When practitioners make calls to the appropriate agencies in order to request consultation about reporting duties, it is normally unnecessary to disclose patient-identifying information.

Practitioners' Confidentiality Contracts

Prudent practitioners should inform themselves of conditions under which they may be required to breach confidentiality and all exceptions to confidentiality and privacy should be discussed with patients as part of the ongoing informed consent process to therapy or counseling. See Chapter 2 for discussion of methods for communicating with patients about confidentiality and its exceptions. See the CD and Appendix A which contain a sample "Client Information Form" that explains confidentiality and its exceptions, also Chapter 3 ("Characteristics and Contents of Good Records") for a discussion of methods to document clinical decision making regarding exceptions to confidentiality.

Impact of Reporting on the Therapeutic Relationship

A topic rarely discussed in the literature is the need to consider the impact of reporting on the therapeutic relationship (Levine & Doueck, 1995; Luepker, 1999). Sometimes mandated reporting can have beneficial clinical effects. For example, a mother who had suffered from abuse and neglect as a child was grateful for her therapist's sensitive attention to her feelings of anxiety and shame over being out of control and slapping her own 9-month-old baby when he would not stop crying. She welcomed the therapist's carefully adhering to her duty to report these problems to child protection and appreciated her making the mandated reports in her presence. She told her therapist that she wished someone had stepped in like that to help her parents gain control of their behavior and protect her when she was young.

Mandated reporting can also feel devastating and cause patients to abruptly leave therapy. A patient became alarmed when her therapist followed his state's law and reported (to the former therapist's licensure board) her statements regarding her former therapist's sexual involvement with her. She had come to therapy feeling very anxious, wishing to gradually discuss over time what had happened and how she had felt in her previous therapy. She did not feel ready to take complaint action. She wished her therapist could have waited until she was ready to make the complaint herself. Feeling the therapist had taken control away from her, she abruptly terminated therapy. The therapist in this case, who was practicing in a state where suspected practitioner sexual conduct must be reported to licensure boards, learned it is helpful to alert all patients that if they reveal the identity of an offending practitioner, he will be required to report to the licensure board. In that way, his patients can discuss the situation freely and remain in charge over the timing and revelation of the alleged offender's identity.

PROCESS OF CLINICAL AND ETHICAL DECISION MAKING

When the therapist in the opening case example consulted her supervisor the next morning regarding her dilemma to report or not to report her teenage patient's reports of suspected child abuse to the child protection agency, her supervisor was stunned. This was the most complex dilemma he had faced in his professional career. The therapist and her supervisor considered their ethical and legal responsibilities. Above all, they wanted to prevent harm and do what would be beneficial to the client. They decided the therapist needed to phone the child protection agency to inquire, without identifying the patient or her family, whether the suspected sexual assault as reported by the girl and the girl's perception that she could be killed by her father were necessary to report. The intake worker stated that under state law, the therapist was required to report these situations. After finishing the conversation with the child protective services intake worker, the supervisor and therapist explored the complex cultural issues and identified legal priorities and clinical options. They consulted a member of their professional organization's ethics committee and the clinic's health care attorney and could see no easy answers.

A report to the child protection agency or to the police regarding either of these situations would likely frighten the girl further and could damage her rapport with her therapist irreparably. It could also end in her father discovering the facts the girl desperately wished to hide, which could end in his attempting to murder her or in having her killed. Further, reporting to child protection could end in the agency's removing the girl from her home. Should she return home eventually, she could end up having to run away and live in exile from her family. A report would also likely cause the father to feel helpless and enraged at the therapist for increasing his vulnerability by exposing him and his family to a governmental agency, just as he was suffering from the pain of dislocation from his homeland and trying to establish himself and his family in a new country. Yet, they were aware that it would be unprofessional and unwise for the therapist to assume the role of investigator and protector, which was the responsibility of child protective services.

Ultimately, they determined that the therapist had no alternative but to follow her legal responsibility to report both the sexual assault by the 21-year-old and the patient's fear of being murdered by her father to the child protection agency. The therapist and her supervisor discussed options for proceeding as sensitively as possible. They agreed that a carefully written letter, rather than only a phone call, might help the child protective services intake worker who would be receiving the report to be in a better position to understand all of the complex details and potential ramifications. They agreed they would ask the agency to inform them of the outcome, and they would express their willingness and wish to remain available to be supportive to both the girl and her family. They agreed they would ask the child protective services intake worker if and when they might offer to speak empathically with the father in order to acknowledge and validate the shame he may feel about the therapist's mandated reporting in the context of the pain he is already feeling about dislocation from his homeland. They realized that their professional decision to report the suspected child sexual assault and the patient's perception and fear of danger with her father was fraught with potential harm to the girl. Yet a decision not to report would also involve potential harm to the girl as well as to themselves as professionals. By systematically consulting child protective services about their legal duties and carefully examining the risk and clinical impact of reporting and their clinical options, they did their best to arrive at a professional decision.

SUMMARY

This chapter reviewed exceptions to confidentiality and emphasized the following: to carefully exercise professional judgment when examining options related to handling exceptions by consulting with colleagues, supervisors, and consultants when faced with questions or dilemmas; to understand case law and standards of care in one's own community regarding exceptions; and to be aware of professional codes of ethics, local and federal laws, rules, and guidelines pertaining to exceptions. This chapter also described more recent clinical approaches to preventive intervention with patients who are at risk of violence, the need for remaining consistent with one's contract with patients and being mindful of the impact on patients and the therapeutic relationship when one must breach a patient's confidentiality. Methods for supporting the therapeutic relationship through providing informed consent to patients regarding limitations to confidentiality and documenting disclosures are covered in Chapters 2 and 3. As the case example illustrated, therapists may face difficult dilemmas when determining the best course of action in cases involving their patients' suspected abuse or threats of harm, and it may not always be possible to know the outcome of a report.

6

Developing Policies and Procedures for Protecting Confidentiality and Managing Its Exceptions in an Electronic Era

A naked 18-year-old female college student was screaming loudly, running across the grassy field outside the student center late on a bitter cold Saturday night. Her roommate felt horrified by the sudden change in her behavior and called the young woman's parents for help. When the parents arrived, they were bewildered, frightened, and helpless. They needed help, so they phoned their trusted neighbor, a psychiatrist, who thought their daughter may be having a psychotic episode. She advised them how to get her to the psychiatric service at a local hospital.

By the time they arrived at the emergency room with their daughter they were frightened and anxious about how to help her. They needed reassurance, support, information, and guidance from hospital staff. Instead, a stiff and guarded staff member declined to speak with them. He stated that "due to HIPAA regulations," he could not reveal information about their daughter to them without their daughter's consent. However, due to the daughter's emergency, their daughter was unable to give her consent for staff to speak with her parents about her condition. Another emergency room staff member, overhearing her colleague's disturbing conversation with the traumatized parents, took her colleague aside to speak with him privately.

She observed that as the patient had allowed her parents to take her to the emergency room, it would appear that she had a trusting relationship with her parents. She showed him a new Family Involvement Law brochure from the Minnesota chapter of the National Alliance on Mental Illness

(NAMI) which NAMI had developed for health care professionals to help them handle confidentiality issues in exactly this kind of urgent situation (www.namihelps.org). The brochure spelled out provisions in the Health Insurance Portability and Accountability Act (HIPAA) Privacy Rule that specifically permit covered entities to exercise their professional judgment in determining circumstances under which they are permitted to share information that is "directly relevant to the involvement of a spouse, family members, friends, or other persons who are identified by a patient in the patient's care." She showed her colleague where the brochure specified that HIPAA identifies emergency circumstances, during which patients lack ability to give consent, where professionals are permitted to use their professional judgment regarding whether it would be in the patient's best interest to share information about the patient with family members.

Following consultation with his colleague, the staff member returned to the patient's parents. They were greatly relieved to hear him compassionately acknowledge their distress and receive information from him about their daughter's mental state. They felt reassured to learn from him that staff had experience assessing such situations, that they expected medication could be very helpful, that their daughter would be hospitalized on the fourth floor of the hospital and cared for by experienced mental health nursing staff that the parents could phone if they had any questions. The parents returned home in the early morning, feeling shaken and exhausted from the evening's crisis, but hopeful that they had left their daughter in good hands. The helpful conversation with the staff member provided a soothing container for their fear and gave them strength to continue providing support to their daughter.

As the above case example illustrates, practitioners find themselves in dilemmas where they must identify clinical needs and balance these with ethical and legal requirements in consultation with colleagues in order to determine what is in the best interest of their patients. The purpose of this chapter is to address the need for thoughtful policies and procedures that help to protect patients' right to privacy and confidentiality and manage their exceptions. I discuss strategies that are consistent with HIPAA as well as with professional guidelines. Practitioners need to consult their colleagues, professional associations, and health care attorneys in order to clarify clinical needs and applicable ethical standards, state and federal laws, and whether their policies and procedures appropriately implement them.

CREATING SECURITY MEASURES

Security of Oral Communication

The need for privacy in psychotherapy is even greater than in other types of health care services. Psychotherapists may help to protect their patients' privacy by not calling them by their names in waiting rooms or other occupied areas. For new patients whom the therapist does not know, an alternative might be to ask: "Who are you here to see?" With known patients, an alternative might be a smile, establishing eye contact, and saying "Hello, please come in when you are ready." Even when practitioners have authorization to discuss a patient or certain aspects of his or her case, they should make sure not to do so in the presence of nonauthorized individuals. It can be tempting to discuss a case over lunch, but that may be unwise.

Security of Paper-Based Information

Although practitioners are encouraged to keep electronic records, and many large health care organizations require it, paper records have not gone away. Records are often printed out for various reasons, and then must be either securely stored or destroyed. A major hospital that uses an electronic system was very embarrassed to have lost a large number of paper patient records. A representative was quoted as saying, "You think it's going to be electronic, and then it's a box of paper" (Lerner, 2011). The hospital had to issue a written statement notifying patients of the security breach.

Practitioners need to routinely check to see that a patient's identity is not visible to unauthorized users in one's private practice or other treatment center. Even when individual psychotherapists have gone to a "paperless" office, there may still be papers that identify a patient, such as intake questionnaires, which psychotherapists must scrupulously ensure are not left on counters, desks, floors, or in unlocked files or drawers. All paper files should be immediately returned to locked filing cabinets. Additional precautions include inspecting buildings for adequate locks to entrances, fire alarms, extinguishers, and sprinkler systems.

Security of Psychotherapy Notes

When I have presented conferences on ethics and record keeping to mental health professionals around the United States, they have uniformly expressed confusion over what psychotherapy notes are and how they can be protected more than the regular medical record. As noted in Chapter 4, psychotherapy notes are those notes meant only to be seen by the clinician and kept separate from the medical record. However, because the official medical record includes presenting problems, history, diagnosis, and treatment, there is little in psychotherapy that ends up being protected more than other kinds of treatment records. Psychotherapists

tell me they do not have time to keep two separate sets of records. Thus, as electronic record systems afford greater access of mental health records to other medical care professionals, psychotherapy records have become less private than ever before, which is contrary to the U.S. Supreme Court's opinion in its *Jaffe v. Redmond* decision that confidentiality is essential to psychotherapy. Mental health records can, however, be "segmented" in the electronic record in order to restrict access to them.

Security of Computers and Other Machines That Store Patient Health Information

Practitioners need to develop careful contingency planning for data backup, emergency mode operation, disaster recovery with technology, and prevention of unauthorized access. Reasonable attempts include the following:

- Establishing technical safeguards to detect identity, date, and time of person accessing computer
- Using only computers with passwords to limit access during routine work
- Using at least seven alphanumeric characters to make it difficult to guess passwords
- Never sharing passwords with other users
- Changing passwords frequently and maintaining any written notation of the passwords in a secure location away from the computer
- Checking for computer viruses every few days
- Installing an encryption program (which must be shared with anyone to whom protected health information [PHI] is sent electronically)
- Removing obvious identifying information, such as patients' names, birth dates, postal addresses, and phone numbers*
- Using a secure server when sending information with patient-identifying information
- Using encrypted compact disks or encrypted removable hard drives so that information can be transported and locked in a different location
- Limiting users to only one system log-on at a time
- Having computers log off automatically when they are inactive for a prescribed amount of time
- Installing antivirus software to block external sabotage
- Keeping software up to date by installing upgrades and patches as they are available
- Prohibiting employees from loading unauthorized software onto the organization's computers

Practitioners need to develop ways to determine whether a breach of unsecured protected information has occurred. There is a feature, generally referred to as "break glass" in some electronic health records systems, which requires anyone who is going to access a designated record to record the justification for access. It can automatically trigger an audit of that record to see who accessed it and why. Also, because thefts of computers and mobile devices containing private patient information are common, practitioners must protect computer

---

* Actually, there are 18 identifiers that must be removed before PHI becomes de-identified and is no longer PHI.

equipment from theft. Thus, even though it is inconvenient when I am in a hurry, I take my laptop computer with me whenever I leave my car and lock my laptop in my file cabinet whenever I must leave my office, even for a few minutes. The University of Minnesota's Privacy and Security Officer also suggests tethering computers to desks with a cable lock. He notes that a practitioner with a wooden desk not built for such tethers might consider using a metal plate with a fastener screwed to the underside of the desk, or some other safeguard that would make stealing the computer more trouble than the average thief would be interested in attempting (Ross Janssen, personal communication, May 26, 2011).

What do we do if our billing service lets us know they have had a break-in, their computers have been stolen, and there is reason to believe that patients' identities and private health care information are at risk? The standard is that we must notify our clients so they may mitigate the damage resulting from the breach. Instructions for notifying patients of a breach and sample "breach notification" forms can be found on professional organizations' Web sites (e.g., National Association of Social Workers and American Psychological Association). Following a breach, many covered entities now offer patients credit monitoring for a year if the information included a Social Security number.

Finally, when computers or copiers are to be given away or thrown away, we cannot simply delete files. We must remove the hard drive and arrange for its destruction or for a professional to wipe the memory.

Breach Notification

The Health Information Technology for Economic and Clinical Health Act (HITECH), part of the American Recovery and Reinvestment Act of 2009, has extensive and specific requirements for responding to breaches (American Recovery and Reinvestment Act, 2009). Practitioners must give patients notice of the breach, describe what happened, share the kinds of information involved, explain what is being done about the problem, and give contact information for questions. HITECH says that when a breach involves 500 or more individuals, there must be a toll-free number that patients may call for information; covered entities must put the information about the breach on their Web site, immediately report the breach to the Secretary of Health and Human Services, and possibly do a press release. Practitioners covered under HITECH can contact their professional organizations for a sample breach notification form that they can download and adapt for this purpose. They can also consult their health care attorneys about how to proceed in fulfilling their legal responsibilities.

PRIVACY MEASURES

"Routine" Uses and "Nonroutine" Disclosures

When developing privacy measures, it is helpful to distinguish between routine uses and nonroutine disclosures of patient-identifiable health care information.

Routine uses of patient-identifiable information are those communications that psychotherapists make in order to develop diagnoses and treatment and to conduct other "necessary clinical operations," such as billing and consultations with patients' psychiatrists or other mental health team members. To be consistent with our stringent professional ethical standards, routine disclosures require at least initial, if not updated, written (when possible) authorizations from psychotherapy patients.

However, as psychotherapists know, billing third-party payers is not always routine. Patients cannot know, for example, in the beginning of therapy what their diagnoses are or what they will need to discuss in treatment for healing to take place. Even though patients provide initial consent to their therapists to provide minimal information, such as their diagnosis and dates of services, to third parties for reimbursement of services, they may be unwilling to reveal further information that third-party payers may later require for reimbursement of continued treatment. Practitioners therefore need to be certain that their patients are fully informed of specific disclosures being requested and that patients have authorized these in writing. Practitioners should then submit only the minimum necessary to payers.

Nonroutine disclosures are those communications to third parties that are outside of usual treatment or billing. Examples of nonroutine disclosures may include responses to requests for records from individuals or organizations outside of the treatment team, such as attorneys. To be consistent with mental health professions' codes of ethics, nonroutine disclosures normally require written authorization from the patient, unless the disclosure is legally mandated.

HIPAA now requires practitioners to maintain a record of all disclosures, both routine and nonroutine, and to make an accounting of those disclosures available to patients upon their request. See CD for a sample log of disclosures. Clinicians can also note disclosures in their progress notes, as noted in Chapter 3.

Security of Facsimile Transmission

Psychotherapy offices routinely use facsimile (fax) transmissions, which allow practitioners to exchange clinical information (e.g., with patients, insurance companies, other health care professionals, or attorneys) about their patients rapidly, conveniently, and precisely. There are risks in using fax transmissions that practitioners must take reasonable steps to prevent. For instance, fax transmissions can accidentally be sent to, or received by, the wrong party. Even when they arrive at the right machine, they might be read by a nonauthorized user.

Psychotherapy practices therefore must develop and carefully enforce faxing guidelines that adhere to applicable laws for protection of patient-identifiable health information.

To protect confidentiality of faxed information, offices and organizations should adhere to the following precautions:

- Locate fax machines in a secure area with access only by authorized users.
- Limit faxed information to the minimum amount necessary to meet the needs of the requester.
- Require written consent of the patient or his or her legal representative except in cases of extreme emergency or other legally authorized reasons.
- Include an attached cover page that states the following: "This information is confidential. It is intended for use by the specified recipient only. If this fax has been received in error, please destroy this information and notify this office immediately."
- Contact the recipient of the information to verify who will receive the fax and whether the information will be protected by necessary privacy and security measures.
- Keep a log in each patient's record of all fax transmissions.
- Designate a staff person who will monitor incoming faxes, verify their completeness, and deliver them to the appropriate, intended recipients.

Privacy Officer

HIPAA requires us to designate a "privacy officer," which is prudent even when a clinical practice is not covered by HIPAA. The privacy officer assumes responsibility for ensuring development, implementation, and enforcement of privacy and confidentiality policies and procedures. As HIPAA does not specify criteria for the privacy officer, psychotherapists in independent practices can assume responsibility as privacy officers for their own practices. Changes in law, technology, and even changes in a therapist's work space, dictate ongoing review. Thus it is essential that the role of regularly reviewing and updating policies and procedures be assigned and competently executed on an ongoing basis.

SECURITY OF THE OFFICE

Employee Screening, Privacy Training, and Security Agreements

Employees and business associates who are covered by HIPAA must be subjected to preemployment background checks in order to verify history of reliability and to receive security training. Training must teach staff how to protect security of patient-identifiable health care information and document staff training activities.

All business associates and employees must sign an agreement indicating that they understand and agree to the psychotherapy practice's security policies and procedures for protecting patients' privacy and confidentiality. Computers and software they use need to be protected from theft, vandalism, and unauthorized access, whether the equipment is in the office or home based.

As part of training and administrative procedures to protect the security of patient-identifiable information, employers should give the following information to persons working in their psychotherapy practice setting:

- The legal basis (state and federal) for patients' right to privacy and confidentiality
- Responsibility for protecting confidential information
- Procedures to prevent or report breaches of security
- Notice that the psychotherapy practice's computer is protected against unauthorized access
- Consequences for failure to follow these policies, such as suspension, dismissal, or legal action

Practitioner Agreements

When practitioners join the staff of a psychotherapy practice, they, too, need to sign an agreement indicating that they understand and will adhere to their professional ethics, state and federal laws governing patient privacy and confidentiality, and the psychotherapy practice's policies and procedures for protecting confidential information and patient privacy. The signed agreement also includes consequences for failure to follow the agreement.

Contractor or Vendor Agreements

Contractors, vendors, or other third parties who provide services to psychotherapy offices, such as copying, transcription, microfilming, destruction, or storage of records, also need to sign the same kinds of privacy contracts. These need to indicate that they understand and agree to the office's confidentiality and privacy policies and procedures and that they have direct responsibility to implement them. Agreements also include guarantees that these persons will not deliberately introduce software viruses or other hazards into the psychotherapy practice computer system.

Communication with Patients about Privacy Practices

Conscientious psychotherapists have already been informing their clients about their offices' privacy practices. However, HIPAA has uniform standards that psychotherapists who are covered under the rule must follow. Whether practitioners are covered under the rule or not, it is clinically prudent to present privacy information to patients in writing, preferably before an initial interview, in a form (such as a handout, pamphlet, or brochure) that patients can keep in their own records in order to refer to as needed and can discuss with their psychotherapists. In the initial appointment, therapists need to attempt to obtain patients' written acknowledgment that they have received and read the privacy practices information. See CD and Appendix A for "Client Information," which includes a statement on privacy practices. See CD also for a sample form that clients can sign to acknowledge receipt of this information.

Patients are emotionally distraught when they seek psychotherapy, therefore oral and written communication about confidentiality and exceptions to confidentiality need to be clear, simple, and brief. Walfish and Ducey (2007) noted, unfortunately, that a majority of practices' HIPAA notices that they studied were difficult to read. In order to build trust and a secure working alliance with their therapists, clients must be able to understand and absorb this information. As noted in Chapter 2, the initial appointment is not the only chance. Opportunities for further clarification of procedures to protect confidentiality and to handle legally mandated exceptions to confidentiality often occur at various junctures during the course of treatment.

Under HITECH, clients have a right to request an electronic copy of their records. Practitioners will want to be sure that their method of delivery for any electronic copies of a client's record is secure. There are many varieties of encryption software available, each with its own set of features, benefits, and limits. When choosing software, it is best to consult with an expert knowledgeable about the technical options for securing transmittal of records.

Initial Written Communication

It is helpful when written communications about psychotherapy answer these questions:

- How does this psychotherapy practice use and protect patients' information?
- What are the routine uses of patients' information?
- Under what exceptions would this practice release confidential information without patient authorization?
- Does this practice use patient information to remind patients of appointments?
- Does this psychotherapy practice report patient information to third-party payers?
- What rights do patients have to request how confidential information is disclosed?
- What complaint procedure can patients follow if there are violations of the stated privacy policies?

- Under what circumstances and in which ways can patients access their records and amend information in their records pertaining to their care?

(See CD and Appendix A for a sample "Client Information" form that describes one office's privacy policies and procedures; see also your own professional organizations' sample forms for HIPAA implementation that adheres to your own jurisdiction's requirements.)

Initial Verbal Communication

Verbal communication about privacy practices is necessary because it helps prevent misunderstandings and can be a vehicle for building trust and a strong therapeutic alliance. Some practitioners worry that having such discussions in the initial interview could intimidate, stifle, or intrude upon their psychotherapy clients. As with any other issue the therapist and patient address, the outcome depends on the method. When therapists rigidly dominate the initial interview with technical language and personal agendas about privacy matters, patients may understandably react with anxiety and trepidation. However, if therapists follow the age-old wisdom of "starting where the client is," a climate of learning and trust can be created in which the patient feels comfortable asking about and discussing a broad range of topics. Most patients, in my professional experience, have welcomed therapists' concern that they understand office-related procedures and how the procedures affect their treatment. Giving patients an opportunity to review empathically written policies and procedures prior to their first outpatient appointment gives them a less-hurried opportunity to reflect on the information. In some instances, discussing seemingly innocuous rules and procedures reduces potential patients' anxiety about why they sought help in the first place.

Case Example

The following example illustrates how a therapist stayed sensitively focused on the primary goal of the first interview—understanding why the client is seeking help and establishing a beginning rapport and working alliance—while taking a few moments at the outset of the initial interview to communicate how information is protected and what the exceptions to confidentiality are.

Therapist: Today our goal is to talk about the problems that you have been having that have prompted you to seek my help. Before we begin talking about these, I wanted to check in with you about whether you received the client information I mailed and whether you had a chance to review this information?

Client: [Indicates she has received it and has read it.]

Therapist: One of the most important items of information in that handout is how I will be keeping confidential what you tell me, and what the exceptions to your confidentiality are. [Pauses to see that client understands and sees she appears agreeable to proceeding.] I must keep confidential what you tell me, unless you give me written consent to release your information or unless there are legally mandated exceptions to confidentiality. Exceptions would include, for example, if you are abusing a child, I am legally required to report suspected child abuse, or if you tell me you are planning to kill yourself or someone else, I must act to protect you or the other person.

Client: [Nods, indicating she understands.]

Therapist: The handout also explains how I will be routinely using what you tell me. For example, if you are working with a psychiatrist, I would be speaking with your psychiatrist about your condition in order to help coordinate diagnostic and treatment planning. I also understand you want me to bill your insurance company in order to be reimbursed. When I send bills to your insurance company, I need to send your diagnosis to them. If your insurance company requires more information later, I will tell you what they are asking for so you can decide whether to release further information to them or not. [Feels satisfied from the client's response that she has reviewed the written information and understands so far what the therapist has stated verbally.]

Before I begin asking you about the problems that prompted you to come here and ask you questions about the history of the problems and your life experiences, I want to give you a chance first to ask me any questions.

Client: [Silent, but contemplative, appears to be interested in the therapist's invitation to consider any questions she may have. After a few moments …] Well, yes, I do have a question … I am having problems with my husband, and I am wondering if you have experience working with marriage problems?

Therapist: [Answers client's questions about her professional background and waits for any further questions, but the client says she has no more questions.] Please don't hesitate to ask me any more questions that might occur to you later … If you're ready, let's move now into what brought you here today … what caused you to pick up the phone and call me seeking help?

Ongoing Communications about Confidentiality

It is crucial to communicate with patients about confidentiality and privacy and their exceptions before therapy begins, and continuing discussions at various junctures in therapy may also be indicated. These may be helpful when third-party payers request additional information beyond the diagnosis, or when therapists receive a court order, subpoena, or third-party request for records, or must fulfill a legally mandated duty to report. Clinical tips for sensitively handling some of these situations are discussed elsewhere in this text. (See, for example, Chapter 5 on exceptions and Chapter 12, section on "Handling Attorneys' Requests, Subpoenas, Court Orders, and Search Warrants.")

PROTECTING PRIVACY AND CONFIDENTIALITY OF DIFFERENT CLIENT POPULATIONS

Treatment of Involuntary Patients

Involuntary patients (e.g., those referred by courts, employers, probation officers, or regulatory boards) have built-in disclosure requirements and must be informed of what will be disclosed and to whom. (See further discussion of this in Chapter 5.)

Treatment of Minors

Practitioners providing psychotherapy to children and adolescents need to balance children's needs for confidentiality with parents' or legal guardians' needs for information. Parents or legal guardians generally have the right to see their minors' psychotherapy records, unless doing so could be harmful to the minors. Practitioners must therefore understand their legal obligations to disclose information to parents and legal guardians, while exercising good clinical judgment about whether doing so would undermine treatment or otherwise hurt children.

For example, a biological parent who has lost parental rights might not have access to the records unless the guardian gives permission. Also, minors who can legally give consent to treatment, such as "emancipated minors," normally have control over access of their records. Therapists should consult their state laws to learn the conditions under which children can be emancipated and have different privacy rights. For example, in Minnesota a minor who has (a) borne a child, (b) been married, or is (c) living away from home and making his or her own financial decisions (regardless of source of income) has different privacy rights than other adolescents. A federal mandate may defer to local or state rules. For example, in substance abuse programs covered by CFR 42, the federal rule directs practitioners to follow the state rule (as with reporting of child abuse or neglect). Practitioners must also learn whether their state statutes have provisions for withholding information from parents when it is in the child's best interest to do so. In all cases, practitioners need to consider what is likely to be beneficial and unlikely to be harmful to child and adolescent clients.

Parents and guardians generally have the right to review a child's record if the child is at risk for harming himself or herself or others and the practitioner believes that they can be helpful and not harmful to the child. Beyond this and a few other rare exceptions, practitioners often lack clear guidance as to when parents must be informed about their children. Schoener (2010) suggests three parameters to consider when deciding whether to disclose information to parents:

- Weigh the pros and cons of telling versus not telling the parents, or any other given party.
- Attempt to assess whether the parent would be in a position to help protect the adolescent if he or she knew about the conduct.
- Determine whether the practitioner has advice to give the parent regarding what the parent could do to help prevent harm.

Working with Parents and Guardians

The degree of confidentiality and privacy needed to promote the best clinical outcomes for children depends to a large extent on their age or developmental stage. Adolescents, for example, may request more privacy than younger children. In most instances, therapists can elicit the cooperation of parents and guardians regarding confidentiality when they explain the importance of confidentiality to the treatment outcome and solicit the opinions and advice of the parents or guardians.

Topics that practitioners may wish to discuss with parents in order to gather important information, reduce anxiety, and increase cooperation include the following:

- Their minor child's need for confidentiality in their treatment
- The clinician's need to be able to make professional decisions about what is necessary for parents to know
- Assurance that the practitioner will inform them of any risk with which they can help

Sometimes parents can better understand the importance of confidentiality when practitioners explain it in writing and parents can refer to it throughout the child's treatment. Developing a confidentiality statement that can be signed by the parents, practitioners, and older children and adolescents not only increases understanding and promotes helpful questions but helps to create an atmosphere of trust and support. The CD and Appendix E contains a sample informed consent policy for parents and guardians, which includes the following statement that parents or guardians may sign about the child's need for confidentiality:

As a parent, I understand that I have the right to information concerning my minor child in therapy, except where otherwise stated by law. I also understand that this therapist believes in providing a minor child with a private environment in which to disclose himself/herself to facilitate therapy. I therefore give permission to this therapist to use his/her discretion, in accordance with professional ethics and law, in deciding what information revealed by my child is to be shared with me. I understand that this therapist will inform me of any risk to my child with which I can help.

Issues regarding confidentiality involving minors can arise throughout the course of therapy. In most instances, therapists can refuse to disclose information at any point during treatment if disclosure could cause serious harm to the minor. During therapy, practitioners should continue to reiterate the above principles and continue to weigh whether release of the information might cause serious harm. Whenever possible, therapists should promote direct communication between children and their parents or legal guardian regarding issues of concern to the parents or guardians.

Working with minors usually entails communicating with other professionals, which may provide opportunities to help the minor but may complicate confidentiality further. Therapists should explain to minor patients (as appropriate, depending upon developmental stage) and their guardians that the child's therapy will involve a team approach in which the therapist will be conferring with the child's teachers and other school personnel. Therapists require consent from parents and guardians in order to share information with school personnel, except in an emergency.

It is equally important for practitioners to keep in mind that discussions with teachers and principals can be risky. School professionals may not have the capacity to protect the confidential clinical information or know how best to use it. I agree generally with Schoener's recommendations (Schoener, 2010) that therapists limit discussions with teachers and principals to the following:

- Information necessary for the child's safety (this should be shared with the child also)
- Feedback that counseling is occurring
- General information about prognosis, limited to such things as a statement that they are not likely to see change in the next few weeks
- Assurances that if this does not help, the practitioner will try something else
- What the therapist would like school personnel to do to help the child (this should be shared also with the child)

Group Treatment

Trust that develops within group therapy depends not only upon clients' relationships with therapists, but also upon group therapy clients' relationships with one another. Because multiple clients are present during group treatment and practitioners have limited control over the behavior of clients after they hear one another's confidential disclosures, practitioners are unable to guarantee confidentiality of group clients' communications. Clients in group therapy therefore often feel a

heightened concern about how the confidentiality of their private communications will be protected. Accordingly, group therapists have a duty, both to individual group clients as well as to the group itself, to explicitly communicate and fully discuss their policies and procedures for safeguarding clients' confidentiality.

As with other forms of treatment, group treatment practitioners ideally should communicate expectations about confidentiality and its exceptions in writing as well as verbally in the intake sessions with individual group therapy clients and with all group members.

At the outset of the first group therapy session, while practitioners are reviewing the purpose and norms for the group, they should explicitly state their own duty to safeguard group clients' confidentiality and cite the exceptions to confidentiality. Group therapists also should discuss the need for group members to make a contract with one another to refrain from discussing each other's identity and confidential communications outside of the group sessions, as well as consequences to group members if there are breaches of privacy and confidentiality. Group therapists need to ensure that all group clients understand and have pledged that they will adhere to the group rules regarding confidentiality.

The following is a sample privacy and confidentiality contract for group clients to sign after they discuss it in the first group session:

> I understand that in order to establish trust in group therapy so that group therapy can be helpful to me and other group therapy clients, it is essential that all group members' identities remain private and that all group members' confidential disclosures be protected. This means that while I have the right to choose to speak to others outside of group therapy about my own problems and my own participation in group therapy, I cannot reveal the identity of any other group members or what any other group members have stated in any group session. I agree to take responsibility for protecting the confidentiality of other group members' identities and what they say in group sessions. I understand that should I breach this confidentiality and privacy agreement, accidentally or on purpose, my group therapist has the right to terminate my participation in group treatment.

Therapists need to ensure privacy and confidentiality of group members by keeping an individual record for each group therapy client (Knauss, 2006). Maintaining separate documentation in individual charts involves a few extra minutes after each group therapy session. However, it is the only way to guarantee adequate documentation and to protect group clients' privacy and confidentiality.

Family and Couple Treatment

The same wisdom that guides confidentiality for group therapy applies to couple and family treatment: Complete confidentiality is impossible. However, there is a mutual duty between the two members of a dyad, or among multiple members of a family, to protect one another's confidential disclosures. As with other types of treatment involving multiple parties, practitioners work ethically and systematically to safeguard confidentiality by imbuing treatment with a respect for the privacy of others and providing a role model for the ways in which that respect can be incorporated into the couple's or family's value system. Practitioners should provide written information regarding privacy practices, as well as communicate these verbally to couples and family members.

When practitioners are responding to requests for family or couple records, identities and information from family members who have not given their consent for release of information must be omitted from any copies of the original record. In order to protect privacy and confidentiality and minimize later time-consuming record deletion problems, therapists may wish to keep separate records for each family member as they do for group therapy clients. Practitioners should also document discussions about confidentiality and privacy expectations and clients' confidentiality contracts in their records.

Confidentiality after Death

Professional codes of ethics uniformly support the notion that confidentiality regarding therapeutic records extends after a person's death. Mental health professionals were alarmed when Martin Orne released treatment records, therapy session tapes, and his recollections of his patient, Anne Sexton, to Sexton's biographer, Diane Middlebrook, after Sexton's death. Dr. Orne claimed that Sexton would have authorized him to release her communications in treatment to her biographer. However, the professional community maintained it was callous for him to do so (Schoener, 2010).

Despite ethical and legal requirements that protect clients' confidentiality after death, deceased clients' legally authorized representatives can act on their behalf and have access to their records. In some states (e.g., Minnesota), if the client is married, the spouse has access to the records after death; in most states the patient's legal heir controls records access after death. In substance abuse treatment programs covered by CFR 42, the federal rule is to follow the state rule, as in the reporting of child abuse or neglect.

I suspect that most patients would feel alarmed if they were aware that relatives could eventually review their psychotherapy records. One therapist anticipated this possibility with his client after she developed a life-threatening illness. The client had spoken to the therapist in several treatment sessions about her decision not to tell her adult daughters certain details about her unhappy marriage with their father. Because the client's strong feelings about her wish for privacy had been a focus of her treatment, and she knew her physical prognosis was poor, the therapist inquired whether she might wish to consider the option of preparing an "advance directive" to indicate her wish to prohibit legally authorized representatives from having access to her records after she died. The client considered this option and decided to prepare a notarized statement to the effect that her wish was for no one to have access to her therapy records after her death. Her family members may still pursue a legal right to have access to her records after her death, but at least she felt the directive could inform them of her wishes for privacy.

Confidentiality in Mandated Reporting

As clients' trust in their therapists deepens they may choose to disclose more sensitive information. In some instances, these revelations result in a duty to report illegal activities, such as suspected child abuse, which can sometimes result in disruptions to therapy. How practitioners handle a potential or actual reporting duty can make a difference. The best way to avoid disruption in therapy is to discuss with potential clients in the initial session the therapists' ethical and legal duty to report harmful activities to appropriate authorities. Knowing this from the outset can be a great source of support to clients. In many instances, clients are relieved to find a vehicle strong enough to help them disclose actions about which they are ashamed or over which they feel they have no control. When possible, it is helpful for practitioners to consider whether and how they can involve their psychotherapy clients in making the legally mandated reports. Some clients have chosen to make the reports themselves, in the presence of their therapists. The goal is to balance clients' need for autonomy and control over their lives with others' need for protection. Chapter 5 provides an example of just such a situation, as well as other such situations.

To be ethical, when practitioners must make legally mandated reports they should normally give only the "minimum necessary" to meet the purpose of the report. However, practitioners should also carefully weigh the possible outcomes in determining how much information to disclose. Schoener (2010) has reported unfortunate instances where limited information in telephone calls to an identified potential victim of violence has led to potential victims feeling terrorized.

Suspected abuse reports to agencies, such as child protective services, are easier because these involve calling a professional social services intake worker, not an identified potential victim of violence. These reports can be summarized briefly but precisely and limited to the following:

- The reporting practitioner's name
- The purpose of the report (including the legal duty that makes it necessary for the practitioner to make a report)
- Name and address of the person alleged to have engaged in the abuse
- Name and address of the alleged subject of the abuse
- What the patient told the practitioner about the alleged abuse, specifically "who allegedly did what to whom"

HANDLING THIRD-PARTY REQUESTS FOR RECORDS

Principles to Consider

When considering third-party requests for clients' confidential treatment information, practitioners must keep in mind the following principles:

- The need to verify carefully the legitimacy of the request for disclosure of information
- The importance of ensuring that a client (or a parent or legal guardian, where permitted by law) fully understands the request, its purpose, and has given consent for disclosure
- The importance of disclosing only that information which is requested and required for the intended purpose

- The need to be informed of one's own state statutes and to seek legal counsel from the practitioner's own attorney as needed

It is important for the clinician to discern the type of third-party request for information he or she has received. Requests generally occur in one of three forms, and each type requires a different response.

A Third-Party Request without Signed Authorization

Psychotherapists may not release confidential, patient-identifiable information without the adult client's or minor client's legal guardian's duly signed authorization to release the records, unless there are extenuating circumstances. Such cases include, but are not limited to, a legally mandated duty to report suspected child abuse or to protect an identifiable intended victim of violence. Thus, when practitioners receive telephone calls or letters from parties requesting client records without a release, prudent practitioners refrain from even acknowledging an acquaintance with the client by saying, "I am unable to acknowledge if I know or work with a client without a client's informed written authorization." Or, alternatively, "Without a client's signed informed authorization, I am unable to release confidential records."

A Third-Party Request with Signed Authorization

This type of release of information is signed by a current or past client, or a client's legal guardian, to send records to another person or agency such as a social service agency, another therapist, or insurance company. Practitioners are more comfortable receiving requests for information when they are for purposes of sharing information needed for continuity of care, do not immediately raise the specter of legal action, and are signed by the patient or legal guardian. The relative informality of the form can, however, motivate clinicians to reproduce the entire record and send it as a matter of course to a person or the requesting agency. Practitioners must develop a more discerning response.

First, practitioners must determine whether the release of information form contains sufficient information in order to accurately determine the identity of the patient and specific purpose of the request and whether the release of information form is valid. A checklist of questions that will help practitioners clarify whether the release of information form is appropriate includes the following:

- Does the form contain adequate data to identify the patient (e.g., date of birth or social security number, address, and telephone number)?
- Does it state the specific purpose of the request and to whom the information will be sent?
- Is the date of the signature recent enough to comply with state legal requirements?

- Is it possible to determine whether it was the client who signed the release and whether the client understood its purpose?
- Does it specify an expiration date?
- Does it inform the patient about his or her revocation rights and any consequences of refusing to sign?

After determining that it is a properly executed and signed form, and that the client understands its purpose, the practitioner should summarize only the information being requested (especially important in instances when the individual was seen in the context of conjoint, family therapy, or group therapy, and the names of other clients and their information must be protected). A summary allows the practitioner to aptly condense their perceptions of the relevant aspects of the clinical contacts for the person or organization receiving the summary. The general principle is to err on the side of sending too little rather than too much. If recipients want more information, they can contact the clinician.

If the record, however, contains information about drug treatment, federal laws protecting confidentiality supersede the release, and no information should be released without specific consent on a federal form allowing the release, a court order, or both.

Subpoenas

Subpoenas are another form of third-party request for patient-identifiable information. In order to release information in response to a subpoena, just as with other third-party requests, practitioners must obtain their patients' or patients' legal representatives' signed authorization for release of information. (For further information about subpoenas and how to proceed, see Chapter 12.)

SUMMARY

With the launching of electronic record systems, practitioners are even more challenged today to find ways to limit access to confidential psychotherapy information to authorized users who will have access only to that information that pertains to their legitimate purposes. This chapter presented practical strategies for developing policies and procedures to protect security and privacy of patient-identifiable psychotherapy information in all forms—oral, paper, and electronic. Tips included defining who will have access to what kind of information and how and when information may be accessed. It presented options for ways psychotherapists can inform their clients of policies and procedures pertaining to how their confidential communications will be protected and exceptions to confidentiality in ways that promote trust and a secure treatment relationship.

As thoughtful practitioners seek to protect confidentiality of private, patient-identifiable data, they are mindful that not all good treatment takes place in isolation. Practitioners can be most helpful to patients when they are able to balance adherence to laws with ethical principles and exercise professional judgment regarding what is most likely to be beneficial and unlikely to be harmful to patients in given situations.

7

Boundary Challenges
Impact of Electronic Communication on the Therapeutic Relationship

Therapists today, whether they actively use electronic communication in their counseling or maintain an online-free practice, are concerned about the rapid explosion of electronic communication and its impact on patients, themselves, and the therapeutic relationship.

Electronic communication offers a wide range of treatment opportunities for common mental health problems that patients may be fearful of discussing with their health care and mental health practitioners due to stigma. These can include alcoholism, drug abuse, depression, anxiety disorders, and eating disorders, which are associated with mortality, morbidity, social and psychosocial problems, violence, criminal behavior, or accidents (Postel, deHaan, & De Jong, 2008). Authors report promising benefits from online counseling with various patient populations (Goss & Anthony, 2009; Wagner, Knaevelsrud, & Maercker, 2006; Wootton & Titov, 2010) and recommend integrating it into training curricula (Scott, 2009); even though some researchers note that the quality of online counseling studies varies (Postel et al., 2008) and that future studies are needed (Richards, 2009; Simpson, 2009).

Despite the enthusiasm voiced by some therapists about the usefulness of online therapy, many therapists avoid electronic communications with patients. They worry not only about loss of privacy, but also the loss of the rich visual cues they have in face-to-face office appointments with patients. They might be concerned whether online therapy would benefit or prolong a patient's struggles (e.g., with agoraphobia or social awkwardness). They find it is harder to have a sense of the patient's mood. It is difficult to see whether patients are crying, and they need to ask. They recognize that a sudden breakdown in Internet service or electronic equipment in the middle of an emotional discussion could be unsettling for clients (Anthony & Nagel, 2009). They believe a virtual presence is no substitute for an in-person presence. Yet we welcome telephone and long-distance video options that not only allow us to provide clinical supervision to practitioners in rural areas, but also accessibility to treatment and continuity of care for clients who are unable to come into our offices for therapy appointments. Examples include those who are physically disabled, students leaving for college, soldiers heading off to war, or persons moving away who are not yet settled in their new communities. Increasingly insurance companies are recognizing the value of telemedicine, such as via Skype, and are paying for it.

Whether therapists routinely use online counseling in their practices or confine their practices to face-to-face clients, however, all face a plethora of electronic-related clinical dilemmas and potential ethical boundary problems. The Internet has created a "small town" atmosphere, and therapists and patients may observe one another in ways they previously could not imagine.

Practitioners worry about loss of clients' and their own privacy. Unless encrypted, e-mail and other forms of electronic communication can be seen by unauthorized users, not unlike a postcard sent through the mail (Kolmes, Nagel, & Anthony, 2011; Myers, 2010). Google has been compiling social networking lists based on Gmail address book contacts without notifying users, thereby permitting personal names and e-mail addresses such as those of estranged spouses, current lovers, attorneys, and doctors, to be publically indexed by search engines. Social media sites often mine users' e-mail or cell phone address books and "suggest" users "friend" these people; this can be confusing to clients and raise boundary issues.

Traditionally therapists learned only information about patients that patients chose to reveal to them or gave consent for them to obtain from others. Now, practitioners may use search engines to seek information about their patients, yet feel ashamed about doing so and confused about whether to disclose to their patients or supervisors the searches they have conducted and what information they have found. Given the secrecy, they wonder what they can document in the patient's record about the surreptitious information they discovered (Clinton, Silverman, & Brendel, 2010).

In turn, patients traditionally had access to information about their therapists primarily from their own disclosures (e.g., published biographical information and descriptions of their professional services). Now, they have instant access to their personal information via the Web, information that may or may not even be accurate or may be disparaging. Clinicians can now expect that their patients will have searched electronically for information about them prior to their initial appointment (Gabbard, Kassaw, & Perez-Garcia, 2011). They may hope their patients will share what they know about them and what questions they may have but cannot count on their doing so. They are left wondering, "What does my patient know about me?" A cartoon shared by my colleague Gary Schoener at a workshop effectively captured this. The cartoon depicted a therapist asking "Why do I have this feeling I've been Googled?"

The purpose of this chapter is to discuss evolving clinical and boundary issues confronting therapists as they explore the rapidly emerging modes of electronic communication, determine under what circumstances it may help or undermine the therapeutic relationship, and how they may protect themselves and their patients. What ethical standards must therapists consider in using electronic communication safely with clients? What ground rules can be helpful? Is it ethical to use Google or other search engine research tools to discover information about patients? If therapists do, should they inform their patients? Do therapists need to develop policies for themselves and their patients on whether they can research each other on the Internet? Can therapists safely belong to Facebook or other social networking sites? If so, what privacy precautions do therapists consider? How do therapists establish boundaries on the Internet? How do therapists handle inaccurate or vindictive comments published about themselves on the Internet? What are appropriate protocols for maintaining blogs and having discussion groups? What standards and guidelines for using the Internet in therapy have professional organizations developed? How have electronic record keeping systems changed our ability to provide care that meets our standards of privacy and quality?

This chapter also emphasizes the need for practitioners to be proactive in thinking through and establishing professionally sound policies and procedures regarding electronic communications, including e-mail, texting, cell phones as recording and communication devices, social media, and other related media. In all cases it is useful to examine basic principles of ethical decision making: *beneficence*, is it likely to help the patient?; *nonmaleficence*, is it unlikely to harm the client?; *autonomy*, is it likely to foster the patient's autonomy by respecting the client's choices and role in decision making?; *fidelity*, is it consistent with what we have promised to the client and consistent with client's expectations of our professional role?; *justice*, does it balance the needs or rights of one person versus another (Beauchamp & Childress, 2009)?

The following story introduces some of the clinical questions practitioners face regarding various forms of electronic communication technology, from e-mail to searches, and ways that technology might impact the problems that bring clients to therapy in the first place. One patient's experience with e-mail in therapy and access to personal information about her current therapist on the Web affected the therapeutic relationship and her journey toward knowing and accepting herself. When she gave me permission to use her story, she expressed hope that it would help therapists to understand the complicated impact the Internet can have on therapy.

LESSONS LEARNED FROM A LONG-TERM, DYNAMIC TREATMENT CASE

"Nancy,"* a middle-aged, unmarried, professional woman employed as supervisor in a large bank, sought help from a psychotherapist for anxiety, depression, obsessive fears of harming people, fears of abandonment, and confusion over identity. She was socially isolated and suffered from serious medical symptoms of irritable bowel syndrome. As a child, she suffered from her controlling father's physical and verbal abuse and felt estranged from her mother, whom she described as emotionally and physically distant. Since her early teenage years, she had been in physically intimate relationships with older married women. Nancy's experiences in psychotherapy in her young adulthood were affected by her impulsivity. She had refused to leave one of her former therapist's offices when her session was over and frequently drove by his home.

At the time Nancy chose to enter therapy with the new therapist, she was suffering from difficulty leaving her home except to go to work, was uncomfortable and confused about her sexual identity, and felt she needed help. She understood the therapist was lesbian-identified and wanted to try out a lesbian lifestyle while receiving knowledgeable support from the therapist. Soon she found herself becoming romantically attracted to her therapist. She became preoccupied with whether the therapist reciprocated her feelings of attraction.

She felt shocked when her therapist informed her she had been diagnosed with cancer and would be out of the office for a week or two for radiation treatments. When the therapist resumed their therapy appointments, Nancy was extremely anxious. She began sending daily e-mails to her therapist, usually around 9:30 p.m., expressing ambivalence about whether to continue or to terminate therapy. Her therapist usually responded within minutes, briefly offering guidance. Rather than feeling calmed by her therapist's immediate e-mail responses, her longings for connection and intimacy with her therapist escalated. After hundreds of anxious e-mails and months of unproductive therapy, the therapist expressed hopelessness about her ability to help. She informed Nancy she would need to terminate with her. Her reasoning was that she belatedly realized that the patient had a borderline personality disorder and required another type of therapy called dialectical behavior therapy (DBT). She referred her to a psychologist specialized in boundary issues, who she felt could make an appropriate referral, and who referred the patient to me.

---

* Not her real name.

As Nancy entered my office, she shared her perception that her previous therapist disliked working with patients who had borderline personality disorder. As I explored further her experience in her most recent therapy, she described how preoccupied she became with her therapist. She had felt she was in love with her therapist and also sensed her therapist had felt attracted to her. She believed the therapist could not admit her feelings however. She wished she could know what had been in her therapist's mind. She felt angry her therapist dropped her. She feared it could happen again with me. She assumed I too would not like to work with a client who had a borderline personality disorder. She had been anxious about losing her therapist due to her therapist's cancer. "Don't tell me anything about your personal life," she emphatically told me. "I don't want to know anything about you!" Perceiving myself to be a therapist who believes in the value of not disclosing personal information, except in limited ways, when it might be beneficial and unlikely to be harmful to my clients, I felt confident agreeing with her request that I not disclose my own personal information to her.

In the early stages of our work together she shared she did not know what she was feeling and often said she could not trust to tell me when she did know. She also felt she could not trust the authenticity of what I said. She was cautious about revealing her feelings related to experiences in her life, family, work, her former therapy experiences, and her perceptions of and needs from me. I felt we could gain insights from Nancy's e-mail correspondence with her previous therapist. She was willing to share some of it with me, but not parts that felt embarrassing to her. The extensive e-mail correspondence she did share gave me an unusual glimpse into detailed interactions with her previous therapist. In her e-mails to her therapist, she appeared to me to be flailing for control.

We discussed professional boundaries in our work ahead, including agreeing upon how she and I would communicate. I explained my preference, whenever possible, to communicate with my patients within our scheduled sessions, not in between sessions, except in case of emergency. I stated I was concerned e-mails were not private and therefore did not use e-mail for communication with my patients. If she needed to leave me a message in between sessions, I requested she do so by phone.

I was struck by how this patient, with her history of early attachment disruption and trauma, had entered therapy requiring a very predictable container within which she could clarify her emotional turmoil. She needed help discovering what may be triggering her fears, impulsivity, and self-destructive behaviors.

She needed assistance developing helpful ways of expressing her feelings and needs. The therapist's illness felt overwhelming in the context of her acute fears of abandonment, emotional reactivity, and longing for secure attachment.

Electronic communication seemed to have made this extremely difficult work even harder for her. Later, after years of hard work with me in individual therapy, this patient explained that the e-mail communication with her former therapist gave her a false sense of hope for reassurance. False, because, as she pointed out, she could not detect her therapist's emotions in e-mails. She could only imagine what was in her therapist's mind. She was unable to get the help she needed to clarify what was in her own mind. "I had to read through the lines," she said. Also, e-mail correspondence in between her office sessions with her therapist was intermittent, unplanned, and unpredictable, which had the effect of exacerbating her anxiety rather than helping to soothe it. As I listened to her describe the experience, I wondered if the frequent e-mails may have increased the preoccupation and disorganization she was feeling in her attachment with her therapist (Bennett, 2004).

As our therapy continued, we too faced challenges establishing boundaries in our therapeutic relationship. Soon she was leaving long phone messages on my voice messaging system. Sometimes her messages were so long that my system filled up and other patients with urgent matters were unable to leave messages. I spoke with her about my concerns: I shared that I wanted to give her my full attention. I explained that in my view, I could better understand her needs when I had an opportunity to speak with her in person in our sessions. I shared how the long messages were affecting other people who needed to reach me.

As therapy continued, she shared more about how frightening it felt to share what she was feeling and thinking with me. She courageously revealed her secret that she was causing her own intestinal problems by ingesting aspirin in order to receive compassionate attention from medical professionals. With my encouragement, she took responsibility to share this information with her psychiatrist, who was treating her bipolar mood disorder, and with her internist who was treating her intestinal problems. She described how amazed she felt to experience both of these professionals listening to her nonjudgmentally.

In addition to working hard in individual therapy with me, she had accepted my referrals to work with colleagues. She was learning self-soothing skills in her weekly DBT group sessions and was consulting a psychologist who specialized in obsessive-compulsive disorder (OCD) in order to learn strategies for moving through fears of harming people and riding the bus. Her need to continue to anxiously phone me in between our sessions continued, and I again discussed my wish for her to limit her phone calls. She shared my concerns about her calls with her OCD therapist, who was very helpful to her and to me. In a matter-of-fact way, he acknowledged the reality of limitations in my practice. He gave her permission to call him instead. She never needed to call him and her phone calls in between appointments to me decreased. The opportunity for me to work as a member of a treatment team and for her to benefit from other professionals' ideas about her problems increased my sense of security and safety and hers.

Then, seemingly out of the blue, I received a message that startled me. "I am going to have to end therapy with you because I may have found out something personal about you," Nancy announced somberly in a voice mail message. Per our prior agreement, I took it up with her in our next session.

"What happened? Can you help me understand what you are thinking?" I asked, after I acknowledged receiving her message. She explained she had discovered an article about a young man from our city with the same last name as mine on a national foundation's Web site. "It was an accidental discovery," she said. She went on to explain that she is acquainted with two people with a disability, a family friend and a member of her DBT group, and was in charge of organizing her company's upcoming annual fund drive to support medical research on this disability. She was searching the foundation's Web site in order to learn about the handicap and what the research foundation was doing. "Was the person with your name on the Web site related to you? If he is, I will have to leave therapy," she said.

I felt surprised. Indeed my son has that disability. I surmised she saw the article about his raising money for medical research that the foundation published on its Web site. I then vividly recalled her urgent plea in our first meeting that I never reveal anything personal about myself in order to protect her from feeling worried as she had worried on learning of her previous therapist's medical problems. I was puzzled how to proceed. What made her assume she would need to leave therapy with me if the person she discovered on the Web site were my relative? What would the impact be on her if I were to acknowledge he was? What would the impact be on her if I did not? I felt my immediate task would be to try to understand what was in her mind while I allowed myself to carefully ponder what was in my own mind, including what needs I may have for personal privacy in our therapy relationship.

This unsettling experience awakened me to the potential disruptions to the therapeutic relationship when patients discover personal information about their therapists on the Web. For therapists, the ability to preserve relative anonymity in therapy is a core value. It protects patients and us from intrusions into our work. We have come to understand that patients learn much about us from how we dress, how we decorate our offices, our facial and body expressions, and to what we pay attention as they speak. But, as Gabbard et al. noted in their discussion of professional boundaries in the era of the Internet, we now live in a post-privacy era (Gabbard, Kassaw, & Perez-Garcia, 2011). What is the meaning to both patient and therapist of additional information the patient discovers? How do we preserve the therapeutic relationship as a safe place for work in the face of too much or too invasive knowledge?

In our subsequent sessions, I consulted Nancy about her experience of discovering what she figured could be personal information about a family member of mine. I also consulted with my treatment team colleagues regarding my dilemma about how to respond to her questions. They did not tell me what to do but wondered with me what harm could come from her knowing a public fact, even if she had expressed a desire to know nothing about my life. Ultimately, I felt comfortable leaving my patient in charge of choosing whether to know or not to know.

"Do you want me to tell you?" I asked. "Yes," she said. After I told her it was my son, I asked how it was for her to know. She expressed sadness that my son had a disability and relief that her treatment need not end due to her having this knowledge. She proceeded with her fundraising effort at her work and seemed calmer with me.

As her treatment evolved, she had further conversations with me about sorting out in her mind what boundary violations were. Would it be appropriate for her as a patient to search for information about me on the Web? Naively, I had not foreseen any of my patients seeing my book on record keeping, but she had ordered it and knew a lot already, including the influence my father had had on my professional work. She discussed these boundary questions also with her psychiatrist, who she felt gave her some good guidance. She said his comments helped her to clarify that it would not be helpful to her or to me for her to search further for information about me.

Sometime later, she mentioned having done an Internet search and finding a "lot of personal information about a former lover" on her Facebook page. The former lover, she explained, was her former college counselor, with whom she had lived for a couple of years. "You know people can find out a lot about you if you are on Facebook," she said in what sounded to me like a warning tone. I wondered if she were referring to me. I checked my Facebook privacy settings that evening and found they were still set. It took me courage to ask her directly if she had been referring to discovering something about me on Facebook. Or was she referring only to her friend? "I was referring to her," she said.

As she continued in individual therapy with me, she gradually made progress in establishing more satisfying relationships. She enjoyed practicing respectful ways of communicating with people and was an active participant in her DBT group, learning self-soothing skills. She was no longer confined to her home outside of work hours. She overcame her fears of holding her infant niece and was able to ride the bus into the city for work. When she disagreed with her father, she found she could express her own separate thoughts to him. She was very pleased to be developing a mutually supportive relationship with her mother. Intermittently, when she experienced intense emotion and shame, she reverted to pinching herself, but eventually decided to change to a more self-caring lifestyle. Earlier, she had told me that she felt "victimized" by the psychotropic medications that had been making her hungrier and causing her to gain unwelcome weight; she began choosing fresh fruits and vegetables in her diet and exercising to combat these side effects. After ongoing intermittent periods of shutting down in our sessions when feeling intense emotion, she could eventually share what was on her mind. We could then pool our respective thoughts, gain deeper understanding of her life and how it had shaped her current experience, and explore her options.

For this client, with early attachment trauma and fears of speaking her true feelings, our mutual dilemmas regarding self-disclosure and her unanticipated access to her therapist's personal life were profoundly challenging. We were able to understand the respective intrusions and negotiate helpful ways to proceed in her therapy. Obtaining consultation from colleagues and focusing on what was likely to promote her autonomy, be beneficial, and unlikely to be harmful, as well as how I could protect myself as her therapist to feel safe when she had more information about me than I might otherwise have disclosed, emerged as critical components of this treatment.

AREAS OF ETHICAL AND CLINICAL CONCERN WITHIN AN OTHERWISE IN-PERSON PRACTICE

The following are some of the clinical and ethical issues related to electronic communication and its impact on the therapeutic relationship; several are illustrated by Nancy's treatment with her former therapist and with me.

E-Mail

Nancy's use of asynchronous e-mail communication as a way to express to her former therapist her intense emotions of anger, helplessness, frustration, and confusion felt detrimental to her. E-mail for her, unlike an office appointment, was an undelineated space. It did not provide the structure she needed to facilitate mentalizing, discerning what was in her mind and what was in the mind of her therapist (Allen, Fonagy, & Bateman, 2008). The therapist responding in the late evenings suggests that the therapist may not have been delineating for herself separate space of work time versus personal time. Many therapists confine their online contact with clients to office hours, reinforcing the boundaries of work time. That she responded in the late evenings also stirred Nancy's fantasies of a personal relationship with her therapist.

The e-mail correspondence documented Nancy's and her former therapist's work. Had Nancy's former therapist considered her e-mails to be a record, visible into perpetuity to unknown others, such as Nancy's subsequent therapists? The thought that Nancy's former therapist may not have considered that her e-mails generated a record (Mangalmurti, Murtagh, & Mello, 2010) made me uncomfortable as I reviewed their e-mail correspondence. From discussions I have had with other professionals, many are unaware that e-mail correspondence is a record of their work as much as their evaluation summaries or progress notes.

Another ethical and legal issue that emerges in the above vignette involves privacy. The e-mails with her former therapist contained highly emotional, sensitive, and private material with her full name on them. If they were not encrypted, they could potentially be seen by anyone.

Professional organizations' newly revised ethics codes (American Counseling Association, 2005), mental health online counseling experts (Anthony & Nagel, 2009), and HIPAA's new HITECH electronic security standards all cite the need for encryption of e-mail correspondence with patients so that private, patient-identifiable information cannot be seen by unauthorized people. To protect their patients' privacy, many practitioners are choosing not to use e-mail with their patients aside from scheduling appointments. They request private content regarding problems be shared only by telephone or in person, and make this clear during the informed consent process.

Langlois (2011) recommends that practitioners never discuss a case with colleagues on e-mail, which can be seen by anyone. In order to fulfill his responsibility to protect patients' privacy and confidentiality, he uses only private modes of communication such as phone or in-person consultation. Many practitioners are unaware that services such as e-mail and direct messaging offer, on their own, limited security and privacy (Kolmes, Nagel, & Anthony, 2011).

Jon Allen, psychologist and professor, noted that e-mail correspondence with former patients creates unclear role boundaries and can intrude upon patients' current therapy (personal communication, May 17, 2011). When patients who are being discharged from the hospital express interest in having his e-mail address so they may correspond with him after they leave the hospital, he suggests that if they wish to contact him, they send him a letter and he will respond with a letter.

Clarifying boundaries, using privacy settings, creating policies for patients and colleagues about e-mail correspondence, and taking care to de-identify any private information in e-mail correspondence so patients' names are not visible are all strategies practitioners can implement to fulfill their professional ethical standards related to privacy, confidentiality, and dual roles.

Internet Searches

As the opening case example illustrates, Nancy was a woman with fragile boundaries, who was vulnerable to reenacting previous romantic enmeshments. She was asking me for help learning and practicing appropriate boundaries in part to prevent the abrupt dissolutions in relationships she had experienced previously. It was understandable that Nancy's searching the Internet and unexpectedly discovering information about my son on a national Web site could feel overstimulating, invasive, and threatening to her. Her belief that she would then have to end therapy with me was based in her fears about my potentially leaving her. She and I eventually discovered this was a reenactment of her feelings about persons to whom she had felt attached in her youth, who abruptly left her when she expressed affection for them. Because her Internet discovery felt like a significant risk to her and became a key theme in our treatment, I needed to document it in her progress notes.

Nancy's previous patterns of becoming enmeshed with her therapists compelled her to uncover even more information about me, even as she was aware it could be potentially threatening for her. How is searching for information about a therapist on the Internet unlike driving by a therapist's home or sitting for hours in a therapist's office parking lot?

As uncomfortable as therapists may feel about patients' searching for information about them online, however, Gabbard, Kassaw, & Perez-Garcia (2011) suggest that the ethical principle of respect for autonomy preclude our attempting to place constraints on patients' freedom to pursue public information. They note that clinicians who feel that their personal space is being intruded upon by patients who are using search engines to find information about them must deal with this matter as a countertransference issue for supervision, consultation, or personal treatment while they explore with patients the meanings of their curiosity.

As Kate Croskery-Jones, a social work professor, wrote to me so eloquently, "It seems that our society is more fluid than ever, making boundaries all the more complex. Being rigid about them may not help many therapeutic relationships. It seems that deep self-awareness respecting our own tolerances and clinical curiosity as to what patients want to know, what they think they know and why they want to know, may yield the best clinical results as well as most livable private life" (personal communication, May 29, 2011).

I was glad that Nancy, who had shared with me her history of driving by her previous therapist's home, felt free to discuss the issues of her discovery on the Internet with me. She provided us with the opportunity to explore the rich meaning of her Internet searches and its impact on our work together. Her courage to speak with me rather than remain silent about these online issues helped her not suffer alone, helped her to clarify her feelings, and helped me to be more present with her.

Clients are not the only ones who may struggle with curiosity and the easy availability of information online. I am reminded of consulting in a case involving a woman whose psychotherapist rode by her house on his bicycle and stopped to chat with her while she was working in her garage. She shared with me that she had felt this was an expression of her therapist's romantic interest in her. She had felt excited by his interest. But, understandably, his reaching out to her in this way interrupted her treatment with him. She and he became unable to focus on what brought her to treatment.

As this case example illustrates, we need to consider our motivations in making contact with our patients. Is our motivation based on valid professional reasons for the purpose of helping our patients? Or are we motivated to satisfy our own personal needs, as was the therapist seeking out his patient at her home?

Just as we consider any of our actions in the light of their potential benefit or harm to our clients, we must also consider our actions on the Internet within the same ethical and clinical framework. If we choose to search out information about our clients, we must then deal with whatever we discover on the Internet. What if we believe we have found information that our client, who has been maintaining sobriety over many years, is drinking again but has not informed us? Can we mention that we Googled the patient and learned this information? What impact will that likely have on the therapeutic relationship? What if our client has a common name and the drinker is not our client, but merely shares her name?

Even though the Internet is rich in information, there is a fair amount of misinformation. A therapist, married and living with her husband and small children, wondered what information her patients might discover about her online. She searched herself on Spokeo, a popular site for gaining information about a person's marital status, address, income, and other data. The therapist was surprised to discover that, according to the Web site, she was a single man living with his elderly parents and in a different age bracket. This experience illustrated to her that any information on herself or on her patients would be a mix of true (the site did correctly list her address) and false data.

Although looking up information about one's patient on the Internet is not necessarily unethical, because it is public information, it can create serious clinical complications such as loss of trust in the therapist (Clinton et al., 2010; Gabbard et al., 2011; Kaslow, Patterson, & Gottlieb, 2011). I have difficulty envisioning sound professional reasons for using a search engine to seek information about my clients, unless, perhaps, I would do so together with them, at their request, and for reasons consistent with their treatment goals. For example, an adolescent girl referred to me for help with peer relationship problems might be excited to show me a photo of herself and a new friend on her Facebook page. Could responding to her invitation to look at her Facebook page facilitate our opportunity to discuss her feelings about her new friendship? Or what if an adolescent suffering from cyber bullying suggested she show me examples of the vicious comments she was receiving? Could seeing those with her help me to bear witness to the trauma she was experiencing and help her identify her options to stand up to her attackers in order to gain control and confidence in herself? As a wise colleague aptly put it: "therapy is not about information, or even truth-seeking in any factual sense. Whatever the patient tells us about his or her experience is what we work with together; it is a shared body of communication that takes on meaning between the two people" (Helen Gilbert, personal communication, June 1, 2011).

Social Media: Discovering Disturbing Information about Practitioners

Social networking sites, such as Facebook, LinkedIn, Myspace, Caring Bridge, and others, expand the chances of patients' feeling troubled by witnessing information or behaviors that therapists would not normally disclose to them: not unlike patients' walking into their therapist's dining room in the middle of an intimate family discussion or entering their therapist's living room in the middle of a party. The following example illustrates the discomfort one patient felt after finding personal information about her therapist on a social networking site.

A 40-year-old woman had to end treatment after 10 years when her therapist became ill from cancer. Her therapist sensitively informed her of his illness and explained why he needed radiation treatment. He was honest with his patient that he could not know whether he would live or die. He made a thoughtful referral, giving her the name of Dr. L., a trusted colleague who had agreed to work with her. Even though the patient felt distressed, she felt able to absorb this amount of information and had no further questions. Not knowing at the time she would need support to manage her feelings about the loss of her therapist, she chose not to accept his referral to see Dr. L. at that time. However, 5 months later, she became more anxious to know about her therapist's condition; the only information she could find was on Caring Bridge, a public Web site for families and friends of gravely ill or dying patients. Though she felt compelled to obtain information about her therapist, the therapist's family members' vivid descriptions of his deteriorating condition felt too intimate and intrusive. She felt isolated and on the outside looking in. No one on this Web site was addressing the needs of the therapist's former patients, only the needs of family and friends. In order to deal with her feelings, she contacted Dr. L., the psychologist whom her former therapist had recommended.

Dr. L. was able to help her mourn the loss of her former therapist and the impact of having received more detail about his dying process than she was able to integrate. Dr. L. realized that while it was important for the patient to grieve the loss, it likely would not have been her former therapist's intention that she share in his and his relatives' experiences of suffering and dying. In the relational therapy he had provided, he understood that the therapeutic relationship is an asymmetrical one. She was aware he had shared his subjectivity with his patients only to the extent that it would be beneficial to them. He had thoughtfully provided for this patient's needs by referring her. Dr. L. began wondering to herself what might her own and her family members' process be should she become terminally ill? Would she ask her family members to consider private ways of informing family and friends of personal details (e.g., by using the privacy settings available on such sites as Caring Bridge)? She reflected on how her compassionate dying colleague probably would, if it were within his power, go to the trouble of discerning what level of detail in his private life would be helpful and not helpful to his patients to know.

Other examples of patients' finding deeply personal information about their therapists on social media sites which can potentially be disturbing and disrupt the therapeutic relationship include personal photos of their therapists drinking or using marijuana with their friends or partners or therapists' personal information on online dating sites. Practitioners are free to participate in online dating sites but need to be fully prepared for their patients finding their information (Gabbard, Kassaw, & Perez-Garcia, 2011).

To protect our patients from finding unintended personal information we would choose otherwise not to disclose, we must choose the maximum level of privacy settings on our social media sites such as Facebook (AMA, 2010a). We must also consider that whatever we say on such sites may be seen by anyone (Facebook alone claims over 50 million users), including our clients, employers, or prospective malpractice or other insurance carriers. When we exercise proactive control to the best of our ability, we can help to prevent ruptures in the therapeutic relationship.

"Friending" and "Fanning" Clients, Students, and Supervisees

As the following example shows, ethical boundary and clinical issues also arise in regard to "friending" clients, students, and supervisees on social media sites.

A school social worker, concerned that cyber bullying was seriously harming a middle school student she was counseling, wondered if it would help to become the student's Facebook "friend" for the purpose of monitoring and helping her student protect herself from the cruel messages the student was receiving. She consulted her colleagues. They advised her that while she had professional reasons to "friend" the student, they explored the dangers inherent in entering into a dual role as "friend" and counselor with the student. They brainstormed with her about other strategies she could use with the troubled student to help empower the student to block the cyber messages, confront the demeaning students, and protect herself. As she worked with her student to develop a plan to protect herself, she helped her student to tell her mother about the cyber bullying and its effects on her. Her mother had not known about the devastating experiences her daughter was having and, after learning, was in a position to help. The mother contacted the National Bullying Organization in Bloomington, Minnesota, where a parent advocate assisted her in working with her daughter and the school to develop strategies to help her daughter. They implemented a program at the school whereby it became "cool" for all students to speak up against cyber and other widespread instances of bullying.

This story also illustrates how helpful it can be when practitioners can consult one another about the ethical implications of potential dual roles and privacy when they consider becoming "friends" with clients on social media sites. It is generally believed that being "friends" with a patient drastically changes the relationship (Cook, 2011), and it is easy to imagine similar issues arising between professors and students, supervisors, and supervisees. Discussions among colleagues help practitioners to consider what policies and procedures they may wish to develop to protect themselves, their clients, students, and clinical supervisees.

Texting

A psychologist shared with me new concerns she felt over clinical and potential boundary issues related to texting with clients.

A colleague with whom he was enjoying conversing over lunch suddenly stopped talking and looked down at her mobile phone. She did not excuse herself for withdrawing suddenly from their conversation. She did not explain why she was becoming preoccupied with her mobile phone. Minutes later, his colleague looked up and resumed talking with him. "What happened? I felt uncomfortable when you suddenly stopped talking and you got busy with your cell phone," he said to her. His colleague

explained she was responding to a client's text message. In their discussion, his colleague realized it was uncharacteristic of her to respond so quickly to her client's messages. "I get swept into feeling I must immediately respond when a client sends me text messages," she discovered as she was thinking aloud. She had lost her usual professional bearings. She began wondering how the urgency she felt to respond to text messages from clients affected the usual boundaries she had always valued and felt protected her treatment with them.

As this therapist's experience revealed, the seductive immediacy of texting pulled her into behaving in uncharacteristic ways, raising new questions for herself about clinical boundaries. Finding her bearings again meant thinking through what policies and procedures for communication with patients would be helpful to develop.

Cell Phones as Recording Devices with Sound and Video Capabilities

Concerns over boundaries, privacy, and confidentiality emerge also around the use of cell phones as recording devices. The possibilities of publically and electronically disseminating private conversations from treatment sessions are limitless. For example, YouTube videos that can be seen around the world by anyone can be created by cell phone recordings.

Do clients need to receive permission from their therapists in order to record their individual sessions? Do group or family members have the opportunity to exercise choice over whether to permit recording of group or family therapy sessions? It is wise to proactively consider these questions and develop policies in keeping with standard ethical principles of safeguarding confidentiality and privacy before they are needed. For example, some therapists ask that all devices be turned off and out of sight so as to assure privacy and focus. The following illustrates an example of a therapist who felt unprepared for these serious questions during her discussion with her patient about her formulation of his diagnosis and treatment needs:

"It happened so unexpectedly," a clinical social worker told me anxiously, requesting a consultation about a troubling event she had experienced in a psychotherapy session with a male patient. "As I was sharing with him my understanding of his diagnosis and his progress, he said he was afraid he might not remember what I was saying. He wanted to hold onto what was in my mind. Suddenly, he pulled out his cell phone, turned it on, and asked me if he could record what I was saying. It happened so fast. I didn't have time to think. I believe I did the right thing in allowing him to record what I was saying about my diagnostic impressions, but I felt unnerved. I was wondering whether his recording could be played in his upcoming law case where he may need to talk about how his mental instability may have caused the financial fraud he was being charged for committing in his business. I understood his wish to hold onto what I was saying, but I felt anxious about losing control over my own privacy."

Cell Phones as Communication Devices

The use of cell phones as communication devices raises ethical and safety issues. Results from two surveys of thousands of drivers who were involved in accidents showed a significant increase in accident risk due to cognitive distraction when drivers used either handheld or hands-free mobile phones (Backer-Grandahl & Sagberg, 2011). Thus, when I call my clients on their cell phones and discover they are driving, I immediately suggest we find a time to speak later, when it is safe to talk.

Several critical privacy concerns include the following:

- Cell phones may store client data. What happens to that private data if they are stolen or lost?
- Do patients know if the number is a cell phone number? If so, do they believe it means the clinician is always available, including in evenings and on weekends?
- Some practitioners use a cell phone as a backup "in case of emergency" number. However, most people carry their cell phones wherever they go; during a vacation, would the practitioner who arranged coverage by colleagues to handle emergency calls answer a client's call?

These issues remind me of *What About Bob,* a movie depicting a patient who followed his psychiatrist's family on their vacation (Williams, Ziskin, & Oz, 1991).

Another area of concern with cell phones that function as more than telephones, such as the iPhone and similar devices, is the applications available for them. As with any software, we need to evaluate any application for its privacy and security. For example, an application that creates a Word document as we dictate case notes might seem perfect to use, but do we consider whether the files would be encrypted? Is contact and user information being collected by the third-party provider? When files are transmitted, is this done securely? As with other forms of electronic media, we need to develop policies and procedures regarding use of cell phones in our initial and subsequent informed consent discussions with patients in order to address these and other ethical and clinical issues.

Telephone and Online Therapy

Providing clinical services by phone and Skype is a widely accepted part of standard practice. There are compelling clinical and ethical reasons to provide therapy by phone or online, including when in-office visits are impossible, for example, due to clients' disability or geographical relocation. In the case of relocation, Skype can be used in a "transfer session" to reduce feelings of loss or abandonment, with the client and the new therapist in the room together talking with the former therapist via Skype. The only question is what are the reasonable limits in the service we can provide a geographically distant client? Complications can include verifying the identity of the client, not having visual cues about the patient's mood, not knowing who else may be in the room with the patient, and having less familiarity with the patient's local resources in case of emergency. Audrey Jung, past president of the International Society for Mental Health Online, notes that face-to-face work allows therapists to do more with patients in terms of their care when they are suicidal or depressed. For example, therapists can physically intervene or call someone else to drive them home and make sure someone is with them during the day. Therefore, when providing phone or online therapy to geographically distant patients, she notes it is important to systematically gather emergency contact information and take the extra steps necessary to ensure that the emergency contact information is accurate (Anthony, Jung, Rosenauer, Nagel, & Goss, 2010).

In the same way that practitioners fulfill their ethical duties by planning for and discussing with patients the risks, limitations, and benefits of therapy provided in-person (see Chapter 2), they must fulfill the same ethical duties by planning for and discussing these same parameters with clients with whom they are working online.

Legal Issues in Phone and Online Therapy to Patients Outside One's Own State

Practitioners need to consult their own licensure boards regarding their respective jurisdictions' laws and rules. Most state licensure boards are silent on the issue of practitioners' right to provide phone or online therapy services to persons outside of their states. States such as California and Washington, however, prohibit this practice.

Gary Schoener, a psychologist who provides ethics consultations nationally and internationally, however, sees no reasonable ethical and professional justification for such laws (personal communication, May 29, 2011). He notes that states have the right to forbid practitioners who are not licensed in their states to serve people in their state, but questions whether it is unconstitutional to prohibit practitioners licensed in the state from providing phone therapy and online therapy across state lines in that this would seem to fall outside their jurisdiction and unfairly restrict interstate activities. He states that prohibiting this practice can interrupt practitioners' ability to follow professional standards of care and can be harmful to patients, even lead to a death in the event, for example, of a failure to follow-up with a client who is out of town and suicidal. When practitioners are concerned about potential for harm to patients resulting from such laws, he advises them to first attempt to deal directly with their respective licensure boards, raising these concerns, and if not successful enlist the aid of their local or national professional organizations. They might contact the U.S. Attorney's office and ask for a restraining order and action against the state licensure board. He also notes such state laws (prohibiting phone therapy to patients outside of the state) may potentially violate federal rules regarding restraint of trade so that the Federal Trade Commission is a possible resource. He encourages practitioners to involve their state professional organizations in addressing this issue.

Blogging

Many practitioners include a blog or blog-like presence on their Web sites. Blogs are common ways that professionals can deliver valuable information about health and wellness and can disseminate news about their practices to existing or prospective patients. Blogs can help practitioners or their organizations to build a personal health care "brand" or professional style that people will remember when they need care. They can help to foster online communication between patients and individuals who can interact with each other about health issues and one's practice. Blogs can also help practitioners to connect and interact with colleagues and other professionals who share common interests.

When maintaining blogs, practitioners need to adhere to ethical and legal standards of practice. For example, to protect patients' privacy, practitioners or organizations are ethically and legally precluded from responding publically to an individual patient's posting of personal problems and questions on their blogs.

Blogging practitioners need to adhere to ethical standards of professional integrity and respect for colleagues and patients. When practitioners use words on their blogs that are demeaning of patients and other professionals, it harms the practitioners' professional reputations and disrupts therapeutic relationships. Because blogs may be lengthy, the information on the blog may be unclear, or may not present reliable information (Gabbard et al., 2011). Practitioners must therefore take care to write clearly and present reliable information, just as they take care to develop appropriate treatment records. Blogs also need to be clear regarding whether the blogger is representing only his or her own professional views or the views of his or her organization.

We must remember that whatever we post on blogs, especially when we post under our own names, becomes a permanent public record that reflects our professional work, opinions, and integrity. In the event of malpractice claims or licensure board complaints about our conduct, blogs can be used as a record of our professional work that can be examined in court or licensure investigations. Thus, adhering to professional standards, such as privacy and confidentiality and respect for our patients and colleagues through our actions and language on blogs, and stating only information that is accurate and within our licensed scope of practice, is essential. Even though a blog is not a patient record, it must be composed with the same care. Kaiser Permanente (2009) has created excellent tips on blogging for its staff to clarify sound professional standards of conduct for blogs.

Online Attacks on Therapists

The amount of information about one's self on the Web is astounding. Health care rating sites such as healthgrades.com and vitals.com are likely to continue to grow in use and popularity. The hazards of having inaccurate information that is hurtful to therapists are unprecedented. Hazards unique to the Internet can include fake profiles, Internet harassment, fake e-mails, chat room screen names, and doctored photos. People can also record themselves delivering an angry rant against someone or something and post it to YouTube or a variety of other places—blogs, Facebook, and so on.

An example of the potential for vindictive behavior using a fake Web site is the *Draker v. Schreiber* (Tex.App.-San Antonio, August 13, 2008) legal case. Anna Draker, an assistant principal, discovered that two students had posted a fake MySpace site with fake photos indicating she was a lesbian. School officials sued them and their parents for intentional infliction of emotional distress.

Just as an angry patient can stalk or harass or even physically assault a therapist (see my discussion of this danger in Chapter 5), an angry patient may create a Web site attacking a specific professional or therapy in general.

Practitioners can protect themselves by searching the Web periodically to monitor false information or photographs and by contacting a Web site administrator to request that problematic information be removed.

Removing Information from the Internet

Removing inaccurate and harmful information from the Internet is difficult, however. Experts say it involves asking the person who posted the information to remove it, but that person may be unwilling to do so (Richmond, 2011). What if the person you must contact to remove the information is an angry patient?

Practitioners might wonder if they should control their online presence by expanding it, for example by posting their professional profile. Businesses like reputation.com are springing up to help practitioners protect their reputations. It may be worth seeking their assistance to counteract any false or malicious information.

IMPACT OF ELECTRONIC RECORD SYSTEMS

As we and our organizations adopt entirely electronic systems, critical new concerns about patient privacy and quality of care arise. It is easier to know we have double-locked a single record in our fire-protected file cabinets in our offices, even if it could disappear within moments during a tornado. As we consider ways to electronically store records, how do we determine which remote information storage systems we can trust to meet HIPAA and our respective states' security requirements?

Previously it was easier to describe our patients in human terms and to write case histories that summarized a patient's unique story. The process of writing narratives helped our patients and helped us and our trainees to clarify and better understand clinical issues in a thoughtful way. With electronic templates leaving less room for free narrative text, we may feel constrained from engaging in this productive exercise. We may find we can no longer describe our patients in ways that bring their uniqueness to our minds or to their minds.

Keeping notes electronically may lead us to also confront barriers in the therapeutic relationship. During psychotherapy supervision a trainee and I looked at a video of his sessions with a patient. We discovered the computer was drawing his attention toward the computer screen, away from his patient. As we reflected on reasons for looking away from the patient, we could readily understand his patient's expressing distress that she was not making progress in therapy. In a thoughtful effort to become more emotionally responsive to his patient, the trainee positioned their chairs in another part of his office. He found the new seating arrangement helped him to focus on his patient rather than on the computer screen.

These are only a few of the many issues related to technology that we may confront while striving to conduct psychotherapy in thoughtful and caring ways. How do we make technology work for us, rather than allowing ourselves to work for it (Groopman & Hartzband, 2009)?

EMERGING CLINICAL, ETHICAL, AND LEGAL STANDARDS

Many authors have noted that the relationship between electronic media and therapy is here to stay (Host, 2010; Rummel & Joyce, 2010), but there is an urgent need for professionals to talk with one another about its emerging ethical issues (Myers, 2010; Rummel & Joyce, 2010; Santhiveeran, 2009). There is a pressing need for training (Clinton, Silverman, & Brendel, 2010; Groopman & Hartzband, 2009; Santhiveeran, 2009). Psychotherapy training should include consideration of clinical dilemmas and ethical issues, including potential boundary issues, that emerge with social networking sites, search engines, e-mail, and other electronic communications (Clinton, Silverman, & Brendel, 2010; Cook, 2011; Gabbard, Kassaw, & Perez-Garcia, 2011). Professional organizations have established ethical guidelines specifically to help practitioners safely use the Internet in counseling (ACA, 2005; APA, 2010; International Society for Mental Health Online [ISMHO], 2000; National Association of Social Workers and Association of Social Work Boards [NASW & ASWB], 2005). Professional organizations also have resources, including online courses, to assist practitioners in developing ethically sound procedures and policies for their clinical practices, teaching, and supervision.

Above all, professional organizations uniformly recommend that we continue to understand and adhere to basic ethical standards whether we are conducting online therapy or whether we maintain an in-person practice. The most common professional standards that practitioners must consider in online work include providing informed consent about risks and benefits of online counseling; notifying clients of safeguards, limitations, and exceptions to confidentiality and privacy; establishing emergency response plans for clients who may be in geographically distant locations; verifying the true identity of a patient; operating within the scope of one's license; accurately representing themselves and their licensure status; and systematically considering potential for harm in dual roles. Questions remain about how courts will eventually rule in regard to therapists' jurisdiction when practicing online (e.g., are they under the jurisdiction of the state in which they are licensed or under the jurisdiction of the geographically distant state in which the online counseling client is located). How can we advocate for legal decisions that will support our ability to continue adhering to professional standards of care?

Just as practitioners need to remain current on their professional organization's standards, they also need to keep up to date on local and national laws that affect the relationship between electronic communication and psychotherapy and counseling practice.

SUMMARY

The same clinical and ethical standards that guide our practice during face-to-face psychotherapy need to guide our practice during online therapy and when electronic media interrupts our otherwise face-to-face practices. Confronting the complexity of electronic media's impact on the therapeutic relationship requires taking extra steps. In order to protect ourselves and our patients, we must seek consultation from colleagues. We must develop thoughtful policies and procedures related to the use of technology in our practices and discuss these with our patients, just as we develop policies and procedures related to our face-to-face work and discuss these with our patients. When the Internet or related electronic media impact the therapeutic relationship, in helpful or in harmful ways, this impact becomes part of our therapy record.

Earlier in this chapter I shared the long story of Nancy's experiences in therapy as it illustrated so many of the complex ways electronic media can enter into the therapeutic relationship and record keeping. As it is highly unlikely that electronic communications will become less prevalent in our lives, we must continue to examine the influences, issues, benefits, and pitfalls of new technology and practices.

8

Retaining and Destroying Inactive Records

Imagine yourself in your office opening your mail. A life insurance company has sent you a request for a former client's records. You haven't seen this client in 10 years but know that his inactive record is still in your files. You look at his record. It is a mess. It does not make sense, even to you. Even though your former client has given consent for release of his records to the company, and you might be able to rely on your memory to write a report to the insurance company, you do not want to have to write one more report this week to another third party. Hey—what about destroying the record since it has been a decade since you last saw him? How long must you keep records, anyway? What do you do? You pick up the phone to consult a colleague.

There are no simple answers for how long to retain inactive records. Yet, it is essential that psychotherapists have systematic policies and procedures for retaining and destroying inactive client records, whether stored electronically or on paper. Here are the four general factors that help guide clinicians in this process:

- Legal requirements
- Ethical requirements of professional organizations
- Needs of clients and continuity of care
- Issues associated with licensure board complaints, lawsuits, and litigation

This chapter addresses each of these factors and provides practical guidelines for how to effectively and efficiently maintain and dispose of clinical records.

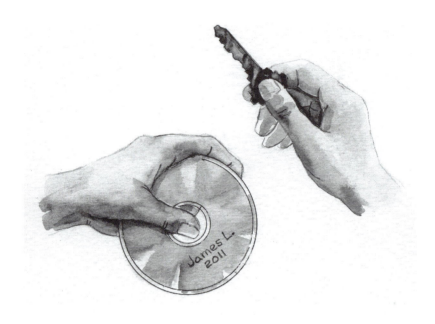

FACTORS TO CONSIDER IN DETERMINING HOW LONG TO KEEP INACTIVE RECORDS

State and Federal Legal Requirements

Therapists should be familiar with state and federal regulations that govern retention and destruction of health care records. State laws vary. In most states, adult patients' files must be kept for at least 7 to 10 years after termination of services. Minor children's files must usually be kept at least until the child's 21st birthday. During this required retention period, clients continue to have the same rights as before to receive copies of their records, either paper copies or electronic copies, when maintained in an electronic record system.

The federal privacy rule (Health Insurance Portability and Accountability Act, HIPAA) does not govern how long psychotherapists must retain records after termination of services. However, it does specify that patients be given the opportunity to see an accounting of disclosures of their health care records for at least 6 years after the disclosure. It also specifies requirements for security and safe destruction of records. The rule directs practitioners to adopt and apply whichever standards—state or federal—for safe storage and destruction of records are more stringent in a given state.

Professional Organizations' Ethical Guidelines

Most mental health professional organizations address the need for careful policies and procedures regarding retaining and disposing of records, and emphasize the need to maintain client confidentiality in both practices. However, in most instances mental health professional organizations echo or defer to statutory requirements. Practitioners can consult their respective mental health professions' ethics codes' requirements for storage, retention, and destruction of records.

Needs of Clients and Continuity of Care

Governmental regulations and ethical guidelines are two factors to consider when developing practice policies and procedures for maintaining and disposing of records, and therapists and their organizations should also keep in mind the importance of their patients' potential clinical needs and continuity of care. For example, a state regulatory board rule may require therapists to maintain patient records for only 7 years after a case has been closed. But therapists may decide to keep records longer, even indefinitely, in case the patient seeks care again after 7 years, either from the original therapist or a different therapist located elsewhere. Similarly, a client who has terminated therapy may experience a crisis long after the 7-year retention requirement has expired and require additional mental health treatment. It can be tremendously helpful to therapists assessing the client's current needs to be able to refer to previous records.

Although the following example was unusual because South Dakota state law required psychiatric hospitals to retain records for 30 years, it illustrates how helpful it was to a subsequent therapist when she was able to obtain the former psychiatric records from her new client's psychiatric hospitalization over 20 years earlier.

A 53-year-old woman, mother of three adult children, who was suffering from depression and marital problems, sought psychotherapy again after nearly 30 years. She indicated to her new therapist that when she was 24, and her children were very young, she had become overwhelmed. At that time she developed a serious depression, became suicidal, was admitted to the psychiatric hospital, and received shock treatments. Because the law in her state required hospitals to keep medical records for 30 years, the new therapist was able to obtain this patient's former records. Through reading the former psychiatric record, the new therapist gained a deeper understanding of her new patient. For example, the new therapist was struck by the fact that while the patient had suffered a severe major depressive episode in the past, she had, nevertheless, been able to function reasonably well, free of depressive symptoms for nearly 30 years, had successfully raised her children, and had maintained friends and meaningful activities in her community. In this instance, the opportunity to review the former record gave the therapist and her new patient valuable information—both about the patient's vulnerability to depression and her resilience. It was also helpful to the new therapist and the patient to note that some of the patient's concerns in her past, as documented in her hospital record, were resurfacing in the present, so these issues could be clarified and become a focus in treatment.

The next example involves a client whose intermittent need for therapy over a 25-year period meant that her therapist never destroyed her record. Contents of her record ultimately provided the narrative the client needed to gain perspective on her life and identify strategies to care for herself.

A 53-year-old woman, in a Southern state, returned for treatment with a psychotherapist whom she had initially consulted for premarital counseling 25 years ago. Intermittently, over the past 25 years, the woman had returned for brief therapy (only three to five sessions) in order to discuss her feelings of helplessness and her needs in her marriage. Each time, her presenting problems involved her wish to persuade her husband to take a job and contribute to the household expenses. When she turned 53, she became moderately depressed. She felt tired of supporting herself and her husband. She wanted to be able to retire within 10 years but was frustrated by her husband's increasing credit card debts. Consequently, she felt alarmed that she would not have enough financial security in order to retire when she wanted to. When she returned to the therapist to work on these problems, she felt stunned to hear excerpts from her record. Her therapist's progress notes revealed she had struggled with the same marital problems for over 25 years. The fact that her records were still available was invaluable. After listening to excerpts from her records she was able to better see her longstanding pattern of problems. The insights she gained strengthened her resolve to do things differently. As a result, she was able to establish and follow through on goals for her life.

Protection in the Event of a Lawsuit or Other Allegations

Another factor to consider when deciding whether and for how long to keep inactive records, and the best manner by which to destroy them, is the possibility of lawsuits or other complaints. Complaints against therapists generally come through one of two vehicles: regulatory board complaints or malpractice lawsuits. In my experience consulting with practitioners who have received complaints against their practices, those who have kept and retained clear, accurate, ethical, and comprehensive records find it much easier to avoid lawsuits or successfully defend their work on the basis of client files.

Because there is usually no time limit as to when patients can file complaints against practitioners through regulatory boards, some attorneys advise therapists to keep records indefinitely.

Malpractice suits are constrained by statutes of limitations, usually 2 years from the termination of therapy or from the time the patients realized that the practitioner's conduct harmed them. For these reasons, too, some attorneys have suggested that therapists maintain records indefinitely, or at least keep a summary statement of diagnosis and treatment, to be able to demonstrate the care they provided.

Inappropriateness of Destroying Records with Intent to Avoid or Influence Judicial Proceedings

It is never appropriate to alter or destroy records with intent to avoid or influence judicial proceedings. The following case example illustrates a family court judge's anger, and a therapist's and mental health clinic's embarrassment, after the therapist destroyed a portion of the client's case in an effort to influence judicial proceedings involving his client.

A 30-year-old divorced woman, who lived with her 7-year-old son in a Western coastal town, had been receiving psychotherapy in a private mental health clinic to deal with parenting and other adjustment problems following her divorce. After a year of psychotherapy, she decided she wanted to move to another city, 1,000 miles from her home. Because the child's father had liberal visitation rights and lived in the same town, she needed to get the court's permission to move with her child away from the father. The woman therefore filed a petition in family court and the child's father disagreed, claiming the child needed more contact with him than would be feasible after the move.

The father was aware of the mother's previous problems controlling her anger, and the father's attorney decided to seek evidence of the mother's psychological imbalance to support the father's claim that it was in the child's best interest to remain geographically close to him. The father's attorney served the private mental health clinic with a subpoena for the mother's records and asked the mother's therapist to testify in court regarding the mother's psychological status.

At the time she petitioned the court to move, the mother was psychologically stable and had been functioning well in her mothering of her young child for several months. She was worried, however, that her clinic record could potentially be harmful to her chances of gaining the court's approval to move away with her son. Initially, when she first sought help from the clinic, she was asking for help to control her impulsive behavior—she was hitting her son, causing bruises. Her clinic record contained a summary of these problems and a copy of the therapist's legally mandated report of suspected child abuse that the therapist had submitted to child protective services. The therapist's progress notes summarized the patient's treatment, which had focused on her goals of controlling her abusive behavior, and her excellent progress.

The therapist felt sympathetic to the mother's fears that the court would deny her request to move if the judge read references in her clinic record describing her previous abusive behavior with her child. Even though the therapist's documentation of the mother's abusive behavior was relevant and integral to the treatment plan, the therapist chose to delete the portions of the record pertaining to the mother's history of abusive behavior.

When the judge learned that the therapist had destroyed this portion of the record, he reprimanded the therapist, the mental health clinic, and its board of directors. He stated that the therapist's behavior was not only unprofessional, it could harm children. Even though the judge ruled in the mother's favor, permitting her to move with her child to the new city, the clinic's credibility and reputation were tarnished. As a result of this unfortunate incident, the clinic learned it needed a policy on retention and destruction of records.

DEVELOPING POLICIES AND PROCEDURES FOR THE RETENTION/DESTRUCTION OF INACTIVE RECORDS

Although it is helpful to have an internal rule about records retention, there is nothing to prevent practitioners and their organizations from retaining records longer than their own internal rule specifies. In one example, an agency chose to retain the counseling records of a client longer than their 7-year standard because she had a history of making complaints against health care professionals. The client was aware the agency's record retention policy was 7 years. Eight years after terminating counseling, she filed a complaint against the agency. By retaining the record beyond its usual retention policy, the agency was able to show the counseling she received and that the complaint was groundless. The state licensure board dismissed the complaint.

Practitioners need to protect the confidentiality and physical integrity of inactive records as carefully as they do active records. All too often, CDs that contain inactive files may not be stored securely. Or, piles of paper records end up in flimsy cardboard boxes in inadequate storage spaces where they are subject to damage by the elements or access by unauthorized users. CDs containing electronic records and records that are paper based should be kept in strong, locked, fireproof containers and stored in secured, climate-controlled facilities. (See Chapter 6.)

Safe Destruction of Inactive Records

Equally important as secure storage is the need for safe destruction procedures. I have heard of disturbing situations that could have been prevented with more careful planning. Even in this era of electronic record keeping, there are still reports about losing paper files. For example, a private practitioner who was moving to another office told me that his secretary accidentally shredded a box of current patients' active files rather than the box of his former patients' inactive files that he was ready to destroy. In another example, a hospital packed up a box of 1,200 patient records for shipping across town and then the box disappeared (Lerner, 2011). A manager at another health care clinic with responsibility for privacy of her clinic's records told me she had conscientiously chosen a reliable company to pick up and shred her clinic's psychotherapy records, but the company's procedure was to ask her to leave closed boxes of records to be shredded in the alley behind the clinic so that the truck driver could retrieve them and take them to the company's shredder. Even though she felt confident that the company was reliable, she was concerned that confidential records could accidentally spill out of the boxes when the driver loaded them onto the truck or that passersby in the alley could get into the closed boxes. She insisted the clinic hire a company that would shred records in her presence.

In another example, practitioners in a private practice were diligently collecting psychotherapy records that needed shredding but leaving them in piles on counters in their office where they were visible and accessible to anyone visiting the office, including evening cleaning staff. Patients felt uncomfortable as they entered the suite of offices, wondering if someone could carelessly glance at their own charts.

Appropriate methods of destroying records will depend upon the mode in which they are stored. Practitioners and their organizations need to determine whether paper records will be shredded or burned. Electronically stored patient-identifiable health care information remains in the memory of computers and facsimile or copying machines; this memory needs to be professionally erased or hard drives removed and destroyed.

Staff Security Agreements and Consequences for Violations

Even when practitioners and their organizations are not covered under HIPAA's workforce security requirements, all staff, including independent contractors and their subcontractors, should be informed of, and sign, staff or business associate agreements in order to protect the security of inactive files. Agreements should include consequences for violations of security policies. When psychotherapy offices hire independent contractors to retain or destroy inactive files, these persons, too, must agree to policies and procedures for protecting privacy and security of inactive records. For HIPAA's workforce security requirements and sample business associate forms, we can go to the Department of Health and Human Services (HHS) Web site or our respective professional associations' Web sites.

Policies and procedures that are consistent with HIPAA rules include the following:

- Clear job expectations to protect privacy and security of inactive files for all staff who have access to or will use patient records
- Consequences for staff for violations of inactive record privacy expectations
- Signed agreements by all staff and independent contractors that they assume responsibility to protect privacy and security of inactive files
- Secure places for keys that unlock cabinets that contain inactive paper files
- Secure places for passwords for authorized users of electronically stored files
- Length of time inactive files will be kept
- Method for destruction of inactive files, whether stored electronically or on paper
- Manner in which clients will be informed of record retention and destruction policy

In addition, background checks are common. (See CD and Appendix A for sample "Client/Patient Information," which includes a sample statement for clients regarding privacy, record retention, and destruction policy and procedures.)

SUMMARY

Four factors that practitioners need to consider when determining how long to retain records, and when they can destroy them, are legal requirements, ethical requirements, clients' needs, and issues associated with lawsuits and regulatory board complaints. Practitioners are encouraged to develop consistent policies and procedures for record retention, but nothing precludes practitioners and organizations from retaining records longer than their internal rules. Therapists are cautioned never to destroy records with the intent to alter judicial proceedings, but instead to develop consistent policies and procedures for destruction. HIPAA requires practitioners who generate patient-identifiable health care information electronically to have written agreements (with consequences for violations) for all business associates, including independent contractors, by which the business associate and contractors provide assurances that they have implemented administrative, physical, and technical safeguards to protect the health information they have access to or use on behalf of the practitioner. HIPAA also requires subcontractors of business associates and contractors to enter into written agreements with substantially similar terms and assurances. For further information and sample business associate agreements, practitioners can visit HHS's or their respective professional associations' Web sites, or may consult their own health care attorneys and regulatory boards to learn about legal requirements for given situations.

9

Using Patients' Records as Therapeutic Tools

My colleagues' eyes usually glaze over when I enthusiastically mention using record keeping as a therapeutic tool. Most therapists see record keeping as a necessary evil—a boring burden that distracts them from the heart of their work. I once felt the same way. But as I developed as a therapist and learned to use every aspect of the therapeutic relationship, I saw that faithfully creating a chronicle of clients' courageous and often arduous journeys can be a powerful tool that hastens their healing. Seeing and discussing records validates their hard work and allows them to see themselves, their problems, their goals, and their gains. Reflecting on notes ratifies their role as collaborators in the therapeutic process. Involving clients in the chronicle of their work enhances self-determination, insight, responsibility for healing, and the integrity of the therapeutic relationship. Record keeping thus can be a dynamic aid to therapeutic intervention—an indispensable tool for growth.

Though involving clients in observing and using the record keeping process can be valuable, therapists must be aware of several parameters. Practitioners (or their work settings) own the records. They are responsible for creating the records and maintaining them in their offices. They must be judicious in deciding how, when, and to what extent to use records in therapy. Timing is crucial. Therapists must use professional discretion when responding to clients' requests and be keenly attuned to clients' mental and emotional status in order to make good decisions about whether or not to employ notes and records as a tool at a particular juncture. Finally, when choosing this or any other therapeutic tool, they must stay true to their own style.

This chapter will examine (a) the history of clients' access to records; (b) use of records as a therapeutic tool; and (c) management of complex, challenging situations, such as when patients request that portions of their records be deleted, or when they insist their therapists keep no records.

HISTORY OF CLIENTS' ACCESS TO RECORDS

The U.S. Freedom of Information Act of 1966 and Federal Privacy Act of 1974 introduced patients' rights to examine and comment upon their own records in federally funded institutions. This caused therapists great consternation. They worried that opening up records to clients' scrutiny could harm the therapeutic process, result in loss of practitioner control over the record, and even "degrade the helping relationship by introducing argumentation and disagreements" (Freed, 1978). However, a few pioneering practitioners in social work, psychiatry, and marriage and family therapy embraced the idea and endeavored to use the new rule as an opportunity. They were surprised to find the process of discussing records with clients to be helpful. Most of their trepidation was unfounded. Some of the positive outcomes of allowing clients to examine their own records included increased communication between clients and professionals and clients seeing this demystification as a symbol of mutual trust, acceptance, and interest (Freed, 1978; Townes, Wagner, and Christ, 1967). Freed astutely suggested that fears associated with not using records in the therapeutic process were a paper tiger and a missed opportunity for better treatment (Freed, 1978).

Patients' legal right to access their own records is now commonplace in the United States. Many state laws, as well as the federal privacy rule (Health Insurance Portability and Accountability Act, HIPAA), require psychotherapists to allow their patients or patients' guardians to examine and comment upon their own records upon their request, unless in the practitioners' professional judgment the contents of the record could be harmful to their patients. However, despite clinical evidence suggesting that engaging clients in record keeping is not harmful and can be therapeutic under most circumstances, practitioners have continued debating the issue. Furlong (1998), a psychoanalyst, for example, warned against patients reviewing their own records. She viewed the clinical record as "analytic mental space," the privacy of which "must be respected ... even by the patient whose discourse contributes to it, in order for it to function effectively." Yet others within the analytic community have suggested that therapists have a professional responsibility to establish clear goals that can be understandable to the patient (Gabbard, 2010; Renick, 2006). Researchers continue studying the impact health record access has on patients and their providers (Cimino, Mendonca, Sengupta, Patel, & Kushniruk, 2000).

Interestingly, most of my patients have expressed no desire to see or discuss their records, even when I have invited them to do so. However, many have taken an active role in examining and discussing my intake summaries and progress notes. With few exceptions, these clients have experienced no discomfort from seeing their record, but instead have found the process to be an evocative learning tool. In my own professional experience, sensitive, factual, nonjudgmental records can inspire clients to greater curiosity about their problems and enhance their participation, sense of safety, and security in the therapeutic relationship.

The debate over the efficacy of involving clients in record keeping is not likely to be resolved in the absence of a significant paradigm shift. For the purposes of this discussion, I will focus on the ways that records can become therapeutic tools.

HOW RECORDS MAY BE USED AS THERAPEUTIC TOOLS

It is worth noting that using records as therapeutic tools, especially when they are used to construct a narrative, becomes more difficult when electronic records force practitioners into using preset templates and impersonal language. When electronic record systems are being designed, it is important for practitioners to be part of that design process to ensure that records may still be kept in a way that preserves the individuality and humanity of each client. When using templates and settings designed by someone else or without input from therapists, we must keep in mind our duty to our clients' stories and uniqueness for the record to be of therapeutic value.

Evaluation Phase

The initial evaluation records help establish a treatment alliance, set the stage for the work ahead, and continue to be of benefit to patients and therapists throughout the course of treatment. Records can be used therapeutically in the following ways.

To Provide a Guide for an Unpredictable Journey

Psychotherapy is a process of discovery, much like writing a book. Even when authors have an outline, there is no certain way to anticipate all that lies ahead. For therapists, too, it is not possible to predict the course of therapy with each unique patient, even when therapists have knowledge and previous clinical experience treating a variety of people suffering from similar kinds of emotional and mental disorders. Therapy parallels writing in that "Putting an idea into written words is like defrosting the windshield: The idea, so vague out there in the murk, slowly begins to gather itself into a sensible shape" (Zinsser, 1988).

Psychotherapy, thus, is largely an inductive process in which records become a map that shows where one has been and where one can go. The initial evaluation starts the process of charting the patients' problems, goals, and progress. With each session, information becomes more detailed, helping to illuminate a path that practitioners and clients may rely upon together.

To Help Organize and Provide a Supportive "Container"

Typically, patients with mental health problems experience extreme anxiety, especially in the initial evaluation, about how they may effectively express themselves. It is common for clients to report feeling overwhelmed or as if they were in a vacuum. They fear they will sound disorganized or incoherent, and wonder how a therapist could possibly understand the complexity of their problems and their debilitating confusion and fear.

Recording what our patients say about their problems and life experience helps us start to identify and organize what initially may sound like disjointed fragments of information. To use Winicott's concept (Winnicott, 1960), records can help create a "holding environment"* for our patients' experience, providing strength to us and our patients. Seemingly disparate experiences and symptoms gradually congeal into a language we can understand and use. The record helps clarify our patients' needs and goals; what they have tried before, successfully or

---

* See also Claire Winnicott's comments on the value of "holding" within the therapeutic relationship: "… we take deliberate trouble to remember all the details about the client's life … Not only do we hold a consistent idea of the client as a person, but we hold the difficult situation that brought him to us by tolerating it until he either finds a way through it or tolerates it himself" (Kanter, 2004, p.15).

not, to solve their problems; and what might or might not be helpful to them; and helps us further define our respective roles and responsibilities in their treatment.

To Provide a Bridge to Further Exploration

When we can refer to our notes on a previous session, and ask our patients about their subsequent thoughts, we build bridges between sessions. Concepts and experiences discussed in previous sessions become the basis for further exploration and also may point to additional information or assistance we may require in order to better formulate accurate diagnosis and treatment plans. It also makes real for patients that even therapists need tools like record keeping to build a bridge because they are human too and need material aids to remember.

To Enhance Trust and Confidence in the Therapeutic Process

On hearing their therapists refer back to what they told us in a previous session, patients may feel relieved to learn they have been understood. Records can become a reflection of their successful communication, increasing their self-esteem and confidence that they have the skills to help heal themselves.

Similarly, clients benefit from seeing their therapists use consulting notes. In response to a follow-up study I conducted asking patients what was helpful in their therapy, patients mentioned the mutually respectful collaboration between professionals. They said it was helpful to them to watch professionals pool knowledge and skills to help them solve problems; the interdisciplinary collaboration honored the complexity of their problems and taught them how they, too, could ask others for help and benefit from collective wisdom (Luepker, 1999).

To Promote Accuracy of Records

Equally important, clients can help themselves and us along the way by correcting factual inaccuracies in our notes. Therapists are human and are learning the "story line" for the first time. Understandably, we can misreport some facts, especially in initial evaluations when we are inundated with information. When patients review their records, they can identify factual mistakes and make a list (on a separate page) of corrections that can be inserted into their record. In addition to ensuring the accuracy of records, this exercise conveys our commitment to thoroughly understanding our clients and making them an integral part of our learning process.

To Promote Self-Determination in Establishing Treatment Plans

Using the record to establish treatment plans with our patients promotes client self-determination and assures that treatment contracts are mutually understood and agreed upon. Participating in the process encourages patients to clarify what they want to work on and what they are not ready to work on and illuminates other important clinical information, such as what they believe about themselves and their lives.

After we have enough information from our evaluations to develop diagnoses and treatment plans, we can summarize with our patients the problems, diagnoses, goals, objectives, procedures, and estimated time for treatment. Keeping it as clear and simple as possible, staying away from jargon and close to our clients' own words, we can usually complete treatment plans on one page that anyone can readily understand. (See CD and Appendix B for sample form.)

We may choose to write treatment plans prior to sessions or during sessions. Either way, by enlisting our patients' participation in clarifying and documenting treatment plans, we promote their self-determination and strengthen the treatment alliance.

Here is an example of a discussion between a therapist and client as they jointly develop a treatment plan:

Therapist: As we discussed last week, I think we are ready to establish our treatment plan. Here is a one-page treatment plan form I have found useful to document problems, goals, procedures, and outcome in treatment. It is like a road map that helps us stay clear and focused in our work together, and able to see what progress we are making toward your goals. Before you arrived today, I got started writing down the problems you described in our first two sessions which you said you would like help with. Here they are [reads them to client]. Are these correct? Did I leave anything out?

Client: Yes, these are all the problems I told you. But I think I want to start only with the first four problems and put this last problem on hold for now. I think this is all I can manage to work on right now.

Therapist: That makes good sense to me given what you've told me. You can always decide later when and if you want to tackle this last problem. I think you are wise to clarify what you feel is manageable now, and to consider timing and pacing yourself.

Let's look at the goals now and put them in your words. As you look at these problems, what are you hoping can be different in your life ... or what would we be seeing if you achieved the goals you described?

Client: Well, looking at the first problem, "trouble deciding whether to stay married," I want to be able to make a decision ... whether to stay in my marriage and try to salvage it or else divorce my husband.

Therapist: O.K. [Writes down goal "make decision whether to try to salvage my marriage or divorce husband."]

Client: That sounds fine.

Therapist: You also said you were anxious having your husband in the house because he chooses to remain involved with the other woman; and you have been having trouble thinking clearly, focusing, concentrating, have been unable to get to sleep and stay asleep, and cannot eat.

Did I understand these problems? [Client indicates they are accurate, and therapist writes them down on the problem list.]

In my experience with similar situations, before we can help you clarify what to do about your marriage in the long run, I am thinking that the first task would be to work together to help you feel more comfortable and be able to eat, sleep, and think clearly. Does that priority make sense to you? [Client agrees.] O.K., so I will write those down as your first goals. [Therapist writes down goals to "think more clearly; to be better able to focus and concentrate; to be able to get to sleep and stay asleep, and to eat." Client agrees.]

From what you have told me, it sounds like your husband's living in the home is a constant hurtful reminder that he is being unfaithful to you and you therefore feel you could feel more secure if your husband were not in the home, and you have decided you would like to ask him to move out. Is that your goal? [Client agrees.] O.K., so I'll write that asking him to leave is one of your goals, too.

Let's look at other thoughts about self-care you and I might have. We talked about how caring for yourself is crucial in feeling less anxious and depressed. You mentioned you are not getting any exercise these days because you have been feeling so bad. Getting exercise a minimum of three times a week is important for everyone to maintain good mental health. But when anxious and depressed, we require more. It is important to set goals that you feel you can really manage so you will have success. Do you feel you can begin doing something this week in the way of exercise? [Client indicates she could.] What shall we put down as what you feel your goal can be for this coming week?

Client: Well, I like to walk. I think I could set a goal to walk two times this week. [Therapist adds "self-care: walk 2×/week" to list of goals.]

Therapist: Now that we've completed the problems and goals, let's turn to diagnosis. A diagnosis is simply a name for a problem. It helps us to know what is going on and gives us ideas about possible remedies. Your insurance company also requires diagnosis in order to pay for treatment.

It looks like your distress started when you found out about the affair your husband was having with another woman. You said you were hurt, anxious, felt betrayed and confused, and started to feel really down in the dumps. You said it was like the floor dropped out from under you. You were hit from left field and now you are trying to adjust to the sudden change in your understanding of yourself, your husband, and your marriage. This constellation of problems or "symptoms" is most consistent with a diagnosis called adjustment disorder with anxiety and depressed mood. I am thinking we could start with that to see if it is the best fit. If you want me to bill your insurance company for your treatment, this will be the diagnosis I will use. If we need to change the diagnosis as we go along, we'll use what we are learning to fine-tune our hypothesis.

Client: [Indicates agreement with this diagnosis to be sent for billing purposes to her insurance company.]

Therapist: Now, turning to our procedures column, I am recommending we continue with 50-minute sessions once a week. Do you feel comfortable with that? [Client agrees and therapist writes that down.] If we need to change it later, we can, but let's start there.

Also, as we discussed last week, I would like to see if some of your symptoms, such as trouble focusing, concentrating, sleeping, could be caused by depression. I recommended that you consult my psychiatrist colleague for an evaluation to see if you are depressed and, if so, whether an antidepressant might help. [Client states she doesn't want to take psychotropic medications but agrees to see the psychiatrist for an evaluation, and therapist writes down in procedure column: "referral for psychiatric evaluation to clarify diagnosis and options."]

We also talked last week about the importance of my being able to routinely consult with your psychiatrist about your treatment, if you need to work with a psychiatrist, so she and I can clarify your diagnosis and treatment plan. I would like to write that down in the procedures list and ask you to sign a form that authorizes me to consult with her as needed.

Now, looking at the section of our treatment plan that says "estimated time": it is always difficult for me, based upon my experience with similar kinds of cases, to predict how long treatment will take. So what I would like to do is to put a question mark here. We can assess our time frame as we go along. You can always choose to end treatment at any time. If you are making no progress or getting worse, I would have an obligation to end treatment or refer you to more appropriate help. My best guess is that you will make good progress in solving these problems, and that the time it will take to get you where you want to be will continue to come into focus as we work toward your goals.

In regard to billing, I understand you will be using the Fortunate Insurance Company, which does not require me to send in periodic requests for further sessions. Therefore only we will be in charge of assessing what you need, and we will also be considering your psychiatrist's recommendations, too. The only information the insurance company requires is your diagnosis, so I would request that you sign this form giving me permission to send your diagnosis to them for billing purposes.

Client: O.K.

Therapist: I think this completes our treatment plan. But I also wanted to mention our outcome section here on the right side of the page. We will periodically be noting the progress you are making on solving these problems in this column. It will be helpful for us to be able to see tangible evidence of progress. As we reevaluate your goals over time, we can keep track together of whether the work we are doing is helpful to you, or what we might need to be doing differently.

Client: O.K.

Therapist: I ask my clients to sign the treatment plan and I'll sign also, to show we have mutually agreed upon this plan. I will keep the plan in your record, but you are always welcome to have a copy. Would you like to have a copy now? [Client indicates it's enough just to have it in the record, does not need a copy. Therapist places the treatment plan in the record.]

Allen, Fonagy, and Bateman (2008) creatively collaborate with their patients in developing diagnostic findings by writing a second-person narrative. A brief excerpt from the summary section of an evaluation follows:

> Anthony, as I understand it, you feel profoundly that, as a consequence of your parents' inability to take you seriously during your childhood, you feel "defective" in that you feel you do not have the basic tools for managing your interactions with others and for managing life in general. In particular, you feel that you lack the ability to negotiate conflicts with others.... When you feel this in group therapy, we ask you to mention it so that you can contrast your understanding of yourself in the group with how other members of the group see you. (Allen, Fonagy, & Bateman, 2008, pp. 173–175)

Narrative therapists Epston (1994) and Nylund and Thomas (1994) described their method of writing follow-up letters to their patients after the initial session; the letters recount the problems the patient brought to therapy and possible solutions they discovered together.

Treatment Phase

After laying the groundwork in the evaluation phase, records continue to be useful throughout treatment. During treatment, practitioners can use records to enhance therapy in the following ways.

To Monitor Progress

Progress notes allow us to see tangible progress. In the example above, the therapist appropriately realized her client could not benefit from psychotherapy until she was feeling more secure and physically and mentally stable. To assess her client's progress, the therapist referred to the initial treatment plan and discussed with her how the plan was working.

Therapist: Our first goals were to help you feel more secure, and to improve your sleeping, eating, and concentration. You had decided you would ask your husband to leave the home since he was choosing to remain involved with another woman; your other steps were to begin caring for yourself by beginning to get some exercise, and to consult my psychiatrist colleague about the possible need for an antidepressant. I understand that you did ask your husband to leave, that he has taken an apartment, and that you and he are cooperating in taking care of your children. It sounds like you made good progress in that area. Have you had a chance to make an appointment with the psychiatrist yet?

Client: Yes, I have. My appointment is scheduled for next Thursday.

Therapist: [Recording that progress in the record] Good for you. Were you able to begin exercising?

Client: I was able to walk three times this week.

Therapist: How did that feel?

Client: Walking made me feel better.

Therapist: Good.

In subsequent sessions, this therapist continued inquiring about and documenting her patient's sleeping and eating habits, and her ability to focus, concentrate, and think clearly, all of which gradually began to improve. Even though the patient was still having marital problems, the visible signs of improvement in her symptoms of depression helped her appreciate how she was choosing not to be a victim and was more in control of her life. She and her therapist were then able to make use of therapy to explore her thoughts and feelings about herself and her marriage.

To Serve as a Bridge between Sessions

Keeping progress notes after each session (even only two or three sentences) provides continuity from one session to the next. A chronicle of interventions and progress allows us to move more mindfully to the next step of treatment. It creates a context within which both the client and therapist can understand the client's problems from different perspectives and make better decisions about priorities. Having a bridge between sessions also helps clients internalize their therapy and thus be able to make use of it in between sessions.

In the following example, the therapist has been working with a patient who has suffered from lifelong fears of abandonment and difficulty stating her true feelings and needs to others. She came to therapy to build self-confidence, and develop communication skills so she could express her feelings and needs to her husband, rather than continue to protect her true self. Before the client arrived for her appointment, the therapist reviewed progress notes from the previous session. When the client arrived, the therapist noted themes from the previous session as a bridge to identify and explore topics of discussion for the current session.

Therapist: I recall in our session last week, you were exploring what you wanted to say to your husband... as you were walking into the office today, you seemed tearful...and said you were feeling anxious.

Client: I did follow through with my decision to tell him what was really on my mind...how I was feeling and what I needed. I realized after our session last week that I couldn't live anymore with myself if I didn't tell him what I was really feeling. It was hard, but I got it all out and felt relieved. But his response made me upset and anxious. He became very angry and cold. It took a lot to get the courage to communicate honestly, and now I feel rejected and alone. That's why I am upset today.

To Offer "Mirroring" Opportunities

Our patients may be ashamed of their problems or feelings of helplessness. In their minds, going to a therapist only confirms their defect. What's more, they may believe the therapist views them as inept and weak. Records can be invaluable to reframe erroneous assumptions as clients read the therapist's factual, non-judgmental language. This allows clients to view their problems more objectively, serves as a model for self-acceptance, and encourages more openness.

Reviewing the record with our patients also reveals differences between therapists' perceptions of patients and how patients see themselves. For example, the record may reflect that the therapist has more confidence in the patient's problem-solving skills than the patient. This may lead to discussions about the different perspectives and open doors for the client to see himself or herself in a more positive and generous light, especially when the therapist gives examples of how the client has demonstrated good problem-solving skills. It may also lead to opportunities to explain how cognitive distortions are associated with the client's major depressive disorder, or trigger questions about how he or she learned to discount his or her own value.

A striking scene in the French movie *The Little Thief* (Vannier, Berri, & Miller, 1988) illustrates dramatically how records can become a mirror that helps shape identity development. The protagonist, a troubled adolescent girl with a history of maternal abandonment, other childhood trauma, and compulsive stealing, finds herself alone at night in the director's office of a juvenile detention center. She discovers her record on the director's desk and reads the notes. As she silently absorbs the adjectives, she sees herself through the eyes of others. This experience appeared to be life-changing for the girl because it allowed her to see herself in an entirely different way.

To Support the Process of Mentalizing*

Narratives written by therapists to their patients to share diagnostic formulations and treatment recommendations support mentalizing, a fundamental ingredient for successful therapy regardless of what therapeutic modality the practitioner uses. Mentalizing can only occur within a secure attachment with the therapist (Allen, Fonagy, & Bateman, 2008):

> Providing a formulation in writing is helpful for patients who have difficulty holding your mind in mind; they benefit from having something tangible and physical—something real. The written formulation can be a basis for mentalizing inasmuch as it can be reworked conjointly; the patient can question or challenge your view, or simply correct factual inaccuracies. This is an example of explicit mentalizing work: you present to your patients the representation that you have of them in your mind; your patients in turn represent their view of themselves back to you; and then you can demonstrate your own ability to reappraise your understanding of them. (Allen, Fonagy, & Bateman, 2008, p. 176)

A second-person narrative helps to provide a clear and explicit formulation and helps patients feel cared for by their therapists. Such a narrative, in which the therapist refers to himself or herself as "I" and to the patient as "you," might begin in the following way: "I thought it might be helpful for our work to summarize my understanding of the problems we are working on together in psychotherapy. Consider this a work in progress, based on our initial sessions."

I like to consider second-person narratives as an alternative to my usual practice of collaborating with patients in discussing our respective thoughts about their problems, diagnosis and treatment goals, and putting them on the treatment plan forms (see CD and Appendixes B and C). Narratives provide clients and therapists another vehicle for understanding what each other has in mind, which supports the therapeutic relationship.

To Provide Perspective

As narratives, records can help patients gain perspective and develop distance from the gripping immediacy of their distress. Patients suffering from traumatic

---

* Mentalizing is being aware of and thinking about feelings in one's self and feelings in others (Allen, Fonagy, & Bateman, 2008).

stress, for example, often say they experience the memories of the traumatic events as though they are occurring in the present (Herman, 1992). In self-protection, they may reflexively avoid speaking, feeling, or thinking about the traumatic events. They need, but may also fear, our help sharing what is in their mind or body and moving through a gamut of emotions in order to grieve unspeakable losses. Narratives, both verbal and written, allow patients to gain control over the events by creating distance from the trauma.

The usefulness of the therapists' notes can be enhanced by having clients write a specific account of the traumatic events or draw pictures of the traumatic events to place the trauma in a context of before, during, and after. Externalizing trauma—naming it—diminishes its timeless hold over clients and expands clients' perspective about what happened. Moreover, when clients feel ready to allow therapists to bear witness to their pain and suffering, therapists' attunement to feelings and creation of records can help validate clients' experiences and promote healing.

To Reveal Lack of Progress or Deterioration

Records assist therapists in identifying when patients are not responding to treatment or are getting worse. In either of these circumstances, we have a responsibility to recognize the problem, reevaluate our professional services, and determine what alternative action we may need to take in our patients' interest.

In one case example, a practitioner was able to make good use of his notes to explore why his client was worse. The therapist noticed that his client's relationship with his partner had been deteriorating over a few weeks' period after a remarkable period of increasing intimacy between the client and his partner. By reviewing the client's treatment record, the therapist was able to pinpoint the onset of the client's tailspin. He was able to ask his client to tell him more about what had been going on at that time that may have precipitated the deterioration in his relationship. This kind of tracking back helped the client reveal disturbing events that had precipitated his hopelessness in the relationship, which then became the focus in treatment.

When practitioners cannot find ways to help clients make progress, options include obtaining consultation, ending treatment, or referring our patients for an alternative intervention. Many therapists have asked me how to handle difficult treatment situations with patients, such as when patients are not complying with their part in the treatment contract. Many times they have found the answer in the records. By tracking patients' lack of compliance with their treatment plans and the reasons behind noncompliance, therapists have been able to open meaningful discussions with patients and determine the best option to pursue.

For example, one practitioner learned that her patient, who had requested therapy for problems precipitated by a person's harmful actions, was not being honest about secretly continuing to meet with the alleged perpetrator. The therapist made a contract with the patient to be honest with her about her behavior. When the therapist discovered months later that the patient was secretly pursuing the relationship for which the patient was asking the therapist for help, the therapist called the problem to her patient's attention. The therapist reminded her that the therapy she was requesting could not work if the patient continued these behaviors. At this juncture, she informed the patient if she chose to continue these behaviors and conceal them from the therapist, therapy would need to end. The patient acknowledged the problem and agreed to be honest. The therapist documented the problem and put the renewed contract in writing in the record, and gave a copy to the patient and to her psychiatrist.

When the therapist discovered later that the patient was continuing to conceal the truth about her behaviors, she felt surprised. The therapist was aware she was struggling with countertransference feelings (e.g., disbelieving her own perception of reality and wishing to continue to work with the patient). Fortunately, by reviewing the record, the therapist could help herself to more clearly see the patient's pattern of deception in treatment. The therapist consulted the patient's psychiatrist, who agreed that therapy was untenable under the circumstances and suggested to the therapist a safe transition for the patient. The psychiatrist agreed to continue providing medications and to handle emergencies as needed, but supported the therapist's plan to initiate termination of therapy. The therapist contacted the patient, who understood her actions constituted her choice to end therapy. The therapist had a closure session with the client, presented referral options, and documented the consultation and status of the termination for the record, with copies for the patient and her psychiatrist.

Taking Notes during Sessions: Questions to Consider

Even though taking notes is often helpful during an evaluation in order to assure that historical facts are noted correctly and to retain essential information for developing a treatment plan, note taking during a psychotherapy session may interfere with the development of rapport and empathy and our ability to listen to our own feelings in response to our patients which are valuable diagnostic tools (Gabbard, 2010; Luepker, 2010). It can be tempting to type notes on a computer during sessions as a way to deal with the time pressure and volume of clients and appointments many practitioners face. In Chapter 7 I mentioned the trainee who, on viewing a video of his sessions with his patient, was dismayed to see how often he looked at his laptop screen instead of his client. He noticed he was not bearing witness to the patient's emotional pain over early childhood trauma and her current experiences of feeling less important to her mother than her sister. The patient had tearfully expressed hopelessness about her lack of progress in therapy. As my trainee discovered, note taking during psychotherapy sessions

can lead practitioners to turn away from patients and focus on their computers. When clients interpret this as inattention or a practitioner's devaluation of the client's problems, the therapeutic relationship is harmed.

I have mentioned elsewhere the advantages of writing progress notes after clients leave our offices. This permits time for reflection and development of perspective on themes and meanings which may not have been clear during the session. Jotting down a few significant details on a pad of paper during sessions can help jog our memories when we write progress notes later. Some therapists report developing an ability to write down significant words and phrases without breaking eye contact with clients. Some therapists make clear to clients the role their note taking plays and report that clients may ask them to note specific things for later discussion.

Termination Phase

Bringing closure to treatment in a sensitive manner is as important as a good beginning. Records play a vital role in termination. Many clients have never had an opportunity in their lives to end a relationship constructively, which, in part, includes expressing what the relationship has meant to them. The termination phase provides a key therapeutic opportunity to review with our patients what has transpired in treatment, the extent of their progress, and what they found to be helpful and not helpful parts of treatment. Documenting the status of termination with our patients, just as we created the initial or subsequent treatment plans together, is a vital part of this therapeutic task. By encouraging active participation, we help patients to conclude treatment effectively and feel free to return to treatment in the future if they need to. (See CD and Appendix D for a sample "Closing Summary.")

Writing Directly to Patients in the Record or a Letter

Narrative therapists Epston (1994) and Nylund and Thomas (1994) described the positive impact of writing letters to their patients following treatment sessions. Epston reported that letters allowed his thinking about his clients and about the therapy to be as transparent as possible, which he found beneficial to himself and his patients. "I have had clients tell me that they regularly reread letters I sent them years ago to remind themselves what they endured, how far they had advanced their lives, and the extent to which they considered themselves to have changed" (Epston, 1994, pp. 31–32). The form and impact of addressing patients directly in the treatment record appears to have a similar effect. Because our patients have access to their records, and because writing directly to them rather than in the third person appears to support the therapeutic alliance, I am wondering why do we not experiment with addressing our patients directly in the records rather than writing about them in the third person?

MANAGEMENT OF COMPLEX, CHALLENGING SITUATIONS

In most instances, patients understand that records are an integral part of professional services. However, on rare occasions, patients demand at the beginning of initial evaluations that therapists keep no records. Sometimes, clients who are in the midst of treatment request that their therapists omit facts from their records. We need to make clear to our clients at the outset the reasons for record keeping and why these options are neither acceptable nor ethical. Establishing appropriate professional boundaries regarding the purposes and protocol for record keeping establishes and maintains a safe therapeutic relationship and protects practitioners from the appearance of impropriety.

SUMMARY

Record keeping has therapeutic value. When clients choose to have access to their own records, and when therapists can use records as a routine part of therapy, practitioners can promote patients' self-determination and enhance their collaborative participation. Reflecting on records helps clients feel cared for and understood. Records help practitioners and patients remain focused on addressing the patients' problems and treatment goals. They help clinicians and clients see progress or lack thereof. Records serve to clarify our respective roles, boundaries, and responsibilities. They provide a vehicle for communicating and mentalizing with our patients, provide helpful bridge-building between sessions, and contribute to our patients' positive self-image. Despite time pressures and challenges to allowing adequate time for taking notes, it is important for each practitioner to find a way that is effective and does not hamper or damage the therapeutic relationship.

10

Clinical Supervision Records

Imagine you are a clinical supervisor in an outpatient psychiatry department of a university teaching hospital. One of your trainees, a mature woman with professional experience working with infants and preschool children, is providing supportive treatment to a 30-year-old married man. His wife was recently admitted to the psychiatric unit of the hospital and diagnosed with major depressive disorder that began 12 days after the birth of their first child. He reported his wife became disorganized, unable to care for the baby, and ultimately attempted suicide. He was distressed, tired, and overwrought, attempting to care for his infant son, while working full-time as an insurance agent in his home office. For reasons that are unclear to you or your supervisee, he declined offers of help from relatives. Your primary concerns are the father's ability to competently care for the child and whether further intervention is needed. You therefore pay careful attention to your trainee's evaluation and treatment of this man and his family crisis. You are satisfied with her meticulous assessment of his mental status and descriptions of his feelings about daily activities with his child. You concur with her conclusion that he is adequately coping with the considerable stress associated with his wife's condition, the needs of his infant, and his job demands.

Your supervisee follows your recommendation to encourage her client to accept the assistance of home visits from a public health nurse. He complies with this suggestion and a nurse routinely assesses both his and baby's needs. Your trainee confers with the visiting nurse and reports to you that despite the unexpected adversity he appears to be coping adequately. As a result, you are stunned when the chief resident in psychiatry informs you your supervisee's client has been arrested for the death of his child and his family members may file a lawsuit against you and the clinic for mismanagement of the father's treatment and negligent supervision of a trainee. You are devastated about the death of the child and filled with fear and self-recrimination. You are responsible for your supervisee's patient care. You understand your vicarious liability for her treatment of this man. You are mortified as you realize you did not document your conscientious, detailed, and consistent supervisory conferences with your trainee. What do you do now?

Unlike consultants, whose contractual arrangements are usually voluntary, supervisors are responsible for their supervisees' work. In fact, inadequate or improper supervision is among the most common causes for disciplinary actions by psychology boards (Association of State and Provincial Psychology Boards, 1998). It is also a growing cause of action in malpractice lawsuits (Reamer, 1995). Many clinical supervisors, however, are unaware of fundamental responsibilities associated with competent supervision. Among these are the need for written contracts between the supervisor and supervisee that explicitly detail the requirements for mastery of learning objectives, including protecting patients' confidentiality and developing relevant treatment plans. Many state boards require supervision plans for prelicensure clinical supervision to be approved and expect supervisors to keep records of supervision in which they describe the patient's assessments, treatment plans, and progress, as well as the supervisee's performance and where remedial efforts may be needed. However, supervisors routinely fail to document supervision sessions.

Lack of documentation is a serious clinical concern. Without a written chronology of the scope and effectiveness of supervision, as noted in the vignette above, supervisors cannot show their reasoning and efforts to help their supervisees improve clients' emotional and mental health, and, more important, to prevent harm to clients. In Gary Schoener's forensic experience, malpractice attorneys routinely subpoena supervision records, but supervisors usually fail to have documented their supervision, unless required to do so by licensing entities. Supervisors then must revert to what they think they remember happened. As an experienced family therapist lamented, "Supervisors are at the same place psychotherapists were thirty years ago—they don't understand the importance of documenting their supervision" (W. Bera, personal communication, 2011).

The purpose of this chapter includes the following: to describe the responsibilities of clinical supervisors, demonstrate how record keeping helps supervisors fulfill their responsibilities, clarify the characteristics and contents of good supervisory records, discuss the distinction between supervision and consultation, and review special issues arising in mandated supervision. Sample supervision forms that supervisors may adapt to their own settings in order to facilitate informed consent and provide systematic evidence of supervision (e.g., face sheet, learning assessment needs, supervision contract, case log, and progress notes) can all be found on the CD and in Appendix G.

CLINICAL SUPERVISORS' RESPONSIBILITIES

Mental health professionals use the apprenticeship model to teach psychotherapy. At all levels (graduate student training, internships, and prelicensure practice) trainees and new therapists learn under the tutelage of supervisors, who are more experienced practitioners and who are responsible for overseeing and directing supervisees' assessment and treatment of patients. Clinical supervisors must be accessible to help supervisees assess patients' problems and needs, plan appropriate intervention, and handle emergencies. Good supervisors carefully identify supervisees' strengths and weaknesses and foster an open, supportive learning environment in which supervisees can explore, grow, and develop confidence. This requires a foundation of trust so that supervisees can feel free to discuss any concerns or dilemmas about their work, no matter how simplistic or embarrassing they may seem.

At the same time, supervisors are an authoritative source for their supervisees. Integral to good supervision is the ability to establish a role model for exemplary professional boundaries and conduct. This is aided by reviewing supervisee records, reviewing other samples of supervisee work such as recordings of interviews, requiring supervisees to discuss a broad sampling of their cases and provide rationale for their clinical decisions, and providing feedback and recommendations to improve patient care. Supervisors also regularly evaluate their supervisees, both verbally and in writing, and discuss their evaluations in supervision. Finally they provide references and make employment recommendations, such as whether to retain or promote supervisees.

While the foregoing goals of clinical supervision are standards of care that supervisors need to know and implement rigorously, often this is not the case. Many supervisors lack sufficient time, funding, administrative support, or skills essential to training competent clinicians and ensuring proper care of patients. Mental health organizations and licensure boards are becoming aware of the need for specific supervision training, systematic review, and means to encourage and evaluate competent supervision skills.

Because supervisors have greater power over their supervisees, they have a fiduciary duty to take proper care of supervisees and supervisees' patients. Mental health professions therefore establish guidelines for training and supervision. Although ethics codes vary, generally they hold supervisors responsible for having sufficient knowledge and skill in the clinical field they are supervising, for refraining from exploitation and harassment of their supervisees to meet supervisors' personal needs, for writing timely and fair performance evaluations, for maintaining respectful and culturally sensitive boundaries, for refraining from providing psychotherapy to supervisees, and for providing acceptable referrals when supervisees are in need of psychotherapy or counseling. Many professions' ethics codes also emphasize the importance of informed consent to supervision (e.g., clarifying the purpose and parameters of supervision), including respective roles, rights, and expectations, all of which provide a foundation for establishing a strong supervisory relationship and for preventing misunderstandings in supervision.

The legal doctrines "direct liability" and "vicarious (or indirect) liability" hold supervisors responsible for proper care of supervisees and their supervisees' patients. "Direct liability" creates the expectation that clinical supervisors will provide appropriate supervision to their supervisees. "Vicarious liability" holds supervisors responsible for their supervisees' care to patients. These expectations are based on the legal theory of *respondeat superior*, a Latin term that means "let the master respond." It implies supervisors are responsible for actions done by their employees, agents, or subordinates when such actions are based upon their assigned duties. It dates back to medieval times in England and a ruling in a complaint against a nobleman who sent a servant out to perform a task and the servant was injured. The nobleman was held responsible for the servant's injury because he sent the servant on the errand. Under these legal doctrines, if supervisees or patients can show that supervisors had a professional responsibility for them, but harmed them due to supervisory negligence, they can, in theory, sue supervisors.

State and commonwealth laws and rules define three major issues: who is qualified to supervise, what constitutes supervision, and who is in need of supervision. Some states include ethical standards for supervision in their statutes.

Statutory approaches to supervision vary between states and may vary between mental health professions within states. For example, in Delaware the state licensing law for psychologists defines "supervising psychologist" as someone who has been licensed for 2 years. But in California, a "qualified primary supervisor" in psychology and psychiatry must be licensed with a minimum of 3 years of professional experience following licensure. In Texas, social workers must complete 40 hours of training in supervision to become certified as supervisors, while in Minnesota it is 30 hours and in Washington, 15 hours. Thus practitioners need to be aware of and document their compliance with their respective jurisdictions' supervision training requirements.

HOW CLINICAL SUPERVISION RECORDS HELP SUPERVISORS FULFILL THEIR RESPONSIBILITIES

Supervisory records benefit supervisors and supervisees in many of the same ways that psychotherapy records benefit practitioners and patients. See Table 10.1 for a list of parallels between benefits of psychotherapy records and benefits of clinical supervision records.

USING SUPERVISION RECORDS AS SUPERVISORY TOOLS

There are parallels between ways supervision records may be used as supervisory tools to facilitate supervision and ways psychotherapy records may be used as treatment tools to facilitate treatment. (See Chapter 9 for discussion of using patient records as therapeutic tools.) The following are examples of beneficial uses of supervision records.

To Provide a Guide for an Unpredictable Journey

Just as therapy is an unpredictable journey, supervision is a process of discovery. There is no way to anticipate what lies ahead in supervision, just as there is no certain way to anticipate a course of therapy. Supervision, like psychotherapy, is an inductive process in which supervision records can become a map that shows where one has been, where one is headed, and what bumps in the road are making the ride more difficult.

To Help Organize and Provide a Supportive "Container"

Supervisees may enter supervision feeling anxious and overwhelmed by new practice settings and difficult patients. Supervision records can assist supervisees to identify and organize what initially felt like disjointed fragments of information and to clarify what has not been helpful or what may be helpful to their patients.

Table 10.1   Parallels between Benefits of Psychotherapy Records and Benefits of Clinical Supervision Records

Benefits of Psychotherapy Records	Benefits of Clinical Supervision Records
Help foster treatment alliance	Help foster supervisory relationship
Provide informed consent to psychotherapy	Provide informed consent to supervision by discussing purpose of supervision, respective roles and responsibilities
Help clarify presenting problems and histories of patients	Help clarify supervisees' professional strengths, weaknesses, previous professional training and experience
Help psychotherapists clarify treatment goals for patients that logically flow from clients' supervisory goals and learning plans	Help clinical supervisors to establish presenting problems and history that logically flow from assessment of supervisees' learning needs
Assist psychotherapists and patients to formulate and mutually agree upon treatment plans, including treatment goals and procedures	Assist clinical supervisors to formulate and mutually agree upon learning plans, including supervision goals and procedures
Help assess progress or lack of progress in meeting treatment goals	Help assess progress or lack of progress in meeting supervisory goals
Provide summary of progress and outcomes of treatment and recommendations that can be used later for continuity of care	Provide summary of progress and outcomes of clinical supervision and recommendations for supervisory evaluations and letters of reference
Help psychotherapists show what they did so they can respond to a financial or quality assurance audit	Help clinical supervisors show what they did so they can respond to a financial or quality assurance audit
Help psychotherapists show that their services met standards of professional care for psychotherapists in their professional community in the event of a regulatory board complaint or in the event of a regulatory board or legal complaint of psychotherapist negligence	Help clinical supervisors show that their supervisory service met standards of professional care for clinical supervisors in their professional community in the event of a regulatory or legal complaint of supervisory negligence

To Provide a Bridge to Further Exploration

When we refer to our notes from a previous supervision session and ask our supervisees about their subsequent thoughts, supervisory notes can help build bridges between sessions. Concepts and observations discussed in previous sessions become the basis for further exploration in supervision and may also point to additional information or assistance the supervisor and supervisee may require in order to formulate a patient's diagnosis and treatment plan. Reflecting on previous supervision sessions may also help to clarify impasses in the therapy relationship between the supervisee and patient or in the supervisory relationship between supervisee and supervisor.

To Enhance Trust and Confidence in the Therapeutic Process

On hearing supervisors refer back to previous supervision sessions, supervisees may feel they have been heard. Supervisors' use of supervision progress notes also provides a role model for supervisees who are learning about the value of creating therapy records.

To Promote Accuracy of Supervision Records

Supervisees can help themselves and their supervisors along the way by correcting factual inaccuracies in supervision progress notes. Supervisors understandably can misreport some facts or supervisees can misunderstand what supervisors believe they said. Just as therapists need to allow patients to amend their therapy records, supervisors need to afford supervisees the opportunity to add their own statements to supervisory evaluations when there may be disagreements or differing views from those of the supervisors on supervision goals or progress.

To Promote Self-Determination in Establishing Supervision Plans

Using the supervision record to establish supervision plans with our supervisees promotes supervisees' self-determination and assures that plans are mutually understood and agreed upon. Participating in the process encourages supervisees to clarify what they are able to work on and what they may not be ready or able to do. In a complex setting, for example, where clinical supervisors must be especially careful not to put supervisees into situations that will overwhelm them and cause them harm, a collaborative approach is critical.

To Monitor Progress or to Reveal Lack of Progress or Deterioration

Contemporaneous supervision progress notes allow us to see tangible progress and patterns, which help us develop realistic evaluations and give us perspective so we may modify our supervision approach as needed. In one instance, a training director noted that a supervisor's supervision progress notes helped him and the supervisor to identify and resolve a trainee's problems in her work. The trainee, who was receiving psychotherapy supervision in an office outside of her training program, was having difficulty bearing witness to her patient's traumatic history of physical and emotional abuse. In her psychotherapy supervision, the supervisor helped her to identify her patients' needs and explored with her how she could become more compassionate with her client. The contemporaneous supervision progress notes helped him see that despite months of systematic effort to discuss problems and establish goals, the supervisee had not followed through with any of the goals she had agreed upon. Supervision progress notes helped him to clarify the parallel process between the supervisory impasse and the treatment impasse. He realized just as he was having trouble finding a way to help his supervisee, the supervisee was having trouble finding a way to help her patient. His supervision notes provided a basis for her quarterly evaluation and helped him to see it was necessary to schedule a meeting with the supervisee and her training director. The meeting helped to clarify the respective impasses, and in turn the supervisee was able to help her patient.

Supervision notes can also help us see when supervisees are not benefitting from supervision and when there may be an ethical responsibility to end supervision. For example, a supervisor had serious concerns about a trainee he was supervising in psychotherapy. The supervisee appeared to be taking the supervisor's recommendations too literally, without understanding how to appropriately apply the concepts with patients and staff. The supervisor documented the situations the trainee reported that caused the supervisor concern, which helped the supervisor gain perspective. He informed the training director of his concerns and his realization that it would be unsafe for the supervisee's patients for him to continue providing external supervision in a community office, where he was unable to observe the trainee's work directly. The training director agreed with the recommendation that the trainee be transferred to supervision within the training department. The training director asked the supervisor to prepare a summary of the events leading to the supervisor's concerns.

In order to respectfully terminate supervision, the supervisor shared the report with the trainee. He explained his professional rationale for referring him back to his training program for on-site supervision. As he read the report to him, he changed the pronouns so that it was as if he were reading a letter written directly to the trainee, which felt more direct, similar to approaches other authors have used in writing letters (Epston, 1994) or evaluation findings (Allen, Fonagy, & Bateman, 2008) directly to patients. The trainee agreed the supervisor's descriptions of events with patients and staff were accurate. He disagreed only with the supervisor's conclusion—that the supervisor needed to terminate the external supervision. In this supervision example, having contemporaneous supervision records made it possible for the supervisor to create an objective report for the trainee and his program that explained the pattern of unsafe professional conduct. It facilitated a respectful termination of the external supervision and plan for transfer to on-site supervision.

To Terminate Supervision

Bringing closure to supervision in a sensitive manner is as important as having a good beginning.

Records assist us to review with supervisees what has transpired in supervision, the extent of progress, and to hear what supervisees found useful and not useful in supervision. The helpfulness of the supervisee's evaluation of the supervisor is often overlooked but is one of the best ways for supervisors to learn and gain further supervision competency, as well as provide modeling for supervisees (W. Haskell, personal communication, March 31, 2011).

CHARACTERISTICS AND CONTENTS OF GOOD SUPERVISION RECORDS

As with clinical records, supervision records need to be clear, concise, specific, germane to the supervision plan, and free from conjectures and value judgments. Good supervisory records include the following contents.

Face Sheet

The face sheet includes important identifying information such as the supervisee's full name, address, phone numbers, name and address of the referring organization and its relevant representative (e.g., academic institution and academic advisor), name and professional address of the supervisor, supervision fee and billing arrangements, if any, and person to contact in case of emergency. (See CD and Appendix G for sample.)

Supervision Contract

Just as written treatment plans help therapists and their patients assure mutual consent and appropriate attention to treatment goals, so written contracts can assist supervisors and their supervisees to assure mutual consent and focus on supervisory goals. Written supervision contracts should include identifying information, purposes of supervision, number of required supervision hours, types of clinical cases needed, criteria for supervisory evaluations, when the supervisor will need to conduct a formal evaluation of the supervisee's work, to whom the supervisor will send a written evaluation, and the rights and responsibilities of supervisor and student. They may be signed by all relevant parties. For example, for students, interns, or residents, graduate school or training program representatives may indicate their approval of the contract. For new professionals who require supervision to meet regulatory board requirements, contracts may be approved by regulatory board representatives and, if applicable, by employers who are permitting the employee to use outside supervision. (See CD and Appendix G for sample.)

Learning Needs Assessment

A key component that informs the supervision contract is the learning needs assessment. Just as psychotherapists begin by documenting an assessment of client strengths and needs, so should clinical supervisors document their assessment of supervisees' professional knowledge, previous training and experience, strengths, and learning needs. (See CD and Appendix G for sample.)

Supervision Case Logs and Progress Notes

Case logs help supervisors and supervisees recall the cases discussed on particular dates, and supervision progress notes describe the content of each session. Case logs typically are brief; progress notes are more detailed. Case logs may include only the supervisor's and supervisee's names, date of supervision sessions, and de-identified patient information, such as age, diagnosis, gender, or case number. (See CD and Appendix G for sample.)

Just as psychotherapists need to document what transpires during treatment in their progress notes, so do supervisors need to document what transpires during clinical supervision in their supervision progress notes. Details in supervision progress notes include the following: cases discussed, specific issues and problems, clinical decisions, options considered, safety concerns (e.g., suicide, violence, or sexual revictimization), recommendations to prevent risk of harm, mandated reports, and referrals needed. Clinical supervisors need to consider ways to document supervisory discussions and any recommendations regarding clinical decisions that have professional boundary implications (e.g., gift giving, client invitations to social events, funerals, weddings, e-mail, instant messaging [IM], and "friending" on social media sites) as well as discussions about multicultural issues (e.g., ethnicity, race, age, socioeconomic class, gender, sexual orientation, religion, immigration status, literacy, mental or physical disability).

Other issues that are helpful to document concern factors that promote or impede the supervisee's ability to establish a strong therapeutic relationship with a client. For example, is the supervisee able to consider cultural differences? Can the supervisee speak in the client's mother tongue or is a translator needed? Finally, we also consider documenting discussions with supervisees regarding policies and procedures for protecting patients' confidentiality and privacy and how they have informed patients of exceptions to confidentiality and privacy, including patient-informed consent procedures for electronic recording of sessions to be used for training purposes. (See CD and Appendix G for sample.)

Organizations may create their own supervision record forms to assist supervisors to remain focused on specific cases and on supervisees' problems and needs with their cases and to document supervisory interventions that promote good quality of care to patients.

Supervisees' Process Recording

Professional schools and supervision training programs have long recognized the value of supervisees creating process recordings of their treatment sessions in order to develop clinical skills (Fox and Gutheil, 2000). Because process recordings include the supervisees' own feelings about their clients and treatment and such notes are intended only for the supervisee's learning, process recordings are normally filed as "psychotherapy notes," separate from clients' or patients' medical records.

Supervisors' Supervision Process Recording

Supervision training programs, such as the Smith College School for Social Work's Advanced Clinical Supervision Certificate Program, recommend it can also be helpful for supervisors in training to do process recording following supervision sessions, in order to enhance their understanding of the supervision process and develop supervisory skills. Given today's time pressures, however, supervisors may lack time for process recording. Thus, supervisors' routine supervision progress notes, when used as supervisory tools, become even more critical in strengthening the supervisory relationship and supporting supervisees to develop their ability to provide quality care to their patients.

Consent Forms

Two types of consent forms initiated at the beginning of the supervisory process may be included in supervisory records. The first type includes statements that inform patients who is responsible for their care and what is involved in supervision of their care, such as supervisory discussions and supervisory review of records or audio- or videotapes. These statements can be incorporated into patients' notice of privacy practices. They include a list of names of all persons who will have access to patient-identifiable confidential information for supervision and how frequently cases will be reviewed. Some agencies, clinics, and licensing boards require patients' consent for supervision, but not all. In Texas, for example, only the Board of Professional Counseling requires their prelicensed counselor practitioners to give their patients a letter providing the name of supervisors (C. Clancey, personal communication, 2011).

The second type of consent forms are those that inform supervisees about information shared with other persons or institutions such as graduate schools, regulatory boards, and employers. These consent forms should include the inclusive dates, name of supervisee, content, purpose of supervisory information to be sent, and the name of the person or organization to whom the supervisory information is to be sent. These forms may be signed by all parties involved (e.g., supervisee, supervisor, and organization requiring the supervision).

At the end of supervision, a third type of consent form may be needed. This type involves subsequent requests for supervisors to authorize release of their performance evaluation information. In lieu of consent forms, former supervisees should put all such requests in writing and sign them. Supervisors should maintain these requests and copies of letters of reference in their files.

CONFIDENTIALITY OF SUPERVISION RECORDS

Because supervision records are confidential, they must be stored with the same security procedures as psychotherapy records. Supervisors need to discuss parameters of confidentiality, related to supervision including its exceptions, with their supervisees.

RETENTION AND DESTRUCTION OF SUPERVISION RECORDS

It is prudent to retain supervision records for as long as applicable rules require retention of the clinical material addressed in supervision. The same standards used to guide the destruction of clinical records apply to supervision records. Supervision records are never altered or destroyed to influence a judicial hearing. See Chapter 8 for discussion of the various factors to consider in deciding how long to retain clinical records (e.g., requirements by institutions, state, federal or provincial law, licensure board rules, insurance companies who are paying for the treatment, and concerns about possible complaint action). Some attorneys may advise keeping supervision records forever, in the event future malpractice or other complaint action might arise as a result of previous supervisory or supervisee failures. In one instance, a supervisee failed to send her documentation of supervision to her state licensing board in a timely manner. The state licensing board requested the supervisor submit documentation to prove the supervisee met the supervision requirements. Had the supervisor not retained documentation of the hours and content of supervision sessions, the supervisee's supervision hours would have been lost, and the supervisee could have sued the supervisor for damages resulting from failing to keep a record of supervision.

OTHER ISSUES

Distinction between Consultation and Supervision

There are important distinctions between supervisors' and consultants' roles. Consultants, in contrast to supervisors, do not have the same responsibilities described above. Practitioners who have full licensing authority and responsibility for their own clinical work may voluntarily choose to seek consultation for expertise in a particular practice area. This voluntary consultation arrangement means they are free to accept or reject the consultant's recommendations. The liability for their work belongs to them, not the consultant. Even though it may be helpful for consultants to document their consultations (e.g., to refresh their memories in case consultees return for further consultation), consultants, unlike supervisors, may choose not to document their consultation. The consultee is responsible for documenting the consultation, not the consultant. As I discussed in Chapter 3, practitioners' documentation of consultation they receive is critical to good clinical practice.

Mandated Supervision

Mandated supervision involves built-in disclosure requirements that carry additional complexity. When practitioners engage in unprofessional behavior, their licensure boards, employers, or courts may refer them for required remedial clinical supervision in order to ensure their ability to practice safely in the future. Before accepting referrals of mandated supervision, supervisors need to consider and to document answers to the following questions.

First, is supervision appropriate to remediate practice problems? Some authors emphasize the need for licensure boards to refer practitioners first for an assessment (Gabbard & Lester, 1995; Schoener & Gonsiorek, 1988, 1989). Assessments can rule out underlying issues such as chemical dependence or serious cognitive or mental illness, and help determine whether supervision will actually be the appropriate method to resolve practice problems. Without a careful prior evaluation, supervision may fail, as noted in the following example.

A retired psychotherapist who was reentering private practice was referred for remedial supervision after her licensure board investigated a complaint and determined she had engaged in inappropriate professional behavior with a former agency client. In its investigation of the complaint, the board found that the practitioner had invited her former patient to have treatment in her private practice against her former agency supervisor's specific request that she terminate with the patient, because the patient needed a higher level of clinical and other care than either her former agency or a private practitioner could safely provide.

Following its investigation and findings, the board did not order the licensee to have an evaluation. It referred her directly for supervision. After reviewing all relevant documents from the board, including the licensee's clinical records of her care of the patient, which were redacted to protect patient privacy, and after having several supervisory discussions with the licensee, the supervisor wondered if the licensee could be suffering from possible cognitive defects that might be impairing her memory and ability to engage in appropriate professional decision making.

The licensee's irritable disregard for the findings of the board and for the professional opinions of other clinical staff who had been involved in serving the needs of the former patient were remarkable. However, assessment of cognitive deficiencies or mental health problems was beyond the scope of supervision. The supervisor learned from this experience that it would have been better had he requested the board order an assessment first before agreeing to provide remedial supervision. He informed the board he lacked enough information and was therefore unable to confidently answer the board's questions regarding the licensee's ability to practice safely in the future.

Second, does the supervisor providing mandated supervision have sufficient professional expertise? Supervisors who agree to provide mandated supervision require additional special skills. They must not only possess knowledge and professional experience regarding the clinical and ethical issues in question and extensive supervisory experience, but be aware of heightened responsibility to define the limitations of supervisee confidentiality. Further, there are special challenges in handling a mandated supervisee's feelings toward the supervisor (anger, distrust, and heightened fears related to the referral) as well as in managing their own reactions.

Careful documentation of informed consent to mandated supervision includes but is not limited to the following:

- Reasons for the referral for remedial supervision
- Purposes of the mandated supervision, including its risks and possible benefits
- Limitations to confidentiality and privacy
- What information the supervisor must review in order to be able to provide the mandated supervision, e.g., including all relevant clinical or investigative records, and findings from the board, de-identified patient records, tapes of sessions
- What information the supervisor will be required to share with the board or referring organization

SUMMARY

Most clinical supervisors today overlook the importance of maintaining supervisory records, which is an urgent problem in clinical care. Had the clinical supervisor in the opening vignette of this chapter known about the importance of keeping supervision records and had she documented her excellent supervision to her trainee, she might not have needed to feel as fearful about the malpractice case her trainee's patient's family unexpectedly brought against her trainee, herself, and the outpatient clinic. She was relieved to discover the visiting nurse had documented in her records the trainee's reasons for referring the father to the visiting nurse association, which showed the careful attention her trainee had given to assure her patient's infant son's safety. The court was able to see the trainee had met the standard of care in her community, and the case was dismissed. Another case example presented in this chapter illustrated how contemporaneous supervision progress notes revealed parallel processes of supervisory and treatment impasses, provided the basis for supervisory evaluations, and led to finding solutions that helped improved a supervisee's ability to provide the best possible care to her patients.

This chapter discussed how clinical supervisors are ultimately responsible for the care that their supervisees provide to patients and for adhering to ethical supervisory standards of appropriate care to their supervisees. It summarized the concept of supervisory liability and how supervision records help supervisors fulfill their responsibilities. It described procedures for assuring patient confidentiality in supervision, for retention and destruction of supervision records, and characteristics and contents of good supervision records. It discussed the importance of facilitating informed consent to supervision through documenting supervisees' learning needs, creating supervision contracts, and maintaining detailed supervision progress notes that clarify supervisory goals, monitor and evaluate progress or lack of progress in supervision, and indicate whether supervisory interventions were timely, promoted good quality care, and reduced risk of harm to patients. It noted that supervisory records form the basis for objective reports and can also be used as supervisory tools to enhance the supervisory relationship. Finally, it described special considerations requiring careful documentation, such as mandated supervision and distinctions between supervision and consultation. To find sample supervision forms (e.g., supervision face sheet, learning assessment and supervision contract, case log and progress note) that supervisors may adapt to their own settings, see the CD and Appendix G.

11

Teaching Record Keeping

Imagine you are the graduate student intern described in the previous chapter. You are horrified when the chief resident in psychiatry grimly appears at your office door to inform you that the police are charging your client with the murder of his infant son. Your heart pounds when you learn the client's family members could sue you for this incomprehensible tragedy. The resident requests you retrieve the client's record. You are stunned to see you did not document the detailed assessment of the client's ability to cope with strenuous job demands, being sole caretaker of his baby, and the stress of his wife being treated on an inpatient ward of a psychiatric hospital. Moreover, there is nothing in your record about your recommendations, such as enlisting the public health nurse for well-baby care or developing a supportive network consisting of family members, friends, neighbors, and church members to reduce the client's severe stress. As your head swirls, you recall that while your supervisor was very supportive in this case, you and she never discussed the critical need for meticulous records.

Graduate students, interns, and new professionals acquire psychotherapy skills not only through intensive course work, but through rigorous training and clinical supervision (Gabbard, 2010; Krasner, Howard, & Brown, 1998). The purpose of supervision is to help students and new professionals apply conceptual knowledge to clinical settings. This includes assuring that students and trainees understand the relevance and necessity of systematic documentation. However, most graduate school curricula lack instruction in record keeping, and clinical supervisors rarely teach it. In a study of psychology faculty providing psychotherapy supervision, respondents reported only 10% of supervision time involved reviewing records (Tyler, Sloan, & King, 2000). The purpose of this chapter, therefore, is first to emphasize the need to make competent documentation of clinical treatment central to all training, and second, to provide specific methods of teaching record keeping. This chapter's general advice is meant to be used

in conjunction with the formats, models, and examples presented in the other chapters of this text.

WHY TEACHING RECORD KEEPING IS ESSENTIAL

As we saw in the example of the overwhelmed client who killed his infant son, well-written records are essential for protecting clinicians from false allegations, as well as for proper diagnosis, treatment plans, and clinical intervention. In the event of a lawsuit or complaint to a regulatory board, a good record is the only way supervisors and supervisees can demonstrate professional and good-faith efforts to assist the client. Thus, one of the more valuable contributions instructors and supervisors can make is teaching students and trainees the importance of maintaining accurate, succinct, and germane records.

There is no substitute for routinely collaborating with students and trainees about patient records. This activity helps students and trainees as well as instructors and supervisors. It helps instructors in practice methods and ethics courses teach applications of clinical and ethical principles to case management. It enables supervisors to identify patients' problems and progress and helps supervisees develop appropriate goals and objectives for therapy. Repeated review of supervisees' records also improves supervisory skills and insight and expands the supervisor's repertoire of interventions with both supervisees and clients. In short, good records help instructors and supervisors become better teachers and help students and supervisees become better therapists.

METHODS FOR TEACHING RECORD KEEPING

Obtain Informed Consent from Clients for Supervisory Review of Records

Clinical supervisors can assure that supervisees provide a written notice of privacy practices and tell their patients in the initial session that a licensed, experienced clinician will be supervising the psychotherapy sessions, will discuss the case regularly with the supervisee, and will review their records. If sessions are videotaped or viewed live by the supervisor and other trainees, the supervisee must obtain written consent from the patient for use of electronic equipment. Obtaining informed consent further defines the limits of confidentiality and allows clients to determine their own boundaries of safety and privacy. Explicit discussions regarding supervision establish a foundation of trust and respect in the therapeutic relationship and foster clients' sense of control and self-determination.

Assess Record Keeping Knowledge and Create Learning Objectives

Teaching record keeping in the classroom or in supervision can be systematic. The first step is to find students' or supervisees' baseline knowledge of the topic. This can be done through preassessments, which ask students and trainees to list what needs to be included in competent records and to describe their philosophy about record keeping, giving a rationale for their position. Assessments show learning gaps and identify what ideas influence students' and supervisees' values and beliefs about the role records play in therapy. After completing the learning needs assessment, the next step is to establish learning objectives. Instructors should include the following in their course syllabi, and clinical supervisors should include these in their supervision contracts:

- Record keeping learning objectives
- Activities the learning objectives require
- Standards for mastery of the learning objectives
- Methods instructors and supervisors will use to evaluate successful completion of the learning objectives

Clinical supervisors can ensure that supervision contracts routinely include careful review of, and feedback about, the interns' or new professionals' records. (See Chapter 10 for further discussion of supervision contracts.) Supervisors can encourage supervisees to read sample records and evaluate their own record keeping abilities. Progress toward increasingly effective record keeping can be discussed and noted. Similarly, persistent problems can be addressed throughout supervisees' training.

Use Contemporaneous Case Material

Teaching record keeping during clinical experience with clients is generally more direct than what can be offered in the classroom. Supervisors have direct access to contemporaneous notes. Also, when clients have consented to supervisory overview, the content of records need not be altered to protect confidentiality. An added benefit of teaching record keeping during direct supervision is greater control over the standard of care and over records for which supervisors are ultimately professionally responsible. However, classroom instructors can use disguised case notes and ask students to critique and rewrite the notes more appropriately. Or, they can present videotaped therapy sessions and ask students how the sessions might be documented. For example, Glen Gabbard has included a DVD in his book on psychodynamic therapy showing actors depicting actual psychotherapy sessions (Gabbard, 2010). Such case vignettes might be used in practice methods and ethics courses to evoke record-keeping exercises.

Provide Outline for Record Keeping

Instructors and supervisors can help supervisees or students by providing an outline of what to include in, or exclude from, records. For example, Chapter 3 presents a detailed discussion of characteristics and contents of good records. Supervisors can use categories from the outline, give specific examples, and explain the basis for each point, emphasizing that consistency in record keeping format makes clinicians' jobs easier and pertinent information more accessible.

Begin with Supervisees' or Students' Observations

Supervisory sessions can begin with exploring what supervisees or students have experienced or observed during their sessions with patients. Once supervisees have freely discussed themes of the sessions and their dilemmas in an initial case, it may be helpful for supervisors to consider with supervisees how supervisees can state the interview material in their records. Teachers can take a similar approach, basing classroom discussion of potential approaches on disguised process notes of a psychotherapy case or on a videotaped interview suitable for classroom use.

Guide Supervisees in Putting Observations in Outline Form

Once supervisees and students have had an opportunity to discuss their observations of the case, the supervisor can guide the student to consider how observations can best be stated in written form. Referring to the beginning of a model record keeping outline, which is presented in Chapter 3, for example, supervisors and teachers can ask their supervisees or students to tell them who the client is: name, age, marital status, race, other characteristics, occupation, and who referred the client. Supervisors can then ask how supervisees or students would succinctly record that kind of *identifying information* in the written record. Supervisors or teachers might give examples of how they record identifying information in their own records.

For the next category in the model outline, supervisors or teachers can ask supervisees and students to state what the client states are his or her problems or reasons for needing help. They then may ask how these *presenting problems* could be stated in the record. Proceeding to the next category, supervisors and teachers can ask supervisees and students to tell the history of problems, starting with their onset, circumstances surrounding onset of problems, and how they would succinctly document the history of problems in the record.

Provide Continuous Realistic Feedback

Continuous realistic feedback promotes learning. When supervisees or students identify appropriate information to include in the record, the supervisor can reinforce the importance of the students' points and note why these are good record keeping practices. Supervisors and teachers can validate supervisees' inclinations to record information that supports their diagnoses and treatment plans.

Reflect on Characteristics and Contents of Good Records

Supervisors can help supervisees or trainees to distinguish between relevant and irrelevant and useful and not useful language by continually reflecting upon a list of characteristics and contents of good records (see Chapter 3). Unlimited opportunities exist for supervisors to seize "teachable moments" to help students become proficient in writing clear, relevant professional records.

For example, if students include irrelevant information in a record entry, supervisors can ask students to consider the outline presented in Chapter 3: "Let's refer back to our record keeping outline that tells us what we state in a record must be limited to what is relevant to the patient's diagnosis and treatment. How is the information you included relevant to the patient's diagnosis and treatment?" Supervisors can help supervisees learn how to discriminate. Struggling with tough questions is an invaluable learning tool. Supervisors can probe the basis of the students' decisions and let them explore even better options.

Supervisors can explain that direct quotes from clients are preferable to paraphrasing because quotes are concrete statements that are less likely to be misinterpreted.

It is critical also for supervisors to teach beginning therapists how to discriminate between problem-centered and value-laden language. Considering examples of each type, and inviting discussion of them, is a good teaching tool. When supervisees or students use jargon or potentially detrimental language, supervisors can turn this into a learning experience by asking further questions to steer them away from this practice.

If supervisees use a comment that sounds prejudicial, supervisors may ask supervisees to consider the following: "What does our outline in Chapter 3 say about the importance of value-free language? How can we determine whether the language in our records comes across as judgmental or prejudicial?"

Supervisors can let their supervisees generate answers, then expand upon these, using follow-up questions: "What happens to our choice of words when we write from the perspective of being in our client's shoes?" "Could the same information be stated in another, less-biased way?" "How would you do that?"

Supervisors can clarify when even relevant material, such as the gender of a client's partner, may be unsuitable to include in the record. Supervisors can suggest alternative ways to address sensitive information in the record.

Instructors and supervisors can also help students and trainees discriminate between information that is important to discuss in supervision yet may be inappropriate to include in patient records. For example, it is crucial for supervisees to feel free to speak to their supervisors about all feelings toward their clients, including sexual attraction. However, stating the therapist's countertransference feelings in the record may not be necessary or helpful. Instructors and supervisors can use the discussion about inappropriate content in Chapter 3 as a resource in the classroom and in supervision.

SUMMARY

Writing and maintaining good clinical records are central to effective psychotherapy and ethical practice. However, graduate schools rarely teach these skills. For these reasons, most student and postgraduate therapists enter supervised clinical experiences with no theoretical or practical framework for understanding or implementing competent record keeping. This lack of skills carries over to institutional settings, where inattention to records deprives patients and students of the best quality in professional services.

The purpose of this chapter is to make students, professors, graduate school administrators, and clinical supervisors outside of the training setting aware of the need for systematic instruction on why and how to write and maintain effective clinical records. Included are examples of the broad implications of inadequate records and methods for teaching specific skills inherent in competent clinical record keeping.

12

Psychotherapists and Records in the Legal System

> Imagine a messenger arriving at your office door with a subpoena for a client's records. Now what do you do? Although your client has asked you to disclose his records in his legal case, you believe that sharing his records with his attorney is inappropriate. Moreover, it could be harmful to your client. What are your options?

Psychotherapists often have trouble answering these kinds of questions because they lack knowledge of the legal system. Consequently, even seasoned practitioners lose their bearings. They begin questioning their clinical judgment and struggle with how to respond when they receive subpoenas or when attorneys pressure them, stating they are "obliged" to release their patients' records. They feel even more confused by the Health Insurance Portability and Accountability Act (HIPAA) "permitting" practitioners to disclose records in patients' legal cases, forgetting that HIPAA also permits practitioners to exercise their professional judgment. An experienced practitioner told me he became so anxious in response to an attorney's demands that he lost his usual composure and handed over his client's entire original record to the attorney. He needed help thinking through his options before acting. He is not alone. Nearly all conscientious practitioners worry about the personal and professional ramifications of being pulled into litigious situations.

Information about the legal system helps practitioners to better serve their clients and protect their practices. It allows them to identify options for appropriate professional relationships with patients and attorneys. Knowledge of the legal process helps them to form their policies and be more systematic about goals, interventions, and documentation regarding clients. When practitioners have patients' authorization and when they conclude, based upon their professional judgment, that they should disclose records in a legal matter, therapists can learn to incorporate the legal experience into the therapeutic relationship. Accruing skills and knowledge regarding therapists' proper roles in the legal process builds confidence and reduces anxiety. In short, with knowledge, neither practitioners nor their clients need to be victims of the legal system.

This chapter provides an orientation to the legal system. It provides practical information and methods to help practitioners function more comfortably inside or outside of the legal system. The first section gives an overview of what makes therapists worry about the legal system. The second section stresses the importance of practitioners' clarifying their roles. The subsequent section offers information and guidance to practitioners for handling various types of requests for patient records, such as attorneys' calls, subpoenas, and court orders. The fourth section presents information about interactions with the legal system and how practitioners can conduct themselves appropriately. The following section describes the process of preparation for testimony in depositions and the courtroom. The next section summarizes techniques for giving testimony, and the final section discusses the management of clinical issues that arise when patients are in legal disputes and when therapists become involved in their patients' legal cases.

THERAPISTS AND THE ADVERSARIAL PROCESS

Why Practitioners Worry: Clinical and Ethical Reasons

The following are clinical and ethical reasons why psychotherapists worry about becoming involved in their patients' legal cases.

Loss of Confidentiality Interrupts Therapy

Therapy is no longer confidential when practitioners release psychotherapy records to the attorneys who are representing their patients in a legal matter. When confidentiality ends, therapy is interrupted. As a result, there are privileged communication laws that give patients the right to decide whether their confidential disclosures in therapy are revealed to courts.

A celebrated example of a client's right to privileged communication in federal courts was upheld by the U.S. Supreme Court in the *Jaffe v. Redmond* (1996) case. This case involved Karen Beyer, a clinical social worker, and her psychotherapy patient, Chicago police officer Marylu Redmond, who was charged with violating the constitutional rights of Ricky Allen, Sr., a man whom she killed while on duty responding to a fight at an apartment complex. Attorneys for the deceased victim's family demanded access to Redmond's psychotherapy record, hoping to unearth further evidence of Redmond's guilt. However, Beyer refused to release her patient's record because Redmond had not authorized her to do so. Beyer's attorneys argued that Beyer had acted lawfully in refusing to release her patient's record without the patient's authorization. Under Illinois law, they

noted, communications between clinical social workers and their psychotherapy patients were "privileged," providing patients with the legal right to choose to keep their psychotherapy records out of court. The lower court agreed with Beyer's position, but a federal appeals court overturned the lower court's ruling. Ultimately, the U.S. Supreme Court heard the case. Numerous mental health professions rallied to support Beyer's position and submitted respective *amicus* briefs with detailed reasons why patients required confidentiality in psychotherapy.

The U.S. Supreme Court recognized the necessity for confidentiality in psychotherapy. "Effective psychotherapy depends upon an atmosphere of confidence and trust, and therefore the mere possibility of disclosure of confidential communications may impede development of the relationship necessary for successful treatment," Justice Stevens noted, writing for the Court (*Jaffe v. Redmond*, 1996). The Court therefore upheld Beyer's patient's right to withhold her psychotherapy records in federal court. Justice Stevens further stated that "The federal privilege, which clearly applies to psychiatrists and psychologists, also extends to confidential communication made to licensed social workers in the course of psychotherapy."

Harm Can Arise from Dual Roles

Psychotherapists also understand their ethical responsibility to refrain from engaging in dual roles that could harm their clients. When therapists serve as witnesses in their patients' court cases, they take on a dual role. Sometimes engaging in both roles as witnesses and therapists can be harmful, at other times it is less harmful, and in some instances, it may not be harmful at all. However, in all instances, it can interrupt the work of current therapy.

Examples of Potential Harm in Different Types of Legal Cases

The following types of legal cases give examples of various levels of potential harm, and how therapy is interrupted when therapists release records and engage in dual roles by becoming witnesses in their clients' legal cases.

Child Custody and Visitation Lawsuits

Parents who are divorcing often ask their children's psychotherapists to release their children's records or testify in custody and visitation disputes. Potentially it can be harmful to the child and family to do so, even when both parents give permission to release their child's therapy records and to testify. During the crisis of their parents' marital dissolution, children under psychological stress require their therapists' supportive neutrality. When therapists testify, parents and children perceive therapists as taking sides or making judgments. This can have a chilling effect on children's comfort in therapy. Judith Wallerstein, an acclaimed researcher on the effects of divorce on children, strongly asserts that therapists' records are usually "irrelevant" in child custody and visitation cases (J. Wallerstein, 2002, personal communication). If courts require mental health evaluations, they should appoint independent examiners.

Personal Injury Lawsuits

Testifying regarding the facts of diagnosis and treatment in personal injury cases also interrupts therapy. However, it can be potentially less harmful for two reasons.

First, in personal injury cases it is routine for the courts to review all medical records. When patients choose to claim damages in a personal injury case, courts must examine all past and current records to determine whether the alleged "events" have caused harm to the patient or have exacerbated preexisting conditions. Therefore, attorneys for patients and defendants gather and review all of the patient's psychotherapy and other medical records. Sometime they also request that therapists provide reports or testimony regarding their patients' diagnoses and treatment. Patients' attorneys hope that records will provide evidence of psychological damages. Defense attorneys hope to prove that the patient's problems are unrelated to the alleged charges.

Second, unlike children in child custody and visitation cases, patients are in control of whether or not to file personal injury suits. If they choose to continue with the lawsuit, they must give their therapists permission to release their psychotherapy records. If they do not want anyone to see their records, they can choose not to file the personal injury claim.

However, even when patients are in control of deciding whether to file the lawsuit, and ask their therapists to release their records or to testify, psychotherapists have good reasons to worry about the potential negative impact on therapy when their clients' records are used in the adversarial system. Defense attorneys attempt to use the information in the records to argue against clients' claims, and clients end up feeling on trial themselves. Psychotherapists sometimes also feel manipulated by patients and attorneys whose apparent primary goals are to "use" testimony about therapy in order to provide supporting evidence that the patients have required therapy to treat the "damage." When a patient's first priority is a positive outcome of his or her legal case, once the legal case is over these patients often discontinue therapy.

Capital Mitigation Cases

In capital mitigation cases, the question before the court is whether to confer a sentence of life imprisonment or death. These cases are rare examples of times when patients have little to lose by authorizing the release of their therapy records. Defense attorneys must be able to find evidence of trauma and mental illness or other impairment to develop "mitigating factors" that would augment their arguments against the death penalty. Defense attorneys, therefore, often ask their clients' therapists to testify regarding their knowledge of clients' life history, diagnoses, and treatment. Thus, unlike other circumstances, when patients in capital mitigation cases have requested that their therapists release records or testify, it may be unethical to refuse to do so.

Why Therapists Worry: Parallel Universes of Attorneys and Therapists

Even beyond ethical and clinical conflicts, therapists also feel anxious because the legal system is unknown terrain. The following describes some of the vast differences between attorneys and psychotherapists.

Therapists and attorneys have different goals and different methods of achieving their goals. The goal of the legal system is to arrive at the "truth." The process is an adversarial process in which there is a "winner" and a "loser." Each "side" declares its position to be "right." The aim is to "win" by proving the merits of one's case and by exposing weaknesses in the opposing party's argument.

By contrast, the goal of psychotherapy is to increase the client's well-being by ameliorating unwanted symptoms. The process is a cooperative one that constructively promotes patients' ability to act in their own best interests and improves patients' mental health and interpersonal relationships. Effective psychotherapy sometimes involves confrontation, but it is not adversarial.

Lawyers are often confused by therapists' jargon and the inexactness inherent in psychotherapy. They become frustrated when psychotherapists answer their questions with "it depends..." and then begin a lengthy discussion about the conditions under which x or y would be true. For their part, therapists cannot understand attorneys' insistence they "cut to the bottom line" and "get to the point." One attorney told a therapist, "If you have a point, I'd appreciate it if you got to it soon."

Therapists see people and their problems as complex. In their view, life cannot easily be negotiated into narrow areas of black and white, but must be lived in the interminable shades of gray that require constant scrutiny and redefining. Therapists lament feeling pressured or "manipulated" by attorneys, while attorneys see this as simply "achieving goals." Therapists often feel that lawyers are being "argumentative," while lawyers insist they are merely "discussing issues" and tell therapists "don't take it personally."

Most therapists feel that forensic work is in conflict with therapeutic goals or simply dislike the adversarial process. They do not want the stress of public scrutiny and the risk to their reputations or livelihoods. At best, working in the legal system is a challenging experience. At worst, it is an overwhelming ordeal. Mental health practitioners who serve as witnesses in depositions or in court are subjected to professional slurs ("how much are you being paid for your testimony, doctor?"). Also, their testimony is memorialized on transcripts and used in subsequent testimony to undermine their credibility ("Isn't it true that in the *Smith vs. Jones* case you said....?").

Growing Trend toward "Forensic" Specialization

Still, a growing number of mental health professionals elect to engage in specialized forensic work (Woody, 2009). Such work includes conducting evaluations for custody, adoption, divorce, personal injury, competence, and sanity. More than ever before, psychotherapists are motivated to expand into other areas, including forensics, to supplement what they can earn providing psychotherapy. In addition, large business-oriented health care management companies are limiting therapy to 6 to 20 sessions and requiring therapists to "justify" additional sessions, even for patients with complex conditions. Thus many psychotherapists have become "refugees," looking for alternative career opportunities.

Some practitioners also see other, more altruistic benefits in forensic work. For these professionals, it is rewarding to use their professional knowledge to educate juries about highly complex matters. For example, a mental health professional who has conducted mental health evaluations and provided testimony in capital mitigation cases feels she has made a difference through informing courts about the impact of pervasive developmental delays and the effects of chronic childhood abuse and neglect on children's loss of control over their violent impulses. Another mental health professional has found it rewarding to educate juries about the effects of psychological trauma in personal injury cases.

Psychotherapists' Need for Information

Even when practitioners are not pursuing forensic specialization, it is important that all therapists have a basic understanding of the adversarial process. Because of the increasing litigiousness in the United States, many experienced practitioners have told me they are receiving subpoenas or letters from attorneys for the first time. Practitioners can now assume that sometime in their careers they are likely to become involved in a legal case. Knowledge is their best tool.

DEFINING ONE'S ROLE

Understanding and Communicating Practitioners' Roles to Patients

When practitioners wish to minimize their involvement in court cases, they should make their policies clear to their patients at the outset. If clients are involved in legal proceedings, or believe they will be, practitioners may best serve such patients and themselves by referring them to therapists whose practice includes forensic work.

Even when psychotherapists circumscribe the boundaries of their practices, this does not guarantee that they will not become involved in a legal case that may arise years later. Patients may become embroiled in legal matters years after termination of their therapy. The following is an illustration of a former patient's legal case and need for records arising years after the patient ended therapy.

Nevertheless, even when such circumstances cannot be foreseen, clarifying policies about forensic involvement helps to define practitioners' areas of expertise and professional focus. (See CD and Appendix A, "Client Information," for a sample policy statement regarding forensic involvement.)

A psychologist who meticulously guards her patients' privacy and confidentiality had treated a patient 5 years before the patient opted to leave an emotionally abusive marriage. In desperation, the patient's spouse made erroneous allegations regarding her mental instability. The patient feared these unfounded allegations could plant doubt about her in the minds of the court-appointed child custody evaluators. She and her attorney therefore asked her former therapist to release her therapy records to the patient's attorney and to write a letter about her psychological status during her previous treatment. The patient's former therapist agreed to summarize the minimum necessary to fulfill the intended purpose in a letter to the patient's attorney, which proved helpful to the patient.

Distinctions between Treatment Witnesses and Evaluation Witnesses*

In addition to clarifying policies regarding their involvement in legal cases, it is crucial for psychotherapists to understand (a) what an expert witness is and (b) the distinction between witnesses who are treatment ("fact") witnesses and those who are evaluation ("expert") witnesses. The following defines *expert witness* and discusses the respective roles of treatment and evaluation witnesses.

Expert Witnesses

Expert witnesses are persons who, by virtue of training or experience, can provide an opinion about a specific topic or question that the court requires in order to make a determination of fact.

Mental health practitioners are used as experts in legal matters because of their professional education, training, and experience in social sciences or medicine.

The Role of Treatment ("Fact") Witnesses

Psychotherapists are often called as treatment or "fact" witnesses because they have worked to assess, diagnose, or treat the client. In this capacity, they may be asked to testify about their assessments of, and interventions with, the client and about the client's progress and prognosis. Treatment witnesses' testimony is limited to such facts pertaining to their assessment and treatment of their clients.

> For example, in a disputed custody case, a mother alleged that the father had a history of having made numerous suicide attempts in front of their preschool-age child. She believed this adversely affected the father's capacity to care for the child. The court requested information from the father's therapist to help determine whether contact would harm the child, including how the father was referred to the therapist; his diagnosis; progress in treatment; the therapist's opinion regarding the father's mental condition, including risk for suicide; and his prognosis. The father gave his therapist permission to disclose the information the court requested. The therapist complied with the mother's attorney's request to submit written answers to the attorney's questions ("interrogatories") and also cooperated after receiving a court order to testify in a court hearing about her diagnostic opinions and the course of the father's treatment.

---

* The terms *treatment witnesses* and *evaluation witnesses* are not used in either law or forensic practice. Only two types of mental health witnesses are described in law and forensic practice: *fact* and *expert*. In order to help the reader understand and to minimize confusion over these two distinct roles, I am taking the liberty of using the terms *treatment witness* to describe a therapist or counselor who is assuming the role of *fact* witness and *evaluation witness* to describe a mental health professional who is assuming the role of an independent *expert* witness.

It is important for therapists to clearly define with their clients and their patients' attorneys their limited role in legal proceedings. Practitioners have often told me, for example, that they feel "responsible" for whether their patients "win" or "lose" their legal cases. It is also easy for clients to feel confused about their therapists' role. Patients and therapists alike need to understand that the patients' attorneys, not the therapists, are responsible for advocating for patients in the legal system. The therapist's role is limited to providing professional opinions based on their professional training and experience and to answering questions about information contained in the clients' privileged file.

Even when therapists carefully define their limited role in a legal case, therapists' professional opinions may be inconsistent with the goals of the legal case or with the client's expectations. When this happens, it may cause serious problems in the client–therapist relationship. This is one more reason why it is critical to discuss candidly with clients throughout the course of therapy the therapist's impressions regarding diagnoses, treatment, and progress, as well as the limits of confidentiality. (See Chapters 2 and 3 for further discussion of these issues.)

For example, if a patient with a diagnosis of narcissistic personality disorder files a personal injury claim and requests that his therapist produce a copy of his records to his attorney, he is likely to become upset if he learns only through court proceedings the nature of his diagnosis and how it may be perceived by the jury. The therapist, client, and client's attorney must be open and honest about the information the therapist will reveal and how it will be presented. When cases go to trial, all parties need to be prepared both for direct examination by the client's lawyer and for cross-examination by the opposing attorney.

It is difficult, if not impossible, to continue therapy when clients are aware that their records will be used in court and that opposing attorneys will attempt to use all of the information in their records against them. It is easy to see how these two roles—therapists as clinical advocates and therapists as fact witnesses—may work counter to one another and how therapists' assuming both roles can seriously strain even the strongest therapeutic alliances.

The Role of Evaluation ("Expert") Witnesses

There are many ways that the role of evaluation, or expert, witnesses differs from the role of treatment, or fact, witnesses. Unlike treatment witnesses, evaluation witnesses' clients are either the attorneys or judges who have hired or appointed them. Evaluation witnesses' role is to provide an independent professional opinion. They are expected to be unbiased, no matter who hired them, in contrast to therapists, who are presumed to be biased toward their own patients. Evaluation witnesses have the responsibility to objectively study a full set of facts, in contrast to therapists serving as fact witnesses who need only to rely on information therapists customarily rely upon. Evaluation witnesses typically must systematically review extensive records (e.g., medical and other records, past and current), as well as depositions and affidavits, in order to formulate professional opinions pertaining to the questions in the legal case. Questions in law cases might concern psychological injuries; causation of psychological injuries; standard of care; competence to stand trial; legal insanity or other matters pertaining to diminished capacity to form the intent necessary for a given crime; and factors that influence a person's response to an event (e.g., rape victim syndrome). Even though evaluation witnesses' mental health examinations are similar to those conducted by therapists, evaluation witnesses' focus, unlike therapists' focus, is on information required to answer questions in the legal case.

Unlike therapists, evaluation witnesses also know from the start that they cannot promise confidentiality to their evaluees. Their job is to either consult with attorneys or prepare and send their evaluation reports to the attorneys who have hired them or to the courts that have appointed them. Evaluation witnesses cannot predict whether their findings will be adverse to their evaluees' legal case. Therefore, to be ethical, the evaluation witness needs to inform the evaluee prior to beginning the evaluation of the purpose of the evaluation, including parameters and limits of confidentiality. The evaluation witness should then obtain informed consent to conduct the evaluation and release the findings. Evaluation witnesses should provide an informed consent form for evaluees to read prior to the evaluation and discuss and sign at the first meeting with the evaluation witness. (See CD and Appendix H for sample consent form used by evaluation witnesses in personal injury cases.) The evaluation witness does not need consent from the evaluee to conduct the evaluation if it is a court-ordered evaluation. The evaluation witness still has an ethical obligation to advise the evaluee verbally or in writing about the purpose of the evaluation and that there is no confidentiality when an evaluation is court-ordered.

The court (judge) can appoint evaluation witnesses to answer questions posed by the court (such as competency or sanity), or to confidentially assist litigants in preparing their cases. In some instances, attorneys may privately hire experts. This is often true in civil litigation, when clients have the means to hire their own attorneys. However, a large proportion of criminal cases involve indigent clients who cannot afford to privately retain attorneys or expert witnesses.

Evaluation witnesses range from educational diagnosticians to psychiatrists. Evaluation experts assess the evaluee. All licensed mental health practitioners who are trained in the diagnosis of emotional and mental disorders can conduct mental health evaluations, but different specialties may use different assessment techniques in a case. A psychologist, for example, may conduct cognitive or personality testing. A neuropsychiatrist may administer the Halstread-Retan Neurological Battery. A psychiatrist may look for medical causes of behavior or evaluate either the appropriateness of currently prescribed psychotropic medications or the need for psychotropic medications. A clinical social worker may conduct a lengthy psychosocial evaluation.

Evaluation witnesses provide their results and professional opinions to the attorney or court who appointed them, and they bill the attorney or the court for their time, not their evaluation. The attorney decides whether the information is helpful. If so, the attorney decides how to incorporate it into the case; if not, the attorney discards it. Courts use evaluation witnesses' findings as a basis for their legal rulings. If the attorney decides to use the confidential expert's information, the results must be divulged to the other side prior to going to court under rules of "discovery."

In some instances, there may be two or more evaluation experts evaluating a client. Some cases boil down to a "battle of the experts," where experts from each side offer different opinions.* In a homicide case, for example, a psychiatrist and psychologist had very different views about a client's competence to stand trial. The psychiatrist, who had seen the client for only 7 days at a local hospital, opined that the client was depressed but able to understand the charges against him and assist his counsel. The psychologist, who had visited the client for a longer period and had seen him under a variety of circumstances, including a period when he was hearing voices and tried to commit suicide, said that his low I.Q. (69), severe childhood neglect and abuse, and escalating depression rendered him unable to assist his counsel meaningfully or act in his own best interest. When such a conflict occurs, the judge or jury must decide what to believe. In this case, the judge said the client was competent and the trial proceeded.

Evaluation experts have a very different kind of professional relationship with evaluees than do the treatment experts. It is short lived. The process can be synthetic and intrusive. The two are not working together to achieve the client's goals or to alleviate the client's suffering. Rather, evaluation experts are objectively observing and assessing evaluees. This may involve asking evaluees to arrange colored blocks or discuss intimate details of their childhoods. Evaluees know that the information will be given to their attorneys or to the courts. In either event, evaluees are not providing information at their own pace, in the context of a trusting relationship that has developed over time, and the information will not remain privileged. Moreover, evaluators may reach conclusions that may or may not be adverse to the client's legal case, and which evaluees may perceive to be incorrect, hurtful, or embarrassing.

However, practitioners who assume the role of evaluation experts should not leave their clinical skills at the door of the evaluation office. They have the same ethical duty to protect the dignity of clients as do treating experts. They must carefully inform the evaluees at the outset of their role and the nature of the

---

* Some attorneys, as a trial strategy, hire more than one expert witness to prevent the opposing counsel from hiring a particular expert witness.

evaluation, including the fact that it is not possible to predict whether the evaluation findings will be adverse to the law case. Evaluation witnesses and referring attorneys must decide which of the two will reveal the results of the findings to the evaluees and how and when this will occur. Evaluees should not have to learn for the first time in court that they have trouble understanding complex situations. They should not hear the details of their sexual abuse in a public setting without first having an opportunity to receive information or explanations about the nature and importance of the evaluation experts' testimony.

HANDLING ATTORNEYS' REQUESTS, SUBPOENAS, COURT ORDERS, AND SEARCH WARRANTS

Requests for patients' records or for therapists' professional opinions or testimony come in many forms. The following are frequent types of requests and ways that therapists can handle them.

Calls and Letters from Attorneys

For both treatment and evaluation witnesses, it is imperative to continuously observe the boundaries of confidentiality. Unless psychotherapists have a signed authorization with specific instructions from their patients, they cannot talk with anyone about them, including their clients' attorneys, especially on the telephone. Evaluation witnesses cannot talk with anyone except the attorney or court who has hired them without the evaluees' authorization. Therapists and evaluation witnesses should tell callers, "I can neither confirm nor deny knowledge of this person without signed authorization." They should then speak with their clients (or former clients) about the calls. Evaluation witnesses should speak with the attorneys or courts who have hired them about the calls.

Practitioners who serve as treatment or evaluation witnesses may consult an independent forensic consultant at any stage of a legal case (e.g., clinicians with forensic experience or attorneys), and it is often immensely helpful to do so—as long as they do not use names or reveal privileged information. For example, a therapist might say to a clinician with forensic experience,

> I have been treating a client for 5 years, and she has recently decided to file a lawsuit about her employer's sexual harassment, which she claims has caused her to lose her job. Her attorney just telephoned me and insists that I send my client's complete file to him. I feel I cannot acknowledge that I even know this client to callers without her authorization, and I do not want to send the records. There are embarrassing details in her file so I think her records could be harmful to her lawsuit. What do I do?

> The therapist learns from the consultant that she must first have a discussion with her client about the case. She learns it is important to discuss with her client the reasons for the legal case. She learns her client may be unaware that if she alleges she has been harmed and is suing for psychological damages, that all of her medical and therapy records must be seen by her own and opposing attorneys and by the court, and that it may be helpful for the client to review her records first in order to know what is in them. If, after further discussion, it is clear the client wishes to proceed with the law case, then the therapist must obtain the client's consent in order to return the client's attorney's phone call.

Evaluation or expert witnesses may also benefit from consultations from independent forensic consultants on various questions that may arise (e.g., issues related to interviewing, writing reports, or testifying). However, they do not face the same concerns involving records. As part of hiring evaluation witnesses, attorneys routinely supply them with all relevant medical records to review.

Subpoenas

A subpoena (the word officially means "under pain of") is a legal mandate issued in the name of the court but generally signed by an attorney or clerk of the court. Subpoenas may be requests for copies of records only, and the practitioner is not asked to appear in person. Other subpoenas (called *subpoena duces tecum*) are requests that the practitioner appear at a legal hearing (e.g., deposition or court hearing) and bring whatever records are specified.

Subpoenas are a process that allows attorneys to collect information and develop their cases in a number of different circumstances with the professional expectation being that they will not abuse this right.

A subpoena is a third-party request that requires a response from a clinician. However, subpoenas should not be responded to in an automatic manner, but with thought and perhaps consultation. Patients are not requesting the information, so subpoenas do not necessarily supersede the clinician's ethical responsibility to protect their patients' or clients' confidentiality. A subpoena, for example, is not sufficient to open substance abuse treatment records and should not be enough to open privileged mental health records. Substance abuse treatment records, for example, require a court order signed by a judge to release them. Other treatment records that might require a court order are outlined in individual state statutes.

Therefore, when clinicians receive subpoenas, they need to contact their clients to determine the following: whether they are aware of the subpoena and understand its purpose, whether the psychotherapy records are actually needed (e.g., psychotherapy records may not be required in personal injury civil lawsuits if the plaintiff's psychological condition is not an issue), and if they wish the information to be released. If the patient or client indicates that he or she wants the information released, the practitioner should obtain a signed release from the client before submitting the information to the requesting person or agency. If there are delays in obtaining informed consent from the client, the practitioner should respectfully contact the person issuing the subpoena to explain the need for time.

Even when clients have signed authorizations for releases of their psychotherapy records in their attorneys' offices, often patients do not understand the implications of what they are signing. Therefore, practitioners can help by suggesting that clients seek clarification from their attorneys about how their treatment records will be used in their legal cases. Only with adequate information can clients give informed consent for release of their psychotherapy records, even regarding their own legal cases.

In matters involving a subpoena, if the client or patient indicates that he or she does not want the information released, then the clinician should contact the attorney representing the patient or client and have this attorney fill in the papers required to quash the subpoena. *Quash* means to "squash" and is the legal means by which to avoid honoring a subpoena. There must be grounds to quash a subpoena, such as confidentiality.

Practitioners should carefully read the subpoena in order to determine the date by which they must respond to a subpoena. When timing is a problem— for example, there is not sufficient time to contact clients for authorization to release their confidential information or clinicians have compelling clinical or personal duties that conflict with the timing of the requested appearances— practitioners may exercise the option to respectfully request that the attorneys or court reschedule their appearances. If the subpoena has a legitimate response date and the clinician has been unable to reach the client or former client prior to the response date, then the clinician can protect the privilege for the client until he or she knows whether the client is willing to waive the privilege.

When submitting confidential treatment information in response to a subpoena, clinicians should compile a summary of the treatment, condensing the information so as best to comply with their ethical duty to provide the minimum necessary. This process, and all communications such as telephone calls or letters, should be documented in patients' records. With their summaries, practitioners should enclose copies of authorizations of releases of confidential information signed by their patients or clients.

Therapists should never release their clients' original records or evaluees' original reports to anyone. They should release only copies. Both treatment and evaluation witnesses should always document any releases of copies of records—

for example, what they have released, and to whom. Documentation of release of treatment records should include dates of treatment covered.

Two final words to the wise: First, it is always important for practitioners to use their professional judgment regarding whether release of records could be potentially harmful to their clients. Second, therapists also need to determine whether the subpoena is bona fide and whether it was properly served. In rare instances, clients have created and issued false subpoenas. The following case example illustrates how a therapist used her professional judgment to protect her client's welfare and paid attention to detail in the subpoena.

A father who had allegedly physically abused his son obtained his son's former treatment records from the boy's former therapist by issuing a fake subpoena to the former therapist. The boy's former therapist erroneously believed that the subpoena was real and mailed copies of the boy's records to the name of the person on the subpoena. Later the father woke the boy in the middle of the night and read the boy's former therapist's notes to him. The father appeared subsequently in the boy's current therapist's office, with another bogus subpoena, asking for her clinical notes. The current therapist had, in the meantime, learned from the boy how his father had misused the boy's previous records. She also suspected that the subpoena was fake. She reminded the father that she had offered already to meet with the father to discuss his questions. She stated she could not, however, release the boy's records because she understood he had misused the boy's records before. She stated that therefore, in her professional judgment, it could be harmful to the boy to share the boy's records with the father. The current therapist also stated she believed the subpoena was not bona fide. At this point, the father backed down and said he would "tear up the subpoena" and did so. Clues to the boy's therapist that the father's subpoena was bogus included that (1) it was printed on regular copy paper instead of the heavier bond paper, and (2) when the therapist called the court to check if the case number was active, the court clerk informed her it was not.

Court Orders

A court order is a document that is signed by a judge. Generally practitioners respond to the request of the judge in the manner indicated in the court order. A clinician cannot quash a court order, because it is the judge making the order. To get the court order reversed, the clinician would need to appeal the judge's decision to the next higher court. Generally, the clinician must have good legal grounds to do so because higher courts look with disfavor on "interim" appeals (i.e., appeals in the middle of the case). Also, appealing the order could anger the judge, which may strategically be unwise, depending upon what the case is. When clinicians choose to appeal a judge's decision, they may wish to consult professional peers and legal counsel.

However, judges are available for discussion, or are at least in a position to read a letter. When clinicians are concerned about sending the information in the form requested by attorneys or judges, clinicians may respectfully explain their concerns to judges. This can be done by telephone or in the form of letters. When practitioners respectfully and clearly express legitimate ethical and clinical concerns, practitioners have discovered judges generally try to heed their concerns.

For example, psychotherapists in several states throughout the country have respectfully written to family court judges about their ethical concerns in becoming involved in custody and visitation disputes of their minor child patients, even at the request of both parents. They have informed judges in the form of a letter about their ethical duty to "do no harm" to their clients. Psychotherapists have explained how they were hired by the family members to serve in a neutral role as therapist. Practitioners have clarified how, in their professional opinion, becoming involved in a custody battle would require them to step out of their neutral role and thereby potentially harm the family. Judges have, in most instances, responded affirmatively to psychotherapists' respectful letters explaining ethical dilemmas and potential harm to children. (See Appendix I for a sample letter to a judge.)

Some practitioners have protected their child patients from potential harm by exercising the option to request that the state's attorney file a motion to "show cause" why the parents should have their psychotherapy records. Practitioners have chosen this option, for example, in instances when a parent is accused of suspected child abuse and issues a subpoena for the child's records through his or her attorney as a way to seek information to discredit the child. In this way, judges can become aware of a parent's intent and be in a position to explore the potential harm to the child and whether the parent's request should be allowed.

In attempting to respond appropriately to these various types of requests for information, clinicians must recognize the dual standards that are at issue: confidentiality and the discovery rules governing criminal and civil action in the courts.

Search Warrants

Search warrants are documents based on "probable cause" that a psychotherapist has evidence germane to a legal case, making it necessary for police or other investigative officials to enter the psychotherapy office and search for information. Agencies, such as prosecuting attorneys or police, write the search warrants and judges must review them and sign them in order for them to be valid. Search warrants include a list of specific items needed.

When judges sign search warrants and police or other investigative officials arrive at therapists' offices to look for records, it is extremely disruptive and can be frightening. Therapists should try to remain calm and be a role model to their patients, who are also alarmed by sudden intrusions of officials arriving unexpectedly with search warrants. Therapists have the right to read the search warrant to see what the police are looking for, to monitor what the police remove, and to respectfully ask for an inventory of what they remove, but they must allow the police to proceed. In the case of a substance abuse program, however, a search warrant is insufficient to open records. Police departments may not know this. Therefore, having a copy available of the federal statute governing substance abuse treatment records to respectfully show the police is important (Schoener, 2010).

Altering Records: A Cautionary Note

It is never proper to alter or destroy records with the intent to influence a judicial proceeding (Brooke, 1994; Weintraub, 1999). Practitioners can best protect their clients, themselves, and the professional relationship by adhering to appropriate record keeping procedures. (See Chapter 3 for discussion of contents of good records, and Chapter 8 for discussion of retention and destruction of records.) In short, psychotherapists must document that which is relevant to the treatment and adhere to a policy regarding record retention and record destruction.

Sometimes clients request that the practitioner either keep relevant information out of the record or omit information that they believe will be "harmful" to them. Therapists can be helpful by discussing with their client the purposes of record keeping and why material relevant to treatment cannot be deleted, as well as options to protect the client.

Summary

In response to legal requests, practitioners must keep in mind the following:

1. The need to verify the legitimacy of the request for disclosure of information
2. The importance of ensuring that a client (or a parent or legal guardian where permitted by law) has fully understood the request and its purpose, and has given consent for disclosure
3. The importance of disclosing only the minimum necessary to fulfill the intended purpose
4. The need to inform oneself of applicable state statutes and rules and to seek legal counsel from practitioners' attorneys (not clients' attorneys) as needed

AFTER BECOMING INVOLVED IN A LEGAL CASE: WHAT NEXT?

Here is a road map for interactions practitioners can expect to happen once they have decided to play a role in a legal case. It offers ideas for handling oneself appropriately as a mental health professional.

Communication with Attorneys

Define Professional Expertise

After therapists have decided it could be appropriate for them to serve as fact witnesses, or while determining whether it is appropriate, it is essential to define for attorneys exactly what the clinician does. Never assume that attorneys are familiar with mental health professions. Some attorneys are well informed and use mental health professionals regularly in a variety of capacities. Others have never worked with a mental health professional and have many misconceptions. In fact, it is not unusual to hear attorneys use the terms *psychiatrist* and *psychologist* interchangeably, or to refer to clinical social workers as psychologists. Mental health professionals get lumped into one generic group. Some attorneys are unaware that many types of professionals are licensed in their states to diagnose and treat mental and emotional disorders.*

To avoid this confusion, practitioners must be clear about the boundaries of their knowledge and expertise. They must explain their training and experience and always provide the attorney with an up-to-date résumé.

A few words about résumés. In some cases, witnesses have several different résumés because they have emphasized different skills or training in order to apply for different jobs. Practitioners should be sure to tell attorneys if they have done this so that attorneys can preempt any questions in a deposition or court about practitioners' veracity. Practitioners should never change or delete information from their résumés for the purpose of testifying. In one case a naïve witness significantly altered her résumé at the request of an attorney. On the witness stand opposing counsel supplied her with a copy of her unedited resume and questioned the witness about it for over an hour. By the end of questioning, the witness's credibility had been destroyed.

Discuss Fees for Witnesses' Time

Psychotherapists who must appear at depositions or in court, or who must write reports for their patients' legal cases, have often asked whether they can bill for their time, and if so, what should they charge. Nothing can ruin

---

* An attorney, for example, found it helpful when a clinical social worker informed her about court cases that had recognized clinical social workers as mental health professionals who were qualified by their professional education and experience to diagnose and treat emotional and mental disorders (*Jaffe v. Redmond*, 1996) and to testify regarding their diagnoses (Court of Appeals of Maryland, 1999).

professional relationships or practices so quickly as not being reimbursed for one's time. Kern states that both types of witnesses are entitled to be paid for their time (Kern, 1996), and other authors suggest helpful steps witnesses may take to ensure their opinions are not determined by financial relationships but by the facts of each case (Dvoskin & Guy, 2008). Witnesses should never work without a contract with an attorney or without a court appointment. Practitioners may choose to donate their time (this is called *pro bono* work, which means "for the good," i.e., free), but this decision should also be stated clearly in a contract. Witnesses should explain their fees and billing procedures with attorneys during the first conversation and establish a verbal agreement or contract on how they will be paid for their time in the case. Practitioners should then request a letter from the attorney or court which states the fee arrangement and agreement. The letter should include the specific type of request, the practitioner's fee, for what types of time the fee will be paid, and when the fee will be paid (on receipt of the witness' bill or within 1 month). Treatment and evaluation witnesses should state to attorneys that it is unethical for mental health practitioners to enter into contingency fee agreements, whereby practitioners are paid for their time only if the attorneys' clients win their cases.

Experts normally bill for any time they must spend in a case: reviewing records, meeting with attorneys, traveling to and from depositions, hearings, or trials, and waiting to testify in court. Frequently, therapists charge more for their time in legal cases than they charge for their time providing treatment in their clinical cases. They do this because legal cases involve more pressures, more knowledge, inescapable deadlines, and interruptions to therapists' schedules.

In litigation for unpaid fees is the last place experts want to end up. Usually attorneys are reliable in complying with payment contracts they make with their witnesses, but occasionally it may be necessary to file a claim in small claims court or through other avenues.

Meet with Attorneys Requesting Witnesses' Time

Whether practitioners are serving as potential treatment witnesses or as evaluation witnesses, it is helpful to meet with attorneys who are requesting their services. Setting aside time to talk communicates the importance of the matter and a mutual commitment to understanding the issues involved and clarifying what role practitioners could appropriately have in the case.

In some instances, meetings with potential mental health witnesses can help attorneys realize that the practitioners are not the best persons to use in their cases. In one case, for example, an attorney representing a man in criminal court met with two practitioners, a psychiatrist and a clinical social worker, who were treating his client. He had presumed that the psychiatrist could best help the jury to understand how his client's egregious history of abuse and neglect and how his mother's severe mental illness had arrested his development and contributed to his problems with perception, judgment, and behavior. Though the psychiatrist was highly esteemed and experienced in both clinical and forensic matters, he lacked knowledge of the adverse effect of cumulative psychosocial stressors on development. Moreover, the psychiatrist's manner was offensive and he appeared biased. During the meeting, he also appeared to dislike his patient and was argumentative and sarcastic as he discussed the case. By the second meeting, the attorney came to believe that this psychiatrist was not the treatment witness for the job. Instead, the attorney asked the clinical social worker to testify, and her testimony went very well.

Meetings also give potential treatment or evaluation witnesses an opportunity to get answers to necessary questions such as: What is the case about? What does the attorney expect the witness to do? What knowledge does the witness have that could help or hurt the case? Do the attorneys' expectations jibe with the witness' scope of knowledge, training, and expertise?

Witnesses' Responsibilities to State Potential Adverse Effects

In addition to addressing the limits of their expertise and their commitment to remain within the facts that they have, potential treatment or evaluation witnesses should also speculate with their clients or evaluees and their clients' or evaluees' attorneys about how exposing sensitive information could be counterproductive to the clients or evaluees in the long run. What is the gain if one wins the battle but loses the war? Consider the case of a 22-year-old female patient who sought therapy for trauma resulting from a date rape and who decided while in treatment to sue her rapist.

> The patient had revealed to her therapist that she had been sexually abused as a child, had become promiscuous in her teens, and had, like many victims of sexual abuse, abused alcohol and drugs to numb her emotional pain. Her moods were mercurial, and she was often angry, fighting with friends and neighbors. The therapist had diagnosed her with posttraumatic stress disorder and borderline personality disorder.
>
> After intensive psychotherapy over approximately a 2-year period, the patient had made tangible progress. Most of her flashbacks were gone; she was no longer cutting herself; she was working; she was attending a 12-step program and remaining sober; and she was no longer having unprotected sex. Her rages were under control, and she was sleeping more comfortably with the help of antidepressants that were being prescribed by her nurse practitioner. The focus of her clinical work had

progressed to her wish to resolve her enduring grief. During this phase of her psychotherapy, she was moving back and forth between debilitating sadness and revenge fantasies. In this context, she was feeling upset about her date rape and learned that she could file a personal injury case against the man who had raped her.

In the therapist's professional judgment, the patient was at a sensitive juncture in her therapy and may be displacing her grief and anger onto the date rape incident. The patient was convinced she could get relief from her emotional pain if she were to win this case. Yet the therapist wondered if filing a law suit would serve her. Being preoccupied with her legal case would likely interrupt her therapy and when the legal case was over, the enormous sense of loss and abandonment might still loom over her.

The therapist understood that all of the patient's records would be needed in court in order to determine whether the date rape had caused new problems or exacerbated old problems. With her client's authorization, the therapist reviewed her client's treatment records with the attorney. She showed him where the patient had recounted previous drinking binges and blackouts, periods of uncontrolled rage, convictions for shoplifting, and episodes of chronic lying, all of which predated the rape. Will it serve the case, the therapist asked the attorney, if these events were to come out in court? If the client's attorney did not bring this information in, was it possible that the opposing attorney would? Equally important, will the court process itself serve to retraumatize this patient? Will she feel harmed again if she loses her case?

Attorneys may be interested only in the law. In most states a rape victim's prior history cannot be used against her, but there are many cases in which information finds its way into the record. Therapists may be looking at the case through different lenses than do attorneys. Therapists are concerned only with the client's emotional welfare. Practitioners therefore have a responsibility to share with their clients and their clients' attorneys their professional thoughts and concerns about harm their clients could experience as a result of clients' legal cases.

Whether to file a legal complaint is up to patients. But when practitioners share their perspectives, they can help clients and their attorneys develop a broader view of the case. Such a conversation may have therapeutic implications as well. Helping clients articulate their aims may help them see other alternatives that do not pose as great a personal risk. Jeannette Milgrom, a clinical social worker, found that a "wheel of options" helped her clients visualize other options available to them to address injustices (Milgrom, 1989).

Carefully Understand the Referral Questions

It is very important for both treatment and evaluation experts to know what the attorneys are asking them to comment on. Therapists therefore need to elicit from attorneys what they will be asking and what treatment information they will need to present. Evaluation witnesses must know what questions they are being expected to answer and what they will need to review, develop, and present. Both types of witnesses must make ethical decisions about whether the attorneys' requests are appropriate and whether they can accomplish the tasks when it is clear what attorneys are asking.

Typical types of questions that attorneys ask potential treatment witnesses are as follows:

How was Ms. X referred to you?

What problems did Ms. X describe to you?

What were her goals for therapy?

Did you develop opinions or diagnoses about her problems? If so, what were these?

Did you develop a treatment plan? If so, what was your treatment plan?

Have you or anyone else referred Ms. X for testing or any other kinds of assessment?

If so, what were the reasons for the referrals and what were the results of that testing?

Have you consulted anyone else about Ms. X? What did they say?

What has been Ms. X's progress? What evidence do you have about that?

Do you have an opinion about Ms. X's prognosis? If so, what is it?

When did you see her and for how long?

Attorneys' questions may not become clear to witnesses until they have learned enough about the case. As they talk further with attorneys and their clients, the issues become more focused. Practitioners should always reflect back to attorneys and their clients what they believe attorneys are asking them to do, and tell them whether or not they can offer the opinions they are seeking. Some cases are uncomplicated and have clear questions; it really boils down to reporting the news. Other cases are more complex. For evaluation witnesses, whose roles are broader than treatment witnesses, there can be many turns and twists as the investigation proceeds. As the emphasis of the cases changes, so can the evaluation witness's role.

Sometimes therapists and evaluation witnesses have wisely requested consultation from professional colleagues familiar with legal work because they are confused about what an attorney is asking them to do. They mistakenly think the source of their confusion is a lack of legal knowledge. This usually is not the

case. More often than not, the source of the problem is that the attorney does not yet have a clear vision of the case, and the therapist or evaluation witness has not asked enough questions.

Reports

Whether attorneys request that experts write reports depends on a number of variables, including whether there is likely to be an out-of-court settlement, the jurisdiction in which the case is being litigated, and whether there have been depositions. The purpose of a treatment witness's report is to summarize the client's diagnosis and treatment. The purpose of the evaluation witness's report is to delineate findings and professional opinions that answer the attorneys' or courts' questions. Either type of witnesses' reports likely will become the basis for their testimony if they are called as witnesses in depositions, hearings, or trials. Witnesses should follow their ethical requirements and include the "minimum necessary" to fulfill the purpose for their reports.

Depositions

In some jurisdictions, attorneys can take depositions, which are sworn statements of potential witnesses. Because most cases are settled out of court, the likelihood of treatment or evaluation witnesses testifying in depositions is greater than the likelihood of their testifying in courtrooms. The purpose of a deposition is to get information about what a witness from the other side ("adverse witness") might say in court. In the deposition, the witness is questioned in the presence of attorneys from both sides.

Both treatment and evaluation witnesses can receive subpoenas for depositions from opposing counsel that include the following: the date, time, and place where the witness is to appear. If the subpoena is *ducas tecum*, therapists are required to bring their patient's records. Usually dates of depositions are not set in stone. Most attorneys will work to accommodate practitioners' schedules. Depositions may take place at a courthouse, in one of the attorneys' offices, or even in practitioners' offices. If cases originate in a different city, depositions may take place in hotel rooms, in borrowed offices of local attorneys, or offices of court reporters.

Depositions usually take place around a conference table. The attorneys requesting the deposition and their client sit on one side of the table. The witness who is being deposed, the attorneys who have retained the witness, and the attorneys' client sit on the other side. A court reporter sits at the end of the conference table and records *verbatim* what is said.

Even though depositions may appear less intimidating and formal than a courtroom, looks are deceiving. Depositions are taken seriously. Witnesses' deposition testimony is an important factor in attorneys' decisions whether or not to settle cases out of court. If the case goes to trial, opposing attorneys rely upon witnesses' deposition testimony in developing their defense arguments. They attempt to find inconsistencies and errors in the deposition testimony. Therefore, witnesses should take extreme care in depositions, as in the courtroom, to answer questions honestly and to base their answers solely on their professional experience and training and on the facts that are available to them. They should always remember that they are only witnesses; they are not responsible for winning the case.

As part of the discovery process in depositions, federal rules require that treatment and evaluation witnesses state names of all legal cases in which they have given deposition and courtroom testimony. Therefore, witnesses need to come to depositions prepared with a list of their previous testimony.

Court rules require that experts have an opportunity to read the transcript of their deposition testimony in order to verify its accuracy. Mental health witnesses should request the transcript of their deposition, read it carefully, and enter corrections on the page provided for corrections. Because attorneys rely on witnesses' deposition testimony during trial, evaluation and treatment witnesses need to be certain that deposition transcripts are accurately recorded.

Witnesses may feel uncomfortable the first time they read their own words. They can use this as a teaching tool. Most witnesses notice that some of their responses look different on paper than how they intended. Because mental health witnesses come from the culture of therapy and speak a specific dialect, they use shorthand that another therapist would immediately understand but that is confusing to "aliens." That's all right. Practitioners will get the hang of how their testimony may be used in direct and cross-examination and the ways they can improve their responses.

Court

Practitioners may be called as witnesses either at preliminary hearings or at trials. The purpose of hearings is to resolve issues integral to a case. Rulings by a judge on issues taken up at a hearing help to define the legal contours of a case. For example, if practitioners are evaluation experts, they may be called to testify as to competency or sanity. If practitioners are treatment witnesses, they may testify to their previous or current clients' past or current mental status. The judges may take their testimony into consideration when they rule on issues.

Hearings may be open or closed to the public. Depending on the situation and the judge's policies, they may be held in open court or in a judge's chambers. For example, in custody suits, it is common for judges to hear testimony confidentially in order to protect children's identity and emotional welfare. This means that the press is not privy to the testimony, although the court file will reflect that the hearing occurred. (For example, the O.J. Simpson criminal trial was open to the public, while the proceedings in his custody battle were closed.) If a hearing is *ex parte* (away from the party) it means that only one side will be heard by the judge. This is much more common in federal court than in state or local courts.

Out-of-Court Settlements

Most cases are resolved before trial. Once the issues are clarified and the parties learn what they stand to lose, and the amount of time, money, and emotional energy involved, they may elect to compromise and settle their dispute out of court. Resolutions often occur after depositions and pretrial hearings.

The proliferation of mediation and restorative justice illustrates the increasing emphasis on out-of-court settlements. In fact, in several states (Florida, for example) people seeking to divorce must take a "divorce class" that focuses on communication, conflict resolution, the legal and economic consequences of divorce, the effects of divorce on children, and so on. Similarly, Florida residents are required to participate in mediation before a divorce is set for trial. Most mediation is successful.

Interestingly, most mediation results in agreements that are similar to what the parties' lawyers predicted would be gained at trial. Moreover, mediated agreements result in better compliance because the parties generate the terms of the agreement instead of having the outcomes imposed upon them by a judge.

The only alternative to settlement is trial. If a case is tried, practitioners will receive a subpoena for trial (this is different from a subpoena for deposition or a hearing). If practitioners are working with attorneys where the agreement to come to court is implicit, they may choose to ask that the attorneys serve them with a subpoena so they can verify for their records that they were called to court. Subpoenas are also helpful if practitioners work in a clinic or agency; they are "excused absences," so to speak. Going to court under subpoena obviates the need to use sick leave or vacation time.

PREPARING FOR DEPOSITION OR COURTROOM TESTIMONY

Whether witnesses are testifying in depositions or in the courtroom, careful preparation is essential. Here are some simple tips practitioners can use to reduce anxiety and reinforce their professional skills.

Schedule

Witnesses should clarify when their testimony will be needed. Attorneys attempt to consider practitioners' clinical and personal demands on their time when scheduling witnesses' court appearances. Practitioners should therefore be sure to inform attorneys or courts who have hired or appointed them about times they will not be available.

Organize

Witnesses should systematically organize their files so they know where to find any documents they may be asked to discuss. It can be stressful to be interrogated, thus it is important to know where to find the information they will need in order to answer the questions. It is helpful to use folders with internal flaps so documents can be easily compartmentalized. For example, a face sheet and consent form is attached to the inside left flap, and records from previous treatment are attached to the opposite flap. Initial evaluation, tests and other diagnostic information, progress notes, correspondence, and billing are attached separately to other sections of the file. Practitioners should find the filing system that works best for them and make sure the file is in order as they are preparing the case. It is important to remember that any notes experts take with them to a deposition or to the witness stand must be made available to the opposing lawyer when he or she asks to see them.

Visualize

Practitioners should reread the file with a fresh perspective. What questions would someone ask about the records who was not a therapist or who did not know the client? Are there any gaps or missing documents? Are diagnoses and the bases for the diagnoses properly noted? Have practitioners summarized any conversations with other professionals whom the client has seen, and have they signed and dated release forms to show their clients' or evaluees' authorization for these discussions?

Practitioners should not worry if their files are not perfect; no such thing exists. They should simply be aware that attorneys may ask them questions that are unanswered in the records or they are not prepared to answer. They can make a note of these questions to discuss with the attorneys with whom they are working or with professional colleagues who have more experience in depositions or court testimony (such as provided by members of the Clinical Social Work Association).

Treatment witnesses should be able to readily find in their records how and when they first met the patient, their patient's identifying information, presenting problems and history of problems, evaluation, diagnosis, treatment plan, progress, and other relevant treatment information, and in addition, how and when they became involved in the patient's legal case. Evaluation witnesses, who normally base their professional opinions on far more extensive records than treatment witnesses, must be able to easily find supporting data for opinions in their files.

Memorize

Testifying in court is like having a highly structured conversation. The more witnesses know off the top of their heads, the better and quicker will be the flow of information. However, during their testimony, it is always appropriate for witnesses to look at their records in order to refresh their memories. It is far better to take the time to do that than attempt to give an answer that may be inaccurate from one's fading memory. Witnesses should try to commit to memory basic facts they may be asked, such as

- A definition of their professions and certifications (What is a clinical social worker? A clinical psychologist? What does it mean to be board certified in clinical social work? Board certified in clinical psychology? Board certified in psychiatry? What are the requirements for board certification? Is an examination required for board certification or licensure?)
- The first and last times they saw the client
- The referral source
- The presenting problems (for therapist witnesses)
- The referral questions (for evaluation witnesses)
- The diagnoses of the patient or evaluee
- The number of hours of therapy (for treatment witnesses)
- The number of hours of the evaluation (for evaluation witnesses)
- Any changes in diagnoses (for treatment witnesses)

A greater command of these and other facts (or at least where to readily find them) not only reduces witnesses' anxiety but communicates their credibility and authenticity in depositions or in the courtroom.

Verbalize

It is usually impossible for therapists to grasp all facets of a legal case without help because the legal system is often foreign to them. However, treatment witnesses can effectively learn their way through the process by using the same techniques they teach their clients. In the same way they show clients how to examine problems from different perspectives, psychotherapists benefit from learning the assumptions, biases, and filters that attorneys, judges, and juries bring to a case. Mental health practitioners know from their therapeutic training and experience that talking helps people gain insight, expand their point of view, and identify options.

Practitioners can simply transfer this knowledge to their forensic cases. When they have been called by attorneys and have agreed to testify, they should talk with the attorneys about their questions and concerns. It is also helpful to find a mental health practitioner mentor with experience in the legal system who can shed light on the next step along the path. The only unhelpful question is the one that goes unasked. The more practitioners can ask, the more they learn and the more mastery they attain. It is like a big jigsaw puzzle: First turn over all the pieces and then start fitting them together. The more practitioners can put together, the more confident and knowledgeable they can become. If they remain curious and stick with it, they will eventually clarify the whole picture. Each time treatment witnesses go through the process, or help their clients to do so, they learn a little more. In time, expert witnesses become as fluent as natives, able to navigate these unfamiliar waters.

Have an Anticipatory Overview

When practitioners are ready to "cross the border" into the courtroom, it can be helpful to get a preview of where they are going. They can ask their patient's or evaluee's attorney to help them visualize the courtroom where they will be testifying. Some practitioners have even asked the attorneys who have hired them to show them the courthouse. When practitioners are court-appointed, they may wish to find an attorney who is not involved in the case to help them with this task. They can usually find a vacant courtroom at lunchtime or during recesses.

When they visit courthouses, practitioners learn the layout. Where is the witness room where they will be asked to wait until they are called to testify? Where is the jury room (witnesses must always avoid contact with jurors)? The telephone? The restroom? The cafeteria? Where are the judge's chambers in the event they are asked to testify *in camera* (judge's chambers)?

Practitioners then can go to the courtroom where they will be testifying and examine the room from all vantage points. It helps to notice the location of each counsel table, where the jury will be seated, and to sit in the witness seat. What do you see and how do you feel? Practitioners' conversations with the attorney may have been limited to telephone calls or discussions at a desk. The courtroom

is a very different environment. Attorneys may seem remote as they speak from a podium or behind the counsel table. It can be helpful for practitioners to think about their testimony while either visualizing or actually sitting in the witness chair. Practitioners might develop new questions or areas of concern as they visualize or sit in the courtroom. They should not be shy. They need to discuss these questions with attorneys with whom they are working. Now is the time for witnesses to ask.

Practitioners should notice any equipment in the courtroom they will be using to illustrate their testimony, such as an overhead projector or other audio-visual aid. Although many courts have new, very sophisticated machines that are used to show evidence, these do not always work well. If practitioners will be asked to demonstrate or discuss evidence (e.g., testing results, copies of records, or genograms), practitioners should request that attorneys make sure equipment works and ask to see what the information will look like on the screen that the judge and jury will be viewing. In order to prevent unnecessary interruptions in the trial, attorneys should also make sure there are extension cords and extra lightbulbs for the projector.

Prepare for Necessities

Treatment and evaluation witnesses should start with the basics. Witnesses should know where the building is, where to park, how early to arrive, where to report, and what they need to bring with them for their personal needs. Many witnesses, for example, have had to run in and out of court to put money in a parking meter because they did not know there was a parking lot around the corner or that they could be exempt from parking charges. In one case, an expert actually stopped in the middle of his testimony to tell the judge that he had to go "feed the parking meter," which is unacceptable court etiquette.

Make Realistic Preparations for Being Away from the Office

Prior to depositions, hearings, or court trials, practitioners should always ask the attorneys involved how much time they can expect to be out of their offices. Then double that time. In most instances, attorneys underestimate the time that will be needed to accomplish a task in a legal case. Sometimes lawyers try to put a positive spin on what is involved and so tell practitioners that they will be "in and out in an hour." Other times the judge is called away to an emergency hearing. In still other cases, practitioners may be called to testify out of order in order to accommodate another witness. Sometimes the testimony of a previous witness may take much longer than anticipated. Whatever the reason, practitioners can avoid disruption in their offices by planning for extra time.

Practitioners should never schedule important appointments or activities immediately after they "think" they will be finished with a court-related duty. Things rarely go as planned. In fact, one of the most important tools in legal cases is patience, followed by flexibility.

Practitioners should be sure to inform patients who are scheduled on the day of their testimony that, while they expect to return to the office in time for their appointments, they could be delayed and may need to contact them. Therapists should verify where and how the patients can be reached if necessary.

Dress Appropriately

Practitioners should select clothing that is consistent with the somber atmosphere of the legal system. Dress matters. It can either enhance or erode mental health witnesses' credibility. Comfortable but subdued professional attire is appropriate. Women should wear conservative business suits, simple jewelry, and closed heels. Men should also wear conservative business suits and ties. The following example illustrates the importance of appropriate dress:

> A psychologist who was testifying in a courtroom as a treatment witness in her client's sexual assault case recalled how uncomfortable she had felt in the courtroom because of her clothing. She was wearing a two-piece suit, in a shocking pink color. She became aware during her testimony that

her stomach was in knots. She was not sure why, because she had previous experience testifying in similar cases. She gradually realized she was feeling out of place seated in the witness box next to the judge, who was wearing a long black robe. She felt out of place in the subdued climate of the courtroom. Her discomfort distracted her from her testimony. She wished she had put on her tailored dark blue suit that morning.

Bring Along Amenities for Comfort

Witnesses should consider whether it would be helpful to bring healthy snacks, such as nuts, fruit, or sandwiches in their briefcases. One expert, aware that he feels less alert in the middle of the morning or afternoon, puts a plastic-wrapped, peeled orange and a bottle of water in his briefcase before heading off to a deposition or courtroom. While waiting to testify, or during breaks, having an orange segment and sip of water helps him maintain focus. Witnesses should always bring with them any prescribed medications that they may require. It can also be helpful for witnesses to have reading materials to keep occupied while waiting to testify.

TESTIFYING

Swearing In

Whether practitioners are testifying as treatment or evaluation witnesses in a deposition, hearing, or trial, they will be asked to swear that the testimony they give is the complete truth. From the moment they begin their testimony until they are dismissed from the deposition or witness stand, a court reporter will record their every word and verbal expression ("uh-huh") and most of their nonverbal responses ("witness nods"). If treatment or evaluation witnesses are testifying in depositions, they will most likely be sitting around a conference table with all of the attorneys, their patients or evaluees, and a court reporter. In the event they are called to testify at a hearing or trial they will be directed to the witness stand or judge's chambers.

Becoming Qualified as an Expert

In the courtroom, both treatment and evaluation witnesses will first be qualified as experts. *Qualified* is a legal term that means that the witness's professional experience and training "qualify" them to render certain types of professional opinions that will be helpful to the court in understanding the case.

Attorneys who have hired mental health witnesses begin by asking the witnesses questions about their professional qualifications. Questions are sometimes more extensive for evaluation witnesses than for treatment witnesses. Questions include graduate schools attended, clinical practica (such as internships, field work placements, or residencies), current and past titles and professional work experiences in clinical or academic settings, organizational affiliations, licensure and other legal or professional certifications, hospital affiliations, honors, and publications that are relevant to the legal case. All of these areas should be detailed in practitioners' résumés. The résumés are then entered into the record. The attorney also asks witnesses to tell how they became acquainted with the plaintiff or defendant and what types of professional opinions they have been asked to provide.

Opposing counsel may elect to cross-examine witnesses about their qualifications as experts. Or opposing counsel may "stipulate" (agree) to their expertise. After hearing from both sides the judges will decide whether witnesses can testify as experts. Experts are usually qualified without comment or argument.

Practitioners must be careful to delineate what kind of testimony they are qualified to give. Treatment experts, unlike evaluation witnesses, cannot provide a professional opinion in a personal injury case regarding whether an alleged event has "caused" psychological damages. (In their role as therapists, they have not been in the role of forensic evaluators.) They can state facts limited to their findings from treatment: that the client sought treatment on a particular date for getting help for a psychological problem, onset of which began after the alleged event. They can testify to the history the client has reported, including whether the client stated that the alleged events exacerbated previous problems. They can testify to the fact that treatment has focused on psychological problems related to the alleged event. Unlike evaluation experts, their knowledge is limited generally to what their clients have reported to them and does not include "corroborating evidence" to support the "truth" of what their clients have reported. In contrast, evaluation experts will have formulated professional opinions, such as (in personal injury cases) whether the alleged events have caused new damages or exacerbated former psychological problems. They will base their professional opinions on their review of data that are normally beyond the scope of therapists' purview in treatment.

Direct Examination

The purpose of direct testimony is to reveal what mental health witnesses believe or know through a series of questions and answers. Treatment witnesses will testify about the course of treatment and their diagnoses. Evaluation witnesses will testify about how they were asked to do a forensic mental health examination and their professional opinions regarding the case. Attorneys who have hired either type of witness will ask them questions in a direct examination. Some questions will require only brief answers, while others will be open-ended questions that allow witnesses to provide a longer, narrative answer.

Mental health witnesses should prepare their direct testimony well in advance of the time they will be presenting it. They should work with attorneys who have hired them, or, if the court has appointed them as expert, they should work with a consultant. When mental health witnesses work with attorneys, they should keep in mind that the way attorneys help mental health practitioners prepare for direct examination depends upon a number of factors: attorneys' experience, how much they have worked with mental health and related experts, their personality types, their attitudes about experts, their understanding of and confidence in the subject matter and in the experts' conclusions, and whether there are other experts in the case who will provide supportive data. Some attorneys are very structured and collaborative and will develop very detailed testimony with practitioners. Others do not meet with or work with experts until just before a hearing or trial, and then discuss expert testimony very generally. In one case an attorney asked the expert as they were walking to court, "So what are you going to say in there?" Unless mental health witnesses assert their needs, they may never hear the questions until they are in court.

In direct examination, the attorney who has called the treatment or evaluation witness cannot ask leading questions—that is, questions that suggest an answer. "Did you attend the University of Colorado?" is an example of a leading question. A more proper way in direct examination for the attorney to inquire about his or her expert's educational background is: "Where did you do your undergraduate work?" Or, "Did there come a time when you were asked to evaluate the Plaintiff?" is more appropriate than "When did you conduct an evaluation of the Plaintiff?" Prior to the trial, therefore, an expert needs to clarify all the information the expert and the attorney believe to be relevant to the case so that the expert will be prepared and the attorney will not have to ask leading questions.

Cross-examination by opposing counsel (discussed later in this chapter) is different because leading questions are allowed. These court rules presume that the expert has discussed the case with an attorney who has hired the expert, and that the expert will know what to volunteer. Working with attorneys to use the clinical information in court is like importing a rare product into a foreign country. Mental health professionals are the experts about the content, while the attorneys know the route. Practitioners can make the journey smoother by helping attorneys to formulate questions that will elicit the most relevant, accurate information from them. They should continually educate the attorney about the limits of their purview. They must be clear about what they can and cannot say and why. Once mental health witnesses know and understand the questions the attorneys will ask, they should check to see if their "story line" flows coherently. Both treatment and evaluation witnesses should be sure they know the attorney's overall objective during the questioning so they can remain focused.

Mental health professionals always need to let professional ethics be their compass. It is not their job to ensure that the testimony they provide is "good" for the client's legal case or helps the client "win." Mental health witnesses' job is to report honestly and clearly what they know, how they know it, and what they do not know (Dvoskin & Guy, 2008). As a psychologist who testifies regularly says, "Just look them in the eye and tell them what you know."

Basic Rules of Thumb for Testimony

Listen Carefully

It is crucial that witnesses listen carefully to the questions and never answer if they do not understand. Many times attorneys roll two or three questions into one, or give circuitous lead-ins to questions. Mental health witnesses need to use their professional skills and take a moment to reflect on the words and make sure they understand the question. If they are confused, they should use reflection or paraphrasing to ask questioners to help them understand the question: "I'm not sure what you are asking me. Are you asking me if he went to school?" Or simply say, "I don't understand the question" or "I don't know the answer." Or, "I can't answer the question in the way you have asked it. I would need to answer it in two parts. Would you like me to answer?"

Use Plain and Simple Language

Witnesses should keep their audience in mind and speak plainly so that juries and judges can understand. Mental health professionals know exactly what is meant by "the patient presented with auditory hallucinations, echolalia, and paranoia," but this is unfamiliar to most people. Instead they should say, "The client was hearing voices or noises, was repeating what other people said, and was suspicious and fearful of others." The word "affect" is typically not known. Witnesses should substitute the word "emotion."

Only Answer What Is Asked

Less is better, especially on cross-examination. Mental health witnesses often err on the side of offering more information than they are asked. Unless attorneys who have hired them have asked them ahead of time to elaborate, the best answers are usually "yes," "no," "I don't know," and "I don't remember."

Avoid Humor or Arrogance

In courtrooms or depositions, humor can backfire and arrogance is out of place. Thus, speaking in a pleasant, nondefensive, straightforward, and professional manner is best.

Remain Calm and Relaxed

It can be difficult for witnesses to remain calm and relaxed when they are fully aware that the job of opposing attorneys is to undermine their credibility. One evaluation witness found it helpful to use meditation techniques both while she was waiting to testify and when she was on the witness stand. It helped her to remind herself that she was only there as one of many parties in the legal matter who held an opinion. She reminded herself that she was there not to "win" the case, but only to give her understanding of reality. When there was a brief interruption in her testimony so that the attorneys could argue an objection in front of the judge, she used the respite to breathe deeply, focus on her out breath, and relax her facial and shoulder muscles. When the attorneys resolved their dispute and she resumed her testimony, she felt composed and her mind was clear for the attorney's next question. She felt so relaxed, in fact, that when the attorney began to yell at her, making it impossible to concentrate on the attorney's questions, she calmly said, "It would help me if you would not yell at me." The attorney yelled back, "I am not yelling," but immediately lowered her voice, to which the witness quietly said, "Thank you." By remaining calm and relaxed, the witness was able to retain her composure in the courtroom, just as she remains calm in tense psychotherapy sessions with her therapy clients. Her calm demeanor in the face of the aggressive lawyer gave her more credibility with the jury.

Cross-Examination

The goal of cross-examination is to elicit the truth and expose weaknesses or errors in the witness's testimony. Thus, it is an attack. Witnesses must respond professionally and gracefully, not defensively or aggressively. They need to understand that opposing attorneys are "only doing their job" to undermine their testimony and credibility. It sometimes helps to think of it like a game. Or, to remember that the more personal the attacks, the more successful the witness has been in remaining focused on the truth. There are many techniques that attorneys use in cross-examination in order to accomplish their goals of exposing weaknesses or errors in the witnesses' testimony.

Attempts to Undermine the Witnesses' Credentials

In the following example, the treatment witness remained calm and did not respond to the opposing attorney's slurs. He simply replied to the questions.

Attorney: Mr. Jones, are you just a social worker?
Witness: I am a clinical social worker.
Attorney: You don't have a doctoral degree, do you?
Witness: No, I do not have a doctoral degree.

Attempts to Show Witness Is a "Hired Gun" and "Paid for Testimony"

In the following example, the witness understood the opposing attorney's tactic to portray him as a "hired gun." The witness was able to make an important distinction between being paid for his testimony and being paid for his time.

Attorney: Dr. Smith, have you testified before?
Witness: Yes.
Attorney: How many times would you say you have testified?
Witness: Approximately 20 times.
Attorney: Are you being paid for your testimony today, Dr. Smith?
Witness: No, I am being paid for my time.

Attempts to Show Witnesses Are Biased

Another tactic is to attempt to show witnesses are biased because they have testified solely for plaintiffs' attorneys or solely for defendants' attorneys. In the following example, the opposing attorney was unsuccessful in using this tactic to demonstrate the evaluation witness was biased. The witness had provided consultation to both plaintiffs' and defendants' attorneys. Had the witness not had both types of experiences, he nevertheless should have simply responded honestly to the question in a nondefensive manner.

Attorney: Dr. Anderson, you testified earlier that you have testified in similar cases over the past 20 years. Were the cases plaintiffs' cases or defendants' cases?
Witness: I have testified in both.

Attempts to Demonstrate Inconsistencies

Another tactic is to "impeach" witnesses by demonstrating inconsistencies between their previous testimony and current testimony or between their testimony and other facts. The following example illustrates how an opposing attorney "impeached" (discredited) a treatment witness by demonstrating a lack of foundation for her professional opinions regarding her patient's diagnosis:

Attorney: Dr. Smith, you have testified today that your diagnosis of Ms. X was major depressive disorder with postpartum onset specifier. Is that true, Dr. Smith?
Witness: Yes.
Attorney: Dr. Smith, you testified in your deposition that the patient first began suffering from symptoms of major depressive disorder 4 months after the birth of her baby. Is that correct?
Witness: Yes.
Attorney: Dr. Smith, could you please tell the jury by when depressive symptoms must begin in order to meet the *DSM* [American Psychiatric Association's *Diagnostic and Statistical Manual of Mental Disorders*] criteria for a postpartum onset specifier?
Witness: It is written in the *DSM-IV*, but I do not recall the exact criteria.

Attorney: I have here a text that may refresh your memory, Dr. Smith. Do you recognize this text?

Witness: Yes.

Attorney: Please tell the jury what the title of the text is and explain to the jury what it is.

Witness: The title is *DSM-IV.* This text delineates symptoms and criteria for diagnoses of mental and emotional disorders.

Attorney: Dr. Smith, on page 386 of this text, do you see the section called "Postpartum Onset Specifier"?

Witness: Yes.

Attorney: Dr. Smith, please read for the jury the first sentence in that section.

Witness: (Looks at the page listing criteria for diagnosis for depression with postpartum onset specifier and sees, to his dismay, that onset of symptoms must fall within 4 weeks after the birth of the baby, not within 4 months as he had stated in his earlier testimony.)

Attorney: Thank you for reading that section to the jury. Now, after refreshing your memory, Dr. Smith, is it still your professional opinion that the patient's major depressive disorder had postpartum onset specifier?

Witness: No, my earlier testimony was incorrect.

(This example underscores again how important it is for therapists to continuously reassess the accuracy of their patients' diagnoses during the course of treatment.)

"Tricks" Attorneys Use

In order to undermine witnesses' credibility, opposing attorneys employ a variety of questions that they hope will confuse or disarm treatment and evaluation witnesses during cross-examinations. Witnesses must be aware of these techniques so they can carefully listen to questions and avoid falling into traps.

Some opposing attorneys attempt to disarm witnesses or cause them to say things they might not otherwise say by being overly informal and friendly. One case involved an interaction between a public defender and an experienced therapist who had never testified in court before. The legal case involved the therapist's psychotherapy client, a 9-year-old girl who had been sexually assaulted by an adult neighbor and friend of her family.

The friendly, engaging public defender smiled warmly at the treatment witness as she walked through the courtroom door: "Oh, hello, Ms. Jones—I understand you do a lot of work with children." The witness, taken by surprise by the public defender's warmth and informality, replied "Well, yes, I do, but most of my clients are adults." In an effort to demonstrate the therapist lacked qualifications to testify as an expert witness in a child's law case, the public defender began the questioning with: "I understand, Ms. Jones, that you mostly work with adults." Ms. Jones had realized earlier that her off-the-record comments to the public defender had the potential of creating an erroneous perception of her practice. She therefore had immediately informed her minor patient's attorney of the informal interchange with the public defender so that he could be prepared to present her many years of experience treating children.

Another tactic attorneys use is to make statements about events that never took place and to ask witnesses to comment on them. Insecure witnesses can become flustered and try to act like they have knowledge about the events even though they never occurred. This underscores the importance of being familiar with the case record.

Attorneys may, in addition, phrase questions in a confusing or negative manner, creating implications that are unfounded. For example, one attorney stated to the witness, "I understand in your deposition that you were unable to distinguish between Ms. Brown's childhood abuse and the abuse she experienced during her treatment with Ms. Y."

Attorneys may also appeal to witnesses' vanity. For example, an attorney might question, "Wouldn't someone with your outstanding credentials and in your position be aware that..." when, in fact, the witness would have had no reason in his or her professional capacity to be aware of that particular incident.

Sometimes attorneys incorrectly paraphrase or misquote the witness's previous testimony. Mental health witnesses must therefore be constantly vigilant in clarifying what they actually said.

Another tactic attorneys use is to ask vague questions: "Dr. Smith, have you been testifying for a long time in lawsuits?" Mental health witnesses must be careful to specify details rather than answer a vague question. A specific response might be: "I have served as a mental health witness in legal cases since 1990."

Sometimes attorneys will imply by their questions that the mental health witness has acted unprofessionally: "Dr. Smith, is it true that you have been providing psychoanalysis to this patient even though everyone knows that psychoanalysis has been discredited for years?" Following such questions, attorneys who have retained the witness should object.

Sometimes attorneys ask questions that challenge the adequacy of the witness's professional conduct (such as in malpractice cases or instances of duty to protect), even when the professional has acted appropriately and within the standard of care.

Sometimes attorneys attempt to trap witnesses into saying that they can do things that no mental health professionals are able to do, such as predict dangerous behavior with certainty.

By using double negatives, attorneys can confuse witnesses and the jury. For example, the question "You did not ask whether he was not planning to kill himself, did you?" could lead an unwary witness to answer incorrectly. Witnesses need to keep in mind that two negatives add up to a positive. Witnesses should clarify the meaning of the question for the jury and respond with a clear answer. "I don't understand the question" is the best response. Witnesses should wait until the question is clear before they answer.

When attorneys preface their questions with "If you remember," it frequently causes witness to forget what the question is about. "If you remember, Dr. Smith, your patient came to you with symptoms of depression. What was the first thing you did to help her?"

Also, when attorneys preface questions with "To your knowledge," or "As far as you know," it can confuse the witness about the meaning of the question. It can also be hazardous for witnesses to preface their answers to such questions with "to my knowledge." For example: "Dr. Smith, to your knowledge, did your receptionist contact the patient to remind the patient of her appointment with you on July 8, the day she made her suicide attempt?" If Dr. Smith replies: "not to my knowledge," then it is unclear to the jury what happened. Does Dr. Smith's answer mean that the receptionist did not make a reminder call to the patient? Or does the answer mean that Dr. Smith does not know whether the receptionist did or did not? A better answer would be precise: "I do not know whether the receptionist called the patient or not."

Attorneys also use the tactic of asking witnesses whether they agree with a long series of oversimplified statements that appear to be entirely true. Attorneys attempt to lead witnesses into agreeing with many such statements with the goal of trapping them into making conclusions that are untrue. A cautious witness can avoid being entrapped by asking attorneys to clarify their questions.

Sometimes attorneys intimidate witnesses by remaining silent for several minutes, causing witnesses to erroneously surmise they should be making further responses. Mental health witnesses should show that they are not afraid of silence. They should not volunteer anything that attorneys do not ask.

In depositions, attorneys may ask witnesses if they have stated everything they know on the subject. Witnesses need to be careful to leave the door open to their future testimony in the courtroom. In order to be cautious, they should say: "I have told you all I can recall at this time." Or, "Can you please be specific with your question?"

Redirect Examination

The purpose of redirect examination is to present further information that will confront or minimize the impact of the cross-examination tactics and strengthen the witness's credibility and testimony. The initial attorney returns to question the witness on issues that were developed in cross-examination.

MANAGING CLINICAL ISSUES DURING LEGAL CASES

Negative Effects of Legal Cases on Patients and Therapists

Litigation is a stressful process that requires time, money, and energy, and can cause a myriad of feelings for patients, including sadness, anger, confusion, shame, betrayal, and intense preoccupation. Being involved in a legal case and evaluated by a mental health professional (evaluation witness) places a person under a microscope, magnifying each deficiency, tearing scabs off old wounds, and leaving patients exposed to those with uncharitable intentions. The two experiences together would tax even the strongest among us, and can be life-changing for clients who are emotionally or mentally burdened.

Similarly, it takes a toll on practitioners. For therapists, too, litigation leaves them exposed to those with uncharitable intentions whose role is to undermine their credibility. Thus therapists' management of their own problems related to their clients' legal cases is of utmost importance.

Techniques for Handling Anxiety

Litigation can become the basis of good therapeutic work. It can be used to develop problem-solving skills. Clients may learn just how courageous and capable they are, and therapists may confront demons only to learn they were paper tigers.

Anticipate Testimony as a Therapeutic Tool

When cases involve clients with whom therapy is ongoing, therapists can use their potential testimony as a therapeutic tool to strengthen their relationship with and empower their clients. They can teach problem-solving skills and lend ego strength to clients when they are forthright and realistic.

Because lawsuits are extreme stressors, they typically feel overwhelming. Clients therefore must be able to speak freely with their therapists about their lawsuits, just as they speak about other problems in their lives.

Therapists therefore should talk about their clients' understanding of the lawsuit (all legal cases are lawsuits, whether civil or criminal), where they think they fit in, how going through a legal process is similar to or different from other experiences in their lives, and how they feel about the litigation. Therapists should ask their patients what they would like the outcome to be and, more important, what they will feel or do if the outcome is not what they would like. If the case is not decided as they hope it would be, what will they decide to think about themselves, the legal system, and their therapy? Have clients make distinctions between what they are and are not in control of, and what therapists who serve as witnesses are and are not in control of. These discussions can be powerful forces in reducing anxiety and helplessness and demonstrating essential interpersonal skills. Clients can turn the "thorns of their crowns" into the "jewels of their crowns" by maintaining an internal locus of control and honoring themselves as they face difficult challenges. Sticking with them through a legal process may be one of psychotherapists' most valuable contributions.

Therapists should document only what is relevant to treatment. They should never record details of discussions their clients have reported having with their attorneys. Specific statements in their records about clients' discussions with their attorneys could undermine clients' attorney–client privilege when the records are seen in court. The following is an example of how a therapist met the requirements of record keeping in a progress note, without recording details that could potentially sabotage her client's privileged communication with attorneys.

12/1: Jane Doe indicated her lawsuit continues to be highly stressful. She discussed her feelings about the lawsuit. We explored her goals and feelings about possible outcomes. She stated that going through her legal case has meaning for her regardless of outcome: "Even if I lose the case, I know in the future I will feel better about myself knowing that I stood up and spoke the truth of what happened to me."

Handling Therapists' Own Anxiety

When psychotherapy clients ask practitioners to provide information to their attorneys, practitioners may be ethically obligated to do so, even when the prospect is distasteful or causes them to feel anxiety. For example, as discussed previously, clinical information may be necessary for defense attorneys to develop arguments in order to save lives, such as in capital mitigation cases. The following case example illustrates how a therapist's anxiety about court impaired her objectivity and ruptured her solid treatment alliance with her former client:

A defense attorney, representing a man who was facing the death penalty in the sentencing phase of his homicide trial, contacted the therapist of the client's mother. The mother had formerly been in treatment with the therapist for over 1 year. The information the therapist could provide about the mother was critical. The severe abuse and neglect her son said he had suffered at his mother's hands was a key component in her son's legal arguments against the death penalty in the sentencing phase of his trial. With the help of her son's attorney, the mother respectfully sent her former therapist a signed, notarized release form, and asked her by phone to provide information about her condition to be used in her son's legal defense.

Initially, the therapist complied with her former client's request. She talked freely with the attorney's investigator over the telephone, electing to return calls and to discuss the mother's previous problems. The therapist remembered the mother well, especially the mother's childhood sexual abuse and her diagnosis of dissociative identity disorder, for which the mother had sought treatment from the therapist. She remembered the mother's progress in treatment and her remorse over her maltreatment of her son which had replicated her own severe childhood abuse.

In an unfortunate turn of events, the son's attorney failed to inform the therapist, as he should have, that he would be including the therapist's name on a witness list and that the opposing attorneys therefore would be eventually contacting the therapist. When the opposing attorney saw the therapist's name on a witness list, he sent the FBI [Federal Bureau of Investigation] to interview the therapist, which shocked the therapist. The therapist responded by becoming uncooperative. She refused to return phone calls from the client's attorney, her former client, or the county child welfare social worker, who also needed the therapist's information.

When the judge intervened and ordered the therapist to submit a report to the judge of her treatment of the mother, the therapist became anxious about the prospect of having to provide a report. She replied to the judge with a scathing letter. Even though the therapist had never asked the attorney, the investigator, the mother, or county social worker to stop calling her, she claimed that all of them had "harassed" her.

The therapist's former client felt hurt and stunned. She could not understand why her therapist would characterize her phone call asking for help in her son's trial as "harassment." She did not know why the therapist, who had been helpful to her in weekly sessions for over a year, was refusing to return her phone call. The former patient not only faced her son's potential death sentence but experienced herself as being abandoned by her former therapist.

The therapist's anxiety over the adversarial nature of the legal case and the unexpected visit from FBI investigators is understandable. Quite likely, the therapist's distress could have been prevented had the son's attorney prepared her for what she could expect. Nevertheless, a more professional and helpful approach to her former client's needs would have been to remain calm and to consider her ethical duty to her former client who had requested the therapist release her confidential information to the court and her legal obligation to comply with the court order.

The rule of thumb is to not overreact to court procedures. Do not create unnecessary battles.

The Need to Recover after Court Trials

It is helpful for practitioners to know that their patients and they need to "recover" after legal cases have ended. Just as patients typically experience a psychological "letdown" after their legal cases are over, it is also common for practitioners to feel exhausted, demoralized, and even depressed following a court case. This is understandable. Many patients do not realize, until the legal case is over, how much energy they have expended in surviving the legal case. Mental health witnesses, too, are not used to the adversarial system and may have experienced attorneys' questioning as personal or degrading attacks. Knowing that these are understandable reactions can be helpful. Just as practitioners assist their patients to care for themselves in the aftermath of a legal case, so should practitioners care for themselves. They need to seek support from colleagues and employ whatever methods help them to soothe themselves.

SUMMARY

Even the most experienced psychotherapists become anxious, confused, and do not know how to respond when they receive calls or subpoenas from attorneys requesting that they release their patients' records or testify in their patients' legal cases. For therapists, the adversarial system is like a foreign culture: they do not understand its language and customs. Even worse, they are unclear about their roles and do not understand their options. However, with information and ongoing consultation from colleagues who have experience with the legal system, practitioners can clarify their roles and become more confident in their interactions with the legal system. This chapter answered the most frequent questions practitioners have asked me about their roles in the legal system. It defined the differences between treatment (or "fact") witnesses and evaluation (or "expert") witnesses, described methods for handling subpoenas or other requests for records in legal cases, and presented strategies for handling clinical issues that arise in therapy during legal cases, as well as ways to clarify one's role and provide testimony in depositions and court.

13

Planning for Interruptions or Closures of Psychotherapy Practices

Imagine yourself in this unexpected nightmare: You are a 51-year-old successful psychotherapist in a busy solo private practice and are taking a much needed vacation with your family in Utah. On the second day, you decide to try skiing down a more difficult slope. Suddenly, you hit a tree. You suffer a brain injury and are without speech. Your unexpected disability abruptly interrupts your career as a psychotherapist. You cannot contact your patients yourself. No one else knows their names or your computer password in order to access your patients' records and upcoming appointments. You cannot help your patients deal with this tragic and sudden loss of your services and cannot help them consider alternative solutions to meet their needs for ongoing treatment. You are especially concerned about those who have experienced deaths of parents when they were very young. For them, losing you without preparation or discussion with you will likely feel like another abandonment.

You always took care to prepare your clients for your vacations. You had planned to prepare them in advance of your retirement, too. Now what will happen? How will your patients have access to their records so other professionals can take over their care? Your husband and adult children are helping you get the urgent medical care you need, but it has always been inappropriate for them to know your patients' names and see their confidential records; they cannot help with your professional emergency. What do you do?

We are clinically, ethically, and legally compelled to take reasonable steps to assure continuity of care for patients when our practices are temporarily suspended or permanently closed. Many practitioners make excellent arrangements when the temporary suspension is anticipated, as in the case of a vacation or

maternity/paternity leave, surgery and recovery time, or periods of medical treatments that make continuing to work with clients difficult or impossible. Therapists with experience planning for such events know it is important to consider what each client may need and, when possible, to allow for the client to have a choice of coverage arrangement. These therapists also often recognize the need to plan for the feelings of clients when the original therapist resumes work with them.

However, many practitioners in independent practice do not carry out this critical responsibility in advance of a drastic, unplanned interruption in services, such as in the tragic circumstances above. This problem was highlighted when several members of the San Diego Psychological Association (SDPA), most of whom were in their early fifties, died or became incapacitated without having developed policies and procedures to ensure the ongoing clinical care of their clients or access to their client records by appropriate agents. Colleagues and family members were left in chaos, struggling to pick up where their late or incapacitated colleagues left off (Holloway, 2003; McGee, 2003). Such traumatic experiences have reminded mental health professionals that establishing proactive procedures for management of tasks involved in suspensions or closures of practices is essential. Having procedures in place protects and comforts everyone who is directly and indirectly involved with the clinician's practice.

The purpose of this chapter is to help practitioners anticipate and make plans for their patients and their patients' records prior to interruptions or closing of their practices in order to promote continuity of care. The first section summarizes the clinical, ethical, and legal reasons why it is critical for practitioners to make contingency plans. The second section presents specific procedures practitioners can have ready to prevent problems that can occur for patients and their records during temporary suspensions or closings of practices.

CLINICAL, ETHICAL, AND LEGAL REASONS FOR HAVING PLANS FOR RECORDS

Clinical Reasons

Continuity of care in psychotherapy is essential. Effective therapy depends largely on the stability and dependability of the therapeutic relationship. In most instances, the therapeutic relationship gradually becomes an extremely important source of strength and validation. It increases the client's self-esteem, confidence, and insight, and reveals a novel understanding of the power of shared wisdom.

While continuity of care is critical, it is impossible to prevent interruptions or even permanent cessation of clinical practices. In most instances patients experience interruptions due to planned events, such as vacations or minor medical procedures. Longer hiatuses include maternity or paternity leaves, prolonged but curable illnesses, therapists returning to school for advanced degrees, or changes in organizational staffing patterns.

Psychotherapy practices may be permanently closed for retirement or other routine reasons. Therapists may move to distant locations (Manosevitz & Hays, 2003; Siebold, 1991, 2005; Walfish & Barnett, 2009). They may change vocations, or leave private practices to work in agencies that do not provide direct therapeutic services. Due to other instances, such as managed care's financial restrictions, other changes in health care politics, or societal economic downturns, practitioners may be unable to earn a living wage. Retirement also explains a growing portion of closed practices. In other cases, therapists die from illness or even suicide, suffer fluke accidents, or must suspend their practices due to regulatory board sanctions.

Clients who receive treatment in institutions (such as academic settings, clinics, employee assistance programs that use interns, or larger mental health organizations) generally have fewer concerns about breaks in treatment or changes in therapists. They may know in advance that these settings are geared toward high turnover of practitioners. They may understand other staff can help them and assist them to have access to their records as needed. Still, clients treated in agencies, clinics, or mental health centers have many of the same concerns and experiences as private practice clients, and clinical and administrative issues should be acknowledged and treated with equal care and concern.

Clients and patients are not alone in their difficulties regarding interrupted, suspended, or closed practices. Clinicians often face the same intricate issues from the reverse side, also experiencing transitions as stressful (Koocher, 2003; Siebold 2004). They must evaluate each client as to how to approach and work through the reasons for and effects of interruptions or cessation in treatment. They may face dilemmas regarding what and how much to disclose to their patients (Siebold, 2011). They may have the added burdens of finding appropriate practitioners to whom to refer clients, working with bureaucratic protocols, properly dispensing records, and wading through morasses of financial matters. Shared practices present additional complex problems. Losing a colleague to life changes or death involves not only emotional stress but also enormous financial, clinical, and administrative responsibilities that may take months or years to resolve.

Even family members can be affected. Family members should be protected from seeing records and having to deal with clinical emergencies whenever possible; they should not have to take responsibility for clinical management of records.

However, spouses of deceased practitioners have called me with the following kinds of questions: "My husband was in solo private practice and died of cancer a few months ago. He left all of his psychotherapy patients' records in his office. It is not my psychotherapy practice, but he did not designate anyone to manage his records. Am I responsible for holding onto his records? If so, for how long? What do I do?" Another distraught spouse called me to say, "My wife died last year and one of her former psychotherapy patients called me, asking for a copy of her record. What should I do?" Adult children of mental health professionals have reported finding patients' records stored in boxes in their deceased parents' attics (G. Schoener, personal communication, 2011). Especially when former patients are well-known, it can be tempting to read their records (Turner, 2010).

Ethical Guidelines

Clinicians are well aware of the painful effects of a sense of abandonment. Therefore, all professional associations agree that practitioners must take steps to prevent abandonment and assure continuity of care in the event a practitioner can no longer provide services. Some professional organizations have updated their codes to include the need for a plan (Kaplan, 2006). The following excerpts from four ethics codes illustrate this professional commitment:

American Counseling Association (ACA)—Code of Ethics and Standards of Practice, Section A: The Counseling Relationship, #11. Termination and Referral. a. "Abandonment Prohibited. Counselors do not abandon or neglect clients in counseling. Counselors assist in making appropriate arrangements for the continuation of treatment, when necessary, during interruptions such as vacations, illness, and following termination" (ACA, 2005).

American Medical Association (AMA)—Code of Medical Ethics: Current Opinions with Annotations, 2010–2011, Section 7.03. "A patient's records may be necessary to the patient in the future not only for medical care but also for employment, insurance, litigation, or other reasons. When a physician retires or dies, patients should be notified and urged to find a new physician and should be informed that upon authorization, records will be sent to the new physician. Records which may be of value to a patient and which are not forwarded to a new physician should be retained, either by the treating physician, another physician, or such other person lawfully permitted to act as a custodian of the records" (AMA, 2010b).

American Psychological Association (APA)—Ethical Principles of Psychologists and Code of Conduct: 3.12 Interruption of Psychological Services. "Unless otherwise covered by contract, psychologists make reasonable efforts to plan for facilitating services in the event that psychological services are interrupted by factors such as the psychologist's illness, death, unavailability, relocation or retirement or by the client's/patient's relocation or financial limitations." 6.02. Maintenance, Dissemination, and Disposal of Confidential Records of Professional and Scientific Work. "c) Psychologists make plans in advance to facilitate the appropriate transfer and to protect the confidentiality of records and data in the event of psychologists' withdrawal from positions or practice" (APA, 2010). See also APA Record Keeping Guidelines (2007).

National Association of Social Workers (NASW) Code of Ethics—Section I. Social Workers' Ethical Responsibilities to Clients. 1.15 Interruption of Services. "Social workers should make reasonable efforts to ensure continuity of services in the event that services are interrupted by factors such as unavailability, relocation, illness, disability, or death." 1.16. Termination of Services. "b) Social workers should take reasonable efforts to avoid abandoning clients who are still in need of services. Social workers should withdraw services precipitously only under unusual circumstances, giving careful consideration to all factors in the situation and taking care to minimize possible adverse effects. Social workers should assist in making appropriate arrangements for continuation of services when necessary...(e) Social workers who anticipate the termination or interruption of services to clients should notify clients promptly and seek the transfer, referral, or continuation of services in relation to the clients' needs and preferences. (f) Social workers who are leaving an employment setting should inform clients of appropriate options for the continuation of services and of the benefits and risks of the options" (NASW, 2008).

Legal or Administrative Guidelines

When practices close for any reason, patients or their legally authorized representatives continue to have rights under state and federal privacy rules and laws for access to their records within the time frame that the records must be maintained. Ownership of the records remains with the retired, deceased, or relocated therapists, even when copies of patients' records have been sent to subsequent therapists at the time practices close. Some regulatory boards, such as in Minnesota, have recognized the need for contingency plans and require practitioners to have plans for continuity of care, including access to records.

PROCEDURES THAT PROMOTE CONTINUITY OF CARE

The following are descriptions of some of the more common ways to prevent problems in suspending or closing practices.

Collaborating with Other Professionals

Practitioners need to develop relationships with other practitioners and construct detailed plans for a range of possibilities, including emergencies during vacations or other leaves of absences, such as maternity or paternity leave, illness or disability, retirement, and death. Practitioners must be sure another trusted practitioner can gain access to important information and documents, such as client files, and the names, phone numbers, and addresses of clients and their designated contact persons. Prior to planned interruptions or retirement, therapists can write a brief synopsis of each client's problems, diagnoses, contact information for client's psycho-pharmacologist, and whether and to what extent the client may be at risk to themselves or others. For unexpected interruptions of services, it is much easier for trusted colleagues to assess clients' current status, potential needs for further care, and what referrals and plans may be indicated when therapists have maintained legible, contemporaneous records. Practitioners may wish to consider consulting an attorney to document the parameters of the colleague's responsibilities.

It is also important to note that in instances involving anticipated temporary suspensions of practice, most notably for maternity leave, it may be difficult for therapists to know in advance how long they will need to be gone. They may need to have the option to extend their leave, as the following example illustrates.

A therapist, pregnant with her second child, arranged for two colleagues in her practice to take responsibility for her DBT [dialectical behavior therapy] group and individual clients during her maternity leave. She carefully prepared her clients by speaking with them about their feelings and needs and arranged for them to meet her colleagues in advance so that the specific transfer, when it happened (which can be unexpected in the case of a pregnancy if the pregnant mom feels comfortable working up to the birth), could go smoothly.

Yet 3 months after the birth of her baby, she found herself feeling very anxious about returning to her practice as planned. She was nursing and felt distressed about the prospect of being away from her baby for a full day. She was torn because she had promised her clients she would return. She was also torn because she imagined her colleagues may be feeling overburdened from assuming responsibility for her work. She therefore felt reluctant to request they extend this responsibility for her. Yet she did not feel ready to leave her baby even for one full day a week.

She therefore proposed to her colleagues that she hire a nanny to hold the baby in an empty room adjacent to her office so she could nurse in between appointments. Her colleagues, including a former supervisor, helped her to clarify her emotional needs to postpone reentry to her practice. They assured her they could continue to assume responsibility for her clients for a longer period. They helped her to see that her patients could understand and accept her being true to herself and her baby after recognizing in the present moment that she and baby needed more sustained time for attachment.

It is easy to see that even routine, temporary closings or interruptions such as in the case above can be a challenging balancing act among the clinician's needs, the client's needs, and the needs of the covering colleagues. This becomes especially true when conditions change, whether because a new mother's needs change or because recovery from an illness takes longer than anticipated. Given that unforeseen changes frequently occur, therapists may consider advising clients of possible variations in their plans. When this is seen as part of the ongoing process of informed consent, therapists can help clients prepare for and work through transitions and changes.

Communicating with Clients about Changes in Practice

Because the therapeutic relationship is the central component of healing from mental health problems, practitioners are mindful of the impact of changes and loss on their patients. Practitioners need to openly discuss the issue of continuity of care with new clients so their clients know and understand their policies and procedures for interruptions in practice. Ideally, clinicians can do this verbally and in writing, as part of both initial and ongoing informed consent processes, using brochures or information sheets that include other information about therapists' practices, such as fees for missed appointments, and so forth, which therapists can place in their records. The more clients are involved in and have some amount of control over their treatment, the less likely they may feel anxiety or abandonment when changes arise during the course of treatment.

During treatment, therapists can share with clients, and document in their records, any specific arrangements they have discussed with their clients in anticipation of either expected or unexpected interruptions of practice. Information about proactive plans for serious and irrevocable events, such as unexpected incapacitation or death of the therapist, can be comforting to patients; especially to more fragile and dependent patients. Knowing the therapist is caring for them in this way can be reassuring. The patient–therapist relationship benefits from direct and realistic communication (Horton, 1995).

Therapists anticipating planned retirements can be careful not to accept new patients for whom an ending may be particularly difficult. In this way, too, they can end with fewer patients to leave behind or need to refer to other professionals.

Information about therapists' contingency plans often arises naturally in the context of preparing for practitioners' vacations or other temporary leaves. The following case example illustrates the emergence of contingency information in the context of anticipating a therapist's vacation.

A 35-year-old female client, whose mother had died of cancer when the client was only 4 years old, had been in outpatient psychotherapy for 1 year to treat her delayed onset posttraumatic stress disorder and major depressive disorder. When she was 30, she had been physically assaulted in her workplace when she was on night duty. In her therapy, the client had benefitted from opportunities to discuss her feelings about the traumatic events related to the assault, her fears of being alone, her intense dependence upon her partner, and her fears of losing her therapist. Over time, her anxiety decreased after creating a narrative of her traumatic events with her therapist and recognizing how her intense fears were related to the childhood trauma of experiencing her mother's sudden death. She began learning how to anchor herself in the present when her fears surfaced so she could clarify her feelings and options. She slowly began practicing being on her own.

As the therapist prepared her client for the therapist's 2-week vacation, the therapist was mindful of the client's childhood history of early maternal loss, her current clinical status, and the importance of using the therapeutic relationship to support her client's emerging autonomy.

Therapist: Before we begin today, I'd like to look ahead with you to the next 3 weeks. As we spoke about last week, I'll be out of the office for 2 weeks starting next week, so our next appointment will be 3 weeks from today.

Client: Yes, I remember.

Therapist: Mary Jones will again be taking emergency calls for me while I am away. Do you still have her number?

Client: I think I still do, but would you write it down for me again on your card?

Therapist: Sure I will. Her number will also be on my voice mail message while I am away. I don't expect you will be having any emergencies, but it's good to have her number anyway.

Client: I don't expect to either...I am feeling much better now than I was before.

Therapist: [Writes the number down and hands card to client.] Glad you have been feeling better, more secure now. Just in case, I appreciate Mary being available to my clients. She and I have very similar approaches to our work, and I trust her completely. As I mentioned a few weeks ago, I am in good health and don't plan to retire for another 10 years, but she is the colleague who has agreed to take responsibility for talking with my clients in the unlikely event I would die or become disabled.

Client: Yes, I remember we talked about that...I had been worried about that. It's good to know there is a plan.

Therapist: [After exploring with the client the worries and questions she had been having.] Now that we've had a chance to speak about plans for my being away for a couple of weeks and how you are feeling about that, shall we turn now to what you want to be sure to cover in our appointment today?

Notifying Current Clients When Practices Close Permanently

When practitioners are in good health, are ready to retire, and close their practices permanently, they can help patients by choosing a specific time to announce their retirement and by allowing sufficient time to prepare their patients for their retirement. Decisions regarding how long to allow for preparation of clients may vary depending on the nature of the practice. For patients in long-term treatment, 6 months can be helpful. For patients receiving short-term therapy, 3 months preparation may be sufficient (Manosevitz & Hays, 2003).

Practitioners may experience heightened emotions as they anticipate their practices closing. Some retiring mental health practitioners have found themselves caught unaware when they began feeling pressure to disclose more personal information with clients than usual or than may be appropriate. They realized these new pressures arose in the context of their own feelings of loss, anxiety, or isolation during the transition. After recognizing the extent of their own stress, they found that arranging for regular consultation or supervision was helpful in supporting their ability to freely listen to their patients' range of feelings and experiences about the transition without intruding their own sense of isolation or guilt and other strong reactions onto their patients. In addition to listening sensitively to the unique impact of the retirement on each patient, another key task is collaborating with patients to determine who may be ready for termination and who may require referrals for ongoing care.

Other essential tasks include conveying clinical information to patients' future therapists, planning for storage of records, arranging for an address and phone (not one's home) for any future contact patients may need to have, making decisions whether to be available to patients by e-mail, deciding whether to keep one's professional license after retirement, and clarifying the limits of what one can do without the license. Practitioners may find it useful to consult with their respective professional organizations regarding recommended procedures, as well as with an attorney.

When therapists must close their practices due to suffering potentially life-threatening illnesses, they often lack their usual emotional or physical energy. Still, in order to meet their patients' needs, whenever possible, it is helpful to give patients information about their conditions, an opportunity to say goodbye, and document they have done so. Daphne Merken, a *New York Times* writer, movingly described painful instances in her own years of therapy when two of her therapists closed their practices due to terminal illnesses without any explanation (Merken, 2010). Her story reveals that in her experience, her therapists and their colleagues were unable to help her in the way that is consistent with our current knowledge of attachment and human beings' need to mourn a loss. "In grief work, we see that grief is eased by preparation and information. Keeping secrets from a patient or refusing to provide information potentially creates a complicated and prolonged grief process" (Siebold, 2010, p. 17).

Keith Horton, MD, a recently retired psychoanalyst in Minnesota, was diagnosed with lung cancer in 1988. He too believed it could be most helpful to his patients if he could be candid with them about his potentially terminal illness. He therefore crafted the following letter for all of his patients:

Dear _____,

On July 11, x-rays taken of my chest during a routine physical exam revealed a mass. On July 18, the tumor mass was confirmed by computed tomography (CT) scan and on July 20, a tissue diagnosis of small-cell tumor of the lung was made. Treatment will begin on July 25.

My surgeon and oncologist say that treatment by chemotherapy and radiation therapy will result in a "very good" prognosis. Scheduling and getting this treatment takes first priority in my life, so our work will be less predictable over the next 6 months or so.

I will be telling each patient as I see him or her about this painful fact. Please let me be the one to inform my other patients. I will also be discussing this data with colleagues as the treatment gets under way.

I will, of course, not work when I feel mentally or physically ill, or if I need psychoactive medication. I will let you know directly of any significant changes in my condition. I will have my own psychiatric consultant to help me objectify my feelings, thoughts, and perceptions during the entire process.

I am sorry for placing this extra burden on our work, but wishing does not make it go away.

Keith A. Horton, MD

Amy Engel (2011) noted how a terminally ill colleague helped her patients by answering only what clients wished to know, made referrals, and assisted them by transferring them to other therapists. Horton noted that after sending his letter (see above), all of his patients indicated they had "known" in some way that something was happening within him (Horton, 1995). In Engel's subsequent work with one of her terminally ill colleague's patients who had chosen not to have any information about the former therapist's health status, Engel found that telling the patient when the former therapist died helped the patient make significant progress. Within the compassionate emotional container Engel provided, the patient became free to grieve her former therapist and ultimately deal with the loss of her mother.

In the event of a practitioner's sudden, unexpected incapacitation or death, notification tasks are easier in institutions such as agencies, mental health clinics, and centers. This is because records belong to the institution, not just to the solo practitioner, and support staff or professional staff are always on site and can locate the practitioner's calendar in order to cancel appointments and make arrangements for continuity of care. In private practices, designated professionals need to be contacted in order to assume notification and assessment tasks with patients.

Notifying Former Clients

Psychotherapists and counselors may wish to make clinical judgments regarding which former patients to notify of their practices' closing. The American Medical Association Code of Ethics requires physicians to notify former patients of their practices closing so they may know how to have access to their records (AMA, 2010b). Patients whose records are no longer being retained but who experienced significant help from psychotherapists may have found security in knowing they could return to their former practitioners at a later date, should they need further help. When they intend to retire or close their practices, practitioners may, therefore, wish to consider sending these patients announcements.

A woman who had terminated therapy with her therapist a few years earlier, felt deeply grateful for the help her former therapist had given her. She was managing fine in her life, but it reassured her to know she could always return to the therapist as needed. Her therapist was relatively young so there was no expectation she would become unavailable. She felt traumatized to read in the newspaper that her former therapist had died of breast cancer. She went to the former therapist's graveyard to speak with her and became so distressed that she needed new therapy in order to grieve the loss. When therapists are able to notify former patients about closure of their practices, it can help to prevent this kind of shock of learning unwelcome news indirectly. Notification can give patients the information to make a choice regarding whether to contact the therapist or request a copy of their records.

When psychologist Helen Gilbert (personal communication, March 24, 2011) was in the process of retiring, she sent the following compassionate letter to her former patients, 2 months before she closed her practice. She reported the letter was welcomed by all:

Dear Former Patients,

I'm writing to let you know that I have decided to close my therapy practice and retire. I gave notice to current patients at the beginning of September and will end on March 1, 2010. There is no crisis, such as poor health, pushing my decision, only the fact that I am getting older and tire more easily and want to spend some time living in a more relaxed way without the schedules and responsibilities of practice.

This decision was not easy to make, because I enjoy my work so much and have appreciated the privilege of working with you, my patients, in the past. It's been a pleasure to feel invested in relating to you and helping you achieve well-being. It's been satisfying work, and I thank you for the trust you put in me for us to work together.

I know that you may have thought you could return some day for more therapy with me, and we may have talked about that possibility, so I feel a need to inform you about my plans. If you would like a referral or would like to talk briefly, I'll be in my office until March, but I won't be able to fit in any appointments. After March 1, messages for me can be sent by mail or phone to the office of my colleague, (name, address, and phone).

As I leave, I will take with me a heart full of memories of people I've cared about, whose emotions I have felt, whose thoughts I have known, and

whose problems I have participated in solving. I hope you are doing well and I thank you for the time you spent with me.
Warmly,

Helen D. Gilbert, PhD, LP

Securely Storing Records

When practices are suspended or closed, it is mandatory under state and federal laws that client records continue to be securely stored and protected. Access to confidential client-identifiable information should continue to be limited to expressly authorized individuals. In most instances, records are obtained and reviewed for one of three reasons:

- To review and respond to requests from clients or their legal representatives for clients' records
- To provide information in the event of a postmortem audit of the therapists' billings to third-party payers (usually the maximum is 3 years, but under some contracts it may be 5 years)
- To provide information to protect the therapist's estate in the event of a lawsuit

In the United States, for example, practitioners cannot be tried after their death; however, their estates can be sued. In Minnesota, two patients sued the estate of their former psychiatrist 2 years after he died from suicide. The estate required the psychiatrist's records in order to defend the estate's assets (Schoener, 2010).

Defining the Role of Designated Agents

We need to have a designated agent (e.g., a person who is legally authorized to assume the tasks of our practices in the event of temporary or permanent cessation). Some practitioners find it helpful to make arrangements with trusted colleagues to "exchange" designated agent services. Designated agents need to have the clinical, ethical, and legal knowledge and experience to manage all aspects of the clinician's practice or know how to gain competent assistance if necessary. It can be a daunting job, especially when a solo practitioner dies or becomes incapacitated suddenly without winding down the volume of patients, and the designated colleague is suddenly responsible for another full practice of patients. Practitioners who assume the care of a colleague's practice face many responsibilities and decisions; preparing for the possibility can make a tremendous difference in both continuity of care for our clients, and for the colleagues who step in to help (Shaw, 2007).

In addition to communicating with clients about their needs and making appropriate plans, one of the most important tasks of a designated agent is managing requests for client records. The designated agent must be able to accurately assess the legitimacy of requests for client records by clients, client guardians, or legal agents of clients, and to know how to legally and ethically respond to requests for copies of records. (See CD for a checklist and a sample "letter or advance directive for designated agent" form.)

Besides protecting the confidentiality of and making decisions about requests for client records, designated agents must be able to adequately attend to other tasks, including

- Financial and clerical matters, such as sorting and responding to important correspondence
- Monitoring client billing and ensuring up-to-date payment
- Communicating with professional organizations and regulatory boards
- Negotiating contracts (or securing an executor or attorney to do so)
- Canceling subscriptions
- Making sure the executor has bills so they can be paid (in the event of the practitioner's death)

Designated agents can perform their roles much more efficiently when we have indicated where they may find essential information and a detailed list of names and phone numbers of people who have agreed to handle certain matters, as well as the specific tasks to be accomplished by each person. Helpful information may include locations of the following:

- Password and directions for how to change voice mail greeting
- List of current and former client names, addresses, phone numbers
- Appointment book with client appointments
- Password and directions for computer access to client records and manual for learning to use the computer software
- Keys to files, mailbox, locked rooms, and so on
- Billing and banking information for deposits, and so forth, if there is no billing staff person to send bills or executor to make deposits
- Managed care and other contracts
- Names, addresses, phone numbers of landlords or tenants
- Professional liability insurance information: names, address, phone number of agent
- Names of professional regulatory boards by whom practitioner was licensed (and contact person if applicable)
- Office insurance contract and name, address, and phone number of agent

- Addresses, phone numbers of important professional contacts and colleagues
- List of professional memberships
- List of dues and subscriptions and records of previous payments
- Description of how designated agents (and others, if applicable) are to be paid for their time and expenses for managing the practice after it closes
- Who, besides the designated agent, is authorized to open and handle mail
- Name, address, phone number of executor of estate (if other than designated agent)
- Name, address, phone number of attorney (if any)

For guidance on preparing advance directives, materials for designated agents, and professional wills, therapists can contact their respective professional organizations. Some professional associations, for example the North Carolina Society for Clinical Social Work (2001) and the San Diego Psychological Association (2006), have developed guidelines for their members on preparing advance directives.

Where to Store "Professional Wills" or Advance Directives

Practitioners often erroneously assume that provisions made ahead of time for patients should be included in their personal wills. However, personal wills are not the appropriate place for such information for several reasons. Wills are usually in the possession of the practitioner's attorney, and many attorneys recommend against disseminating copies of wills to prevent legal problems after death. Wills are rarely obtained immediately after death; they must be approved in probate court before they can be completely operational. Finally, wills are not easily altered; therefore, changing designated agents is extremely costly and time consuming.

We need to leave our advance directives or "professional wills" with (a) persons, such as family members, who would be the first to know of a sudden incapacitation or death and who therefore could notify the designated colleagues; (b) colleagues who routinely provide coverage for us during anticipated temporary leaves; or (c) colleagues who have agreed to assume responsibility for our practices after they close permanently. To facilitate information getting to former clients searching for practitioners who have retired, died, or become incapacitated, professional associations can maintain a voluntary category of "designated colleagues" in their annual membership renewal information. Clients needing to know how to obtain their records after their therapist died, retired, or became incapacitated can obtain necessary information by contacting the professional associations (McGee, 2003).

SUMMARY

Proactive procedures for management of tasks involving suspensions or closures of practices protect everyone who is associated with the clinician's practice. This chapter discussed the clinical, ethical, and legal reasons why practitioners need to prepare in advance for preparation of clients and for disposition of records in the event of temporary suspension or closing of their practices. It recommended specific procedures psychotherapists in any setting could develop in order to adequately protect the confidentiality of client records or provide access to client records by appropriate agents after their retirement, incapacitation, or death.

Epilogue

When I agreed to write this second edition, I had no idea that the experience would be richer, more rewarding, more difficult, and more complex than I anticipated.

One of the great rewards has been connecting with respected colleagues who use the book both in classes they teach and in their own practices. Hearing from them what they found most valuable in the first edition, and what they hoped the second edition would add, energized me. I also found that helpful and unexpected opportunities popped up when I least expected them: being able to meet last winter with faculty who use my book, sitting in on meetings of community mental health service directors who were discussing electronic records, and meeting a national trainer for one of the top electronic record software companies. I also loved being able to consult with and incorporate the wisdom of many colleagues locally and nationally whom I have known over the years and new colleagues I had never met before.

It quickly became clear to me that the emerging area of electronic records and electronic media and communications in general needed to become a central part of the new edition. I found myself learning and thinking about electronic records, e-mail, Facebook, texting, and related topics far more than I ever thought I, as a Baby Boomer–generation therapist, ever would.

As I finished the first edition, HIPAA regulations were just going into effect, and I felt hopeful because of the special protection accorded psychotherapy notes. However, my research for this edition showed me that as therapists are pinched by the demands of time and money, psychotherapy notes are the types of record keeping they are least likely to do. I also felt disturbed by the greatly increased opportunities for breaches of privacy, the threats this creates to the therapeutic relationship, and the extent to which confidentiality and privacy have, in fact, been compromised.

The other issue I struggled with was the electronic records themselves. Efforts to instantly access information have resulted in templates being used, and I noticed that templates can potentially create a great barrier to our ability to tell the complete and unique human stories of our clients. When we cannot construct meaningful narratives within constricted templates and when we have difficulty absorbing client information on a small computer screen, we lose a critical ingredient in forming therapeutic relationships and in communicating our patients' life stories to other professionals who collaborate in their care.

These discoveries and feelings made it very difficult to wade into the material and write those sections, particularly what became Chapter 7 and parts of Chapters 3 and 4. I found in those sections that I was mainly interested in raising the issues and asking questions, rather than providing answers. This approach felt more appropriate given that these areas are still evolving. As this second edition goes to the publisher, I am aware of the National Institutes of Health's preliminary considerations on what the contents of a behavioral health care electronic record need to include. I'm also aware professional organizations are continuing to develop guidelines on electronic communications.

Once I did begin writing on these difficult topics and solicited feedback from colleagues on drafts, it was tremendously helpful to hear their excitement over the new material. Many told me it brought to their minds clinical issues in their own practices. Working on Chapter 7 and reflecting on its contents also enriched my own perspective and practice and awakened my curiosity about ways electronic media can be useful; I began learning about the use of electronic conferencing in supervision training.

My struggle with and determination to persevere through writing about the electronic communications, media, records, and the existential complexity of balancing clinical, ethical, and legal issues in our daily practice, affected me in other ways, too. Throughout the new edition, but particularly in these parts, I felt the presence of my mother, who died a few years ago at the age of 90. My mother, herself a psychiatric social worker, was very excited about the first book. She had gone back to graduate school while raising four children, and her great love for continuing education was an inspiration to me. She was a fierce advocate for civil rights and for diversity of all types. She worked in Topeka, Kansas, to racially integrate neighborhoods before *Brown v. Topeka Board of Education*, and advocated for ordination of gay- and lesbian-identified clergy. She encouraged me to tackle the difficult things in my own life and was my greatest cheerleader. I felt her encouragement and support as I pressed on with my research and writing.

I also felt encouraged by seeing that the concepts central to psychotherapy (confidentiality, the therapeutic relationship) are indeed timeless concepts. Today we may deal with HIPAA and HITECH, e-mail and Myspace, electronic records and encryption, but those are simply the newest clothes on a body that has not changed much over the years. New permutations of communication and record keeping will continue to come and go; the core of our discipline will keep us grounded.

References

Allen, J. G., Fonagy, P., & Bateman, A. W. (2008). *Mentalizing in clinical practice*. Arlington, VA American Psychiatric.

American Association for Marriage and Family Therapy. (2001). *Code of ethics*. Retrieved from http://www.aamft.org/imis15/Content/Legal_Ethics/Code_of_Ethics.aspx

American Counseling Association. (2005). *ACA code of ethics*. Retrieved from http://www.counseling.org/

American Medical Association. (2010a). AMA policy: Professionalism in the use of social media. Washington, DC: Author. Retrieved from http://www.ama-assn.org/ama/pub/meeting/professionalism-social-media.shtml

American Medical Association. (2010b). *Code of medical ethics: Current opinions with annotations, 2010–2011*. Washington, DC: Author.

American Psychiatric Association. (2001a). Technical amendment to the final rule Standards for Confidentiality of Individually Identifiable Health Information (*Federal Register*, February 28, 2001, PP12738-12739). Letter to Secretary Thompson at the U.S. Department of Health and Human Services.

American Psychiatric Association. (2001b). *Urgent action alert: Final health privacy regulation comments*. Retrieved from http://www.psych.org/pub_pol_adv/finalhealthprivacy31303.cfm

American Psychoanalytic Association, American Psychological Association, & The American Academy of Psychoanalysis. (1995). Amicus Brief in support of respondents in case of *Jaffee v. Redmond*.

American Psychological Association. (2007). *Record keeping guidelines*. Retrieved from http://www.apa.org/practice/guidelines/record-keeping.pdf

American Psychological Association. (2010). *Ethical principles of psychologists and code of conduct: 2010 Amendments*. Retrieved from http://www.apa.org/ethics/code/index.aspx

American Recovery and Reinvestment Act. (2009). Public law 111-5.

Appelbaum, P. S. (2000). Threats to confidentiality of medical records: No place to hide. *Journal of the American Medical Association, 283*(6), 795–797.

Anthony, K., Jung, A., Rosenauer, D., Nagel, D. M., & Goss, S. (2010). Interview with Audrey Jung, president of the International Society for Mental Health Online (ISMHO) presented at the Online Counseling and Therapy in Action conference, April 25, 2009. *British Journal of Guidance and Counseling, 38*(4), 483–494.

Anthony, K., & Nagel, D. M. (2009). Ethical framework for the use of technology in mental health. Retrieved from http://www.onlinetherapyinstitute.com/ethical-training/. Published in full in Anthony, K., & Nagel, D. M. (2009). *Therapy online: A practical guide*. London: Sage.

Associated Press. (1997, October 6). McGovern rethinks Eagleton. *Washington Post*, A8.

Association of State and Provincial Psychology Boards. (1998). *Disciplinary data system, August 1983–January 1998*. Montgomery, AL: Author.

Backer-Grandahl, A., & Sagberg, F. (2011). Driving and telephoning: Relative accident risk when using hand-held and hands-free mobile phones. *Safety Science, 49*(2), 324–330.

Barber, G. (2009). Electronic health records and the end of anonymity. *New Jersey Law Journal, 198*(3), Index 227.

Beauchamp, T. L., & Childress, J. F. (2009). *Principles of biomedical ethics* (6th ed.). New York: Oxford.

Bennett, S. (2004). Viewing telephone therapy through the lens of attachment theory and infant research. *Clinical Social Work Journal, 32*(3), 239–250.

Berkemper, E. (2002). Family therapists' ethical decision-making processes in two duty-to-warn situations. *Journal of Marital and Family Therapy, 28*(2), 203–211.

Bond, T., & Mitchell, B. (2008). *Confidentiality and record keeping in counseling and psychotherapy.* London: Sage.

Brooke, P. S. (1994). Legal and ethical aspects of mental health care. In E. M. Varcarolis (Ed.), *Foundations of psychiatric mental health nursing* (2nd ed., pp. 61–66). Philadelphia: W.B. Saunders.

Brooks, M. K. (2004). Legal aspects of confidentiality of patient information. In J. H. Lowinson et al. (Eds.), *Substance abuse: A comprehensive textbook* (4th ed., pp. 861–1382). Philadelphia: Lippincott Williams & Wilkins.

Carter, P. I. (1999). Health information privacy: Can Congress protect confidential medical information in the "Information Age"? *William Mitchell Law Review, 25*(1), 223–286.

Cimino, J. J., Li, J., Mendonca, E. A., Sengupta, S., Patel, V. L., & Kushniruk, A. W. (2000). An evaluation of patient access to their electronic medical records via the World Wide Web. *Proceedings of the AMIA Symposium 2000,* 151–155.

Clinical Social Work Association. (2006). *Clinical Social Work Association code of ethics.* Retrieved from http://associationsites.com/CSWA/collection/Ethcs%20Code%20Locked%2006.pdf

Clinton, B. K., Silverman, B. C., & Brendel, D. H. (2010). Patient-targeted Googling: The ethics of searching online for patient information. *Harvard Review of Psychiatry, 18*(2), 103–112.

Confidentiality of Alcohol and Drug Abuse Patient Records, e-C.F.R. pt. 2 (2011).

Cook, B. (2011, January 14). Facebook "friend" request from patient? French doctors decline. Retrieved from http://www.ama-assn.org/amednews/2011/01/10/bisd0114.htm

Court of Appeals of Maryland. (1999, September Term). #134 *In re:adoption/guardianship #CCJ14746 in the Circuit Court for Washington County.*

Draker v. Schreiber. 271 S.W.3d 318 (2008) Tex.App., San Antonio.

DSM-IV-TR (2000). *Diagnostic and Statistical Manual of Mental Disorders,* 4th Edition (Text Revision). American Psychiatric Association.

Dvoskin, J. A., & Guy, L. S. (2008). On being an expert witness: It's not about you. *Psychiatry, Psychology and Law, 15*(2), 202–212.

Elbogen, E. B., Van Dorn, R., Swanson, J., Swartz, M., & Monahan, J. (2006). Treatment engagement and violence risk in mental disorders. *British Journal of Psychiatry, 189,* 354–360.

Engel, A. (2011). The dynamics of dedication: Treatment of a patient of a terminally ill therapist. Paper presented at the American Association for Psychoanalysis in Clinical Social Work 2011 Conference. Marina Del Rey, CA.

Epston, D. (1994). Extending the conversation. *Family Therapy Networker, 18*(6), 31–37, 62–63.

Ewing v. Goldstein. 120 Cal. App. 4th 807 (2004).

Ewing v. Northridge Hospital Medical Center. 120 Cal. App. 4th 1289 (2004).

Federal Register. (2002, August). Volume 67, Number 157: Rules and Regulations. (53181–53273).

Federal Register. (2009, August). Volume 74, Number 162: Breach Notification for Unsecured Protected Health Information Rule. 45 C.F.R. pt. 160–164.

Fisher, C. B., & Oransky, M. (2008). Informed consent to psychotherapy: Protecting the dignity and respecting the autonomy of patients. *Journal of Clinical Psychology, 64*(5), 576–588.

Foreman, J. (2006, June 26). At risk of exposure. *Los Angeles Times*. Retrieved from http://articles.latimes.com/2006/jun/26/health/he-privacy26

Fox, R., & Gutheil, I. A. (2000). Process recording: A means for conceptualizing and evaluating practice. *Journal of Teaching in Social Work, 20*(1/2), 39–55.

Freed, A. O. (1978). Clients' rights and casework records. *Social Casework, 59*(8), 458–464.

Furlong, A. (1998). Should we or shouldn't we? Some aspects of the confidentiality of clinical reporting and dossier access. *International Journal of Psychoanalysis, 79*, 727–739.

Gabbard, G. O. (2009). What is a "good enough" termination? *Journal of the American Psychoanalytic Association, 57*, 575–594.

Gabbard, G. O. (2010). *Long-term psychodynamic psychotherapy: A basic text* (2nd ed.). Arlington, VA: American Psychiatry.

Gabbard, G. O., & Lester, E. P. (1995). *Boundaries and boundary violations in psychoanalysis*. Arlington, VA: American Psychiatric.

Gabbard, G. O., & Wilkerson, S. M. (1994). *Management of countertransference with borderline patients*. Washington, DC: American Psychiatric Press.

Gabbard, G. O., Kassaw, K. A., & Perez-Garcia, G. (2011) Professional boundaries in the era of the Internet. *Academic Psychiatry* 35:168–174.

Gartrell, N. (1992). Boundaries in lesbian therapy relationships. *Women and Therapy, 12*(3), 29–50.

Gentile, S. R., Asamen, J. K., Harmell, P. H., & Weathers, R. (2002). The stalking of psychologists by their clients. *Professional Psychology: Research and Practice, 33*(5), 490–494.

Gilbert, H. (2010). Letter to former patients. Personal communication, letter published with permission of author.

Goss, S., & Anthony, K. (2009). Developments in the use of technology in counseling and psychotherapy. *British Journal of Guidance and Counselling, 37*(3), 223–230.

Griffith, E. E., Zonana, H., Pinsince, A. J., & Adams, A. K. (1988). Institutional response to inpatients' threats against the President. *Hospital and Community Psychiatry, 39*, 11.

Groopman, J., & Hartzband, P. (2009, August 31). Opinion: Sorting fact from fiction on health care. *Wall Street Journal*.

Groshong, L. W., Myers, R. K., & Schoolcraft, D. G. (2010). *HIPAA seven years later. Compliance with HIPAA privacy and security rules: The impact on clinical mental health practice*. Clinical Social Work Association.

Hartocollis, A. (2010). "Snippets" of patient data are accidentally posted. *New York Times*. Retrieved from http://cityroom.blogs.nytimes.com/2010/09/27/snippets-of-patient-data-are-accidentally-posted/

Hasman, A., Hanson, N. R., Lassen, A., Rabol, R., & Holm, S. (1997). What do people talk about on Danish elevators? *Ugeskr. Laeger, 159*, 6819–6821.

Hauser, H., Cording, C., Hajak, G., & Spiessl, H. (2008). Information and consent in psychiatry and psychotherapy. *Psychiatrische Praxis, 35*(4), 163–169.

Health Policy Institute. Center on Medical Record Rights and Privacy. Georgetown University. http://medicalrecordrights.georgetown.edu

Herman, J. (1992). *Trauma and recovery*. New York: Basic Books.

Holloway, J. D. (2003). Shutting down a practice. *Monitor on Psychology, 34*, 32–33.

Horton, K. (1995). When the therapist is ill: Implications for self-disclosure theory. Presented to the Minnesota Society for Clinical Social Work, October 1995 Minneapolis, MN.

Horvath, A. O. (2005). The therapeutic relationship: Research and theory. *Psychotherapy Research, 15*(1–2), 3–17.

Host, K. (2010, Summer). The interface between technology and the therapeutic relationship. *Access*. Clinical Social Work Association Newsletter.

Hotze, T. Reassessing "minor" breaches of confidentiality. March 2011. *Virtual Mentor*. Volume 13(3): 163–166.

International Society for Mental Health Online (January 9, 2000). Suggested principles for the online provision of mental health services. www.ismho.org (retrieved 11/12/11).

Jaffee v. Redmond. (1996). 116 Supreme Court 1923, 135, L.Ed.2d 337.

Jobes, D. A., & O'Connor, S. S. (2008). The duty to protect suicidal patients: Ethical, legal and professional considerations. In J. L. Werth, Jr., E. L. Welfel, & G. A. H. Benjamin (Eds.), *The duty to protect: Ethical, legal, and professional considerations in risk assessment and intervention*. Washington, DC: American Psychological Association.

Jobes, D. A., Overholser, J. C., Rudd, M. D., & Joiner, T. E. (2008). Ethical and competent care of suicidal patients: Contemporary challenges, new developments, and considerations for clinical practice. *Professional Psychology: Research and Practice, 39*, 405–413.

Kafka, Franz (2009). *The Trial*. (M. Mitchell, Trans.) New York: Oxford University Press. (Original work published in 1925.)

Kagle, J. D. (1991). *Social work records*. Belmont, CA: Wadsworth.

Kaiser Permanente. (2009). *Kaiser Permanente social media policy*. Retrieved from http://xnet.kp.org/newscenter/media/downloads/socialmediapolicy_091609.pdf

Kanter, J. (2004). *Face to face with children: The life and work of Claire W. Winnicott*. London: Karnac.

Kaplan, D. (2006, September 1). New requirement to have a transfer plan. *Counseling Today Online: Ethics Update*. Retrieved from http://www.counseling.org/Publications/CounselingTodayArticles.aspx?AGuid=5533c9ab-318f-480b-abfb-4454622b9309

Kaslow, F. W., Patterson, T., & Gottlieb, M. (2011). Ethical dilemmas in psychologists accessing Internet data: Is it justified? *Professional Psychology: Research and Practice, 42*(2), 105–112.

Kern, S. I. (1996). Responding to subpoenas and other demands for records and testimony. *New Jersey Medicine, 93*(2), 85–88.

Knauss, L. K. (2006). Ethical issues in record keeping in group psychotherapy. *International Journal of Group Psychotherapy, 56*(4), 415–430.

Kolmes, K., Nagel, D. M., & Anthony, K. (2011). An ethical framework for the use of social media by mental health professionals. *Therapeutic Innovations in Light of Technology, 1*(3), 20–29.

Koocher, G. P. (2003). Ethical and legal issues in professional practice transitions. *Professional Psychology: Research and Practice, 34*(4), 383–387.

Krasner, R. F., Howard, K. I., & Brown, A. S. (1998). Acquisition of psychotherapeutic skill: An empirical study. *Journal of Clinical Psychology, 54*(7), 895–903.

Langlois, M. (2011, January 17). How to have a 100% HIPAA compliant online presence. Retrieved from http://mikelangloislicsw.wordpress.com/2011/01/17/how-to-have-a-100-hipaa-compliant-online-presence/

Lerner, M. (2001, November 8). Web posting has health and university officials scrambling: Mental health records of children from twenty families were mistakenly put onto the Internet. *Star Tribune*, p. 1B.

Lerner, M. (2011, May 6). Allina hospitals fire 32 over privacy violation. *Star Tribune*. Retrieved September 2011 from http://www.startribune.com/lifestyle/wellness/121402894.html

Levine, M., & Doueck, J. et al. (1995). *The impact of mandated reporting on the therapeutic process*. Thousand Oaks, CA: Sage.

Lowinson, J. H., Ruiz, P., Millman, R. B., & Langrod, J. G. (2005). *Substance abuse: A comprehensive textbook* (4th ed.). Philadelphia: Lippincott Williams and Wilkens. (Brooks article is pp. 1361–1382.)

Luepker, E. T. (1989). Clinical assessment of clients who have been sexually exploited by their therapists and development of differential treatment plans. In G. R. Schoener, J. Gonsiorek, J. H. Milgrom, E. T. Luepker, & R. Conroe (Eds.), *Psychotherapists' sexual involvement with clients: Intervention and prevention* (pp. 159–176). Minneapolis, MN: Walk-In Center.

Luepker, E. T. (1999). Effects of practitioners' sexual misconduct: A follow up study. *Journal of the American Academy of Psychiatry and the Law, 27*(1), 51–63.

Luepker, E, T. (2010). Records: Purposes, characteristics and contents. In Hanrahan, S. J., & Anderson, M. B. *Handbook of Applied Sport Psychology.* London: Routledge.

Luepker, E. T., Warren, J. I., Conaty, L., Melton, J., Norton, L., & Horton, E. (2000). Handling subpoenas, other third party requests for records, and court orders. *Clinical Social Work Federation Committee on Clinical Social Work and the Law Memorandum.*

Mangalmurti, S. S., Murtagh, L., & Mello, M. M. (2010). Medical malpractice liability in the age of electronic health records. *New England Journal of Medicine, 363*(21), 2060–2067.

Manosevitz, M., & Hays, K. F. (2003). Relocating your psychotherapy practice: Packing and unpacking. *Professional Psychology: Research and Practice, 34*(4), 375–382.

Martindale, S. J., Chambers, E., & Thompson, A. R. (2009). Clinical psychology service users' experiences of confidentiality and informed consent: A qualitative analysis. *Psychology and Psychotherapy: Theory, Research and Practice, 82*, 355–368.

Mayell, H. (2002). Thousands of women killed for family "honor." *National Geographic News.* Retrieved from http://news.nationalgeographic.com/news/2002/02/0212_020212_honorkilling.html

McGee, T. F. (2003). Observations on the retirement of professional psychologists. *Professional Psychology: Research and Practice, 34*(4), 388–395.

Merken, D. (2010, August 4). My life in therapy. *The New York Times Magazine*, p. 28. Retrieved September 2011 from http://www.nytimes.com/2010/08/08/magazine/08Psychoanalysis-t.html?pagewanted=all

Myers, R. K. (2010, Summer). Social media and psychotherapy: Beginning in the middle of the conversation. *Access.* Clinical Social Work Association.

Milgrom, J. H. (1989). Advocacy: Assisting sexually exploited clients through the complaint process. In G. R. Schoener, J. Gonsiorek, J. H. Milgrom, E. T. Luepker, & R. Conroe (Eds.), *Psychotherapists' sexual involvement with clients: Intervention and prevention* (pp. 159–176). Minneapolis, MN: Walk-In Center.

Mishler, E. G. (1979). Meaning in context: Is there any other kind? *Harvard Educational Review, 49*(1), 1–19.

Monahan, J. (1993). Limiting therapist exposure to Tarasoff liability: Guidelines for risk containment. *American Psychologist, 48*(3), 242–258.

Monahan, J. (2006–2007). Tarasoff at thirty: How developments in science and policy shape the common law. *University of Cincinnati Law Review, 75*(2), 497–521.

Moran, M. (2009). Many residents reluctant to report patient violence. *Psychiatric News, 44*(8), 16.

National Association of Social Workers. (2008). *Code of ethics* of the National Association of Social Workers. Retrieved from http://www.socialworkers.org/pubs/Code/code.asp

National Association of Social Workers & Association of Social Work Boards. (2005). *Standards for technology and social work practice.* Retrieved from http://www.socialworkers.org/practice/standards/NASWTechnologyStandards.pdf

National Association of Social Workers General Counsel. (2010). *Legal rights of children: NASW General Counsel law note*. Washington, DC: NASW Press.

North Carolina Society for Clinical Social Work. (2001). *A suggested model for the sudden termination of a clinical social work practice*. Durham, NC: Author.

Nylund, D., & Thomas, J. (1994, November/December). The economics of narrative. *Networker*.

Ornstein, C. (2008, March 15). Hospital to punish snooping on Spears. *Los Angeles Times*. Retrieved September 2011 from http://articles.latimes.com/2008/mar/15/local/me-britney15

Pabst, L. (2010, July 13). Estranged from family, doctor snoops in records. *Star Tribune*. Retrieved September 2011 from http://articles.latimes.com/2008/mar/15/local/me-britney15

Peel, D. C. (2009, September 18). Privacy rights. Written testimony before the Health Information Technology Committee.

Peel, D. C. (2010, October 20). Across the pond: An update on health privacy and health data security: How are American patients faring? Paper presented to a security seminar at the University of Cambridge.

Peel, D. C. (2011, February 18). Poll shows: We trust our doctors, not their systems. Retrieved from http://patientprivacyrights.org/2011/02/poll-shows-we-trust-our-doctors-not-their-systems/

Piper, A. (1994). Truce on the battlefield. *Journal of Law, Medicine, and Ethics, 22*(4), 301–313.

Pomerantz, A. M. (2005). Increasingly informed consent: Discussing distinct aspects of psychotherapy at different points in time. *Ethics & Behavior, 15*(4), 351–360.

Postel, M. G., deHaan, H. A., & De Jong, C. (2008). E-therapy for mental health problems: A systematic review. *Telemedicine and e-Health, 14*(7), 707–714.

Privacy Act of 1974. 5 United States Code 552A.

Reamer, F. G. (1995). Malpractice claims against social workers: First facts. *Social Work, 40*(5), 595–601.

Renick, O. (2006). *Practical psychoanalysis for therapists and patients*. New York: Other Press.

Renzulli, F. (Writer) & Taylor, A. (Director). (1999, February 14). Pax Soprano [Television series episode]. In I. S. Landress (Producer), *The Sopranos*. New York: Silver Cup Studios.

Richards, D. (2009). Features and benefits of online counselling: Trinity College online mental health community. *British Journal of Guidance and Counseling, 37*(3), 231–242.

Richmond, R. (2011, April 13). How to fix (or kill) web data about you. *New York Times*. Retrieved September 2011 from http://www.nytimes.com/2011/04/14/technology/personaltech/14basics.html

Romans, J., Hays, J., & White, T. (1996). Stalking and related behaviors experienced by counseling center staff members from current or former clients. *Professional Psychology: Research and Practice, 27*(6), 595–599.

Rummel, C., & Joyce, N. (2010). So wat do u want to wrk on 2day?: The ethical implications of online counseling. *Ethics & Behavior, 20*(6), 482–496.

Rutherford, B. R., Aizaga, K., Sneed, J., & Roose, S. P. (2007). A survey of psychiatry residents' informed consent practices. *Journal of Clinical Psychiatry, 68*(4), 558–565.

Rutherford, B. R., & Roose, S. P. (2006). Do psychiatry residents obtain informed consent for psychotherapy? *Journal of American Psychoanalytic Association, 54*(4), 1343–1347.

San Diego Psychological Association. (2006). *Guidelines for preparing your professional will: Materials developed by the Committee on Psychologist Retirement, Incapacitation or Death*. San Diego, CA: Author.

Sandberg, D., McNeil, D., & Binder, R. (1998). Characteristics of psychiatric inpatients who stalk, threaten, or harass hospital staff after discharge. *American Journal of Psychiatry, 155*(8), 1102–1105.

Sanford, S. M., Hartnett, T., & Jolly, B. T. (1999, Summer). Lessons from the past: The roots of the informed consent process. *The Monitor.*

Santhiveeran, J. (2009). Compliance of social work e-therapy websites to the NASW Code of Ethics. *Social Work in Health Care, 48,* 1–13.

Schoener, G. R. (2010). Advanced legal and ethical issues for therapists and supervisors. Paper presented to a conference at Bridge for Runaway Youth, sponsored by The Kenwood Therapy Center. Minneapolis, MN.

Schoener, G. R., & Gonsiorek, J. C. (1988). Assessment and development of rehabilitation plans for counselors who have sexually exploited their clients. *Journal of Counseling and Development, 67,* 227–232.

Schoener, G. R., & Gonsiorek, J. C. (1989). Assessment and development of rehabilitation plans for the therapist. In G. R. Schoener, J. H. Milgrom, J. C. Gonsiorek, E. T. Luepker, & R. Conroe (Eds.), *Psychotherapists' sexual involvement with clients: Intervention and prevention* (pp. 401–420). Minneapolis, MN: Walk-In Counseling Center.

Schoener, G. R., Milgrom, J. H., Gonsiorek, J. C., Luepker, E. T., & Conroe, R. (Eds.) (1989). *Psychotherapists' sexual involvement with clients: Intervention and prevention.* Minneapolis, MN: Walk-In Counseling Center.

Scott, W. S. (2009, May/June). Integration of online therapy into a training curriculum. *Family Therapy Magazine.* The American Association for Marriage and Family Therapy.

Shabbir, S. A., & Jian, W. S. (2011). Leaks and threats to patient data. *British Medical Journal, 342*(d1095).

Shaw, J. (2007, July). Op-ed: Should a sex therapist have a professional will? *Newsletter, Society for Sex Therapy and Research, 24*(2), 7–8.

Siebold, C. (1991). Termination: When the therapist leaves. *Clinical Social Work Journal, 19*(2), 191–204.

Siebold, C. (2004). Reflections on premature termination: Is it always goodbye? *Newsletter of the National Membership Committee on Psychoanalysis,* Winter/Spring, 3.

Siebold, C. (2005). Commentary on "Transference opportunities during the therapist's pregnancy: Three case vignettes." *Psychoanalytic Social Work, 12*(1), 13–18.

Siebold, C. (2010, Fall). From the president. *American Association for Psychoanalysis in Clinical Social Work Newsletter.*

Siebold, C. (2011). What do patients want?: Personal disclosure and the intersubjective perspective. *Clinical Social Work Journal, 39*(2), 151–160.

Simpson, S. (2009). Psychotherapy via videoconferencing: A review. *British Journal of Guidance and Counselling, 37*(3), 271–286.

Skeem, J. L., & Monahan, J. (2011). Current directions in violence risk assessment. *Current Directions in Psychological Science, 20*(1), 38–42.

Social Security Act. (1997). 18 United States Code 1852.

Stanberry, B. (1998). The legal and ethical aspects of telemedicine. 2: Data protection, security and European law. *Journal of Telemedicine and Telecare, 4,* 18–24.

Steinbrook, R. (March 19, 2009). Health care and the American Recovery and Reinvestment Act. *New England Journal of Medicine.* 360: 1057–1060.

Tarasoff v. Regents of the University of California. (1974). 529 P 2d 553, 118 Cal. Rptr. 129.

Tarasoff v. Regents of the University of California. (1976). 551 P 2d 553, 334 Cal. Rptr. 14.

Thapar v. Zezulka. 994 SW 2d 635 Tex: Supreme Court (1999).

Time Magazine. (1996, September 2). Where Are They Now? p. 17.

Townes, B. L., Wagner, N. N., & Christ, A. (1967). Therapeutic use of psychological reports. *Journal of American Academy of Child Psychiatry, 6,* 698.

Townsend, M. C. (1999). *Essentials of psychiatric/mental health nursing.* Philadelphia, PA: F.A. Davis.

Turner, C. (2010, June 23). Marilyn Monroe on the couch. *The Telegraph.* Retrieved from http://www.telegraph.co.uk/culture/film/7843140/Marilyn-Monroe-on-the-couch.html

Tyler, J. D., Sloan, L. L., & King, A. R. (2000). Psychotherapy supervision practices of academic faculty: A national survey. *Psychotherapy, 37*:98-101.

UN Population Fund. (2000). *State of World Population 2000.* Retrieved from www.unfpa.org

U.S. Department of Health and Human Services. (2000, December 28). Standards for privacy of individually identifiable health information. *Federal Register, 65*(250), 82461–82510.

U.S. Department of Health and Human Services. (2001a, May 9). Protecting the privacy of patients' health information. Retrieved from http://www.aspe.hhs.gov/admnsimp/final/pvcfact2.htm

U.S. Department of Health and Human Services. (2001b, July 6). Standards for privacy of individually identifiable health information. Retrieved September 2011 from http://aspe.hhs.gov/admnsimp/final/pvcguide1.htm

U.S. Department of Health and Human Services. (2001c). Final Privacy Rule: Regulation text. Retrieved from http://www.aspe.hhs.gov/admnsimp/final/PvcTxt01.htm

United States v. Patillo. (1971). 438 F2d 13. 4th Circuit.

U.S. Office for Civil Rights. (2001, October 18). *Standards for privacy of individually identifiable health information.* Washington, DC: Author. Retrieved from http://www.hhs.gov

Vannier, A., Berri, C. (Producers), & Miller, C. (Director). (1988). *The Little Thief* [Motion picture]. France: Orly Films.

Wagner, B., Knaevelsrud, C., & Maercker, A. (2006). Internet-based cognitive-behavioral therapy for complicated grief: A randomized controlled trial. *Death Studies, 30*(5), 429–453.

Wahlberg, D. (1999, February 10). Patient records exposed on web. *Ann Arbor News,* p. 1A

Walfish, S., & Barnett, J. E. (2009). *Financial success in mental health practice: Essential tools and strategies for practitioners.* Washington, DC: American Psychological Association.

Walfish, S., & Ducey, B. B. (2007). Readability level of Health Insurance Portability and Accountability Act Notices of Privacy Practices used by psychologists in clinical practice. *Professional Psychology: Research and Practice, 38*(2), 203–207.

Weintraub, M. I. (1999). Documentation and informed consent. *Neurological Clinics, 17*(2), 371–381.

Wellspring Family Services. (2008). Notice of privacy practices. Seattle, WA: Author. Retrieved from http://family-services.org

Wiger, D. (2005). *The psychotherapy documentation primer* (2nd ed.). Hoboken, NJ: Wiley.

Williams, B., Ziskin, L. (Producers), & Oz, F. (Director). (1991). *What About Bob?* [Motion picture]. USA: Buena Vista Home Entertainment.

Winnicott, D. (1960). The theory of the parent-child relationship, *International Journal of Psychoanalysis,* 41:585–595.

Woody, R. H. (2009). Ethical considerations of multiple roles in forensic services. *Ethics & Behavior, 19*(1), 79–87.

Wootton, B. M., & Titov, N. (2010). Distance treatment of obsessive compulsive disorder. *Behaviour Change, 27*(2), 112–118.

Yalom, Irvin D. (2002). *The gift of therapy*. New York: Harper Perennial.
Zinsser, W. (1988). *Writing to learn*. New York: Harper and Row.
Zuckerman, E. (2008). *The paper office* (4th ed.). New York: Guilford.

Appendix A

SAMPLE CLIENT/PATIENT INFORMATION FORM

Welcome to my practice. I will be continually working to provide you with appropriate, high-quality services. I believe that a client who understands and participates in his or her care can achieve better results. I have the responsibility to give you the best care possible, to respect your rights, and to recognize your responsibilities as a client. I have prepared this information handout, which includes a notice of my privacy practices, to help you identify these rights and responsibilities.

Your Rights as a Client

Your Right to Privacy and Confidentiality

This notice of privacy practices describes how information I maintain about you may be used and disclosed and how you can get access to this information. Please review it carefully.

I follow the privacy provisions of state and federal laws and rules and of my profession's ethical standards. You have the right to know, through discussion with me and in writing, my policies and practices regarding the uses and protection of the information you will share with me and the limitations of privacy of your information. I may make changes in my policies and practices, but if I do, I will inform you. Please keep a copy of this handout for your records.

The information I collect from you is needed for providing evaluation and treatment to you. I will inform you of the consequences, if any, of refusing to supply information I request. If you choose to not supply such information, I may be unable to determine which services are most appropriate for you and it will make it more difficult for me to carry out an effective treatment plan for you.

Your treatment record is accessible only to me and to personnel whom I have authorized to help me provide services to you. Your record includes your assessment, treatment plan, progress notes, psychological test reports, psychiatric and other medical reports, and closing summary.

Your billing record is also accessible only to me and to personnel whom I have authorized to perform billing services for you.

In order to further protect your privacy and confidentiality, I will not use e-mail to communicate with you in between our office appointments, only the telephone. I also do not "friend" my clients or patients on social networking sites.

It is your choice whether or not to use your insurance coverage for payment of my services. If you request that your insurance company pay for my services, I will share only the minimum information necessary for your insurance company to process claims. I provide the following information to my billing staff for submission of claims to you and your insurance company:

(a) name and address of your insurance company; (b) your subscriber and group plan numbers; and (c) your name, birth date, social security number, diagnosis, dates of service, type of service.

If your insurance company requires further information, I will first consult you about your insurance company's request. I will give you the option to make an informed decision regarding what, if anything, you wish to be released.

All personnel—counseling, support, or billing—whom I authorize to have access to your health care information in this office will limit their access to and use of your health care information to the minimum necessary to fulfill their authorized respective functions for treatment and payment services. They have agreed to abide by the privacy and security practices of this office.

If you are receiving services from other health care professionals, I will need to routinely confer with them about your assessment, counseling plan, and progress for the purpose of coordinating your services.

At times I may also seek out professional consultation about some aspects of my work with you. Usually it will not be necessary to share your identifying information with the consultant(s). The consulting professional(s) also must abide by applicable laws and ethics and protect your confidentiality in all cases.

You have the right to request restrictions on personal health care information that I routinely disclose for purposes of treatment and payment. If, in my professional judgment, the restriction you request could be harmful to you (for example, prevent my ability to provide adequate services to you), I will inform you when I cannot agree to any such restriction you may request.

You have the right to an accounting of certain disclosures of your information I have made after April 14, 2003, not including disclosures for treatment, payment, or health care operations, and disclosures made to you or disclosures otherwise authorized by you or by state law.

Other than the routine disclosures noted above that are necessary to perform treatment and billing services on your behalf, no information will be released to any other persons or agencies outside of this office without your written authorization except by court order. Before you give me written authorization to respond to any other requests for your health information, satisfy yourself that the information is really needed, that you understand the information being sent out, and that giving the information will help you. You have the right to approve or refuse the release of information to anyone, except as provided by law.

Exceptions to the above information release procedures are:

1. When I have knowledge of, or reasonable cause to believe, that a child or elder adult is being neglected or physically or sexually abused, in which case state law requires that such information be reported.
2. Reporting of maltreatment of vulnerable adults.
3. Reporting of alleged practitioner sexual misconduct.
4. Reporting of instances of threatened homicide or physical violence against another identified person. I must report such threats to the appropriate police agency as well as to the intended victim.
5. In cases of threatened suicide and if, in my professional judgment, your health and safety are at risk, I may contact at least one concerned person and/or the appropriate police agency to intervene and for evaluation.

Minors' Right to Privacy

All nonemancipated minor clients under the age of 18 must have the consent of their parents or guardians following an initial intake session to receive further treatment services. State law (check your state law) provides that minors have the right to request that their records be withheld from their parents or guardians. When a minor client requests that records be withheld and/or, in my professional judgment, I determine that sharing the minor's counseling information with parents or legal guardians is detrimental to the physical or mental health of a minor, I may refuse to release it to parents and legal guardians in order to prevent harm.

Right to Read Your Own Records and to Submit an Amendment

You have the right to inspect and request a copy of your own records, paper or electronic. All requests must be made in writing. I will assist you in understanding your records by being available to answer questions and to explain the meaning of technical terminology. I welcome your informing me of any inaccuracies of information in your file. You have the right to put in writing an amendment to the information in your file, which I will keep in your file.

Right to Know How Long I Will Retain Your Inactive Records

After you complete services, your record will be retained for 7 years. At the end of 7 years, the record will be entirely destroyed, leaving only the name of the client and date of record destruction. The time period begins from the date of the last visit. (Or for minors, from the date they reach 18.) Should I provide you with any further direct contact services, the counting period will begin again after conclusion of the new service.

Right to Accounting of Disclosures

Upon written request, you have the right to obtain an accounting of certain disclosures of your personal health care information, excluding those that are necessary to conduct your counseling and payment services as described above and excluding disclosures I have made to you or disclosures you have otherwise authorized.

Right to Determine Alternative Communications

You may request and I will accommodate any reasonable request for you to receive personal health care information from me by alternative means of communication or at alternative locations. For example, in order to protect your privacy, please inform me to what address you prefer that I mail billing statements or copies of records or letters and what telephone number you prefer I use.

Right Not to Be Discriminated Against

You have the right not to be discriminated against in the provision of professional services on the basis of race, age, gender, ethnic origin, disabilities, creed, or sexual orientation.

Right to Know My Qualifications

You are entitled to ask me what my training is, where I received it, if I am licensed or certified, my professional competencies, experience, education, biases or attitudes, and any other relevant information that may be important to you in the provision of services. You have the right to expect that I have met the minimum qualifications of training and experience required by state law and to examine public records maintained by the Minnesota Board of Social Work and Minnesota Board of Psychology, which are the licensure boards that regulate my practice.

My professional competencies include the following: child, adolescent, and adult psychotherapy; couples and family psychotherapy; group psychotherapy; clinical research; consultation; teaching; supervision; and forensic evaluation.

Right to Be Informed

You have the right to be informed of my assessment of your problem in language you understand and to know available counseling alternatives. You also have the right to understand the purpose of the professional services I recommend, including an estimate of the number of counseling or consultation sessions, the length of time involved, the cost of the services, the method of counseling, and the expected outcomes of counseling. You have the right and responsibility to help me develop your own counseling plan. If you are considering medication or other remedies, you have the right to be informed by your physician or other health care professional of treatment alternatives, action of the medication or remedies, and possible side effects.

Right to Refuse Services

You have the right to consent to or refuse recommended services. I can provide services to you without consent only if there is an emergency and in my opinion failure to act immediately would jeopardize your health. In such emergency cases, I will make reasonable efforts to involve a close relative or friend prior to providing emergency services. No audio or video recording of a treatment session can be made without your written permission.

Right to Voice Grievances

You have the right to voice grievances and request changes in your counseling plan without restraint, interference, coercion, discrimination, or reprisal. I encourage you to share any concerns you may have with me directly at the above number, including if you believe your privacy rights have been violated. You also have the right to file a complaint about my services to the Minnesota Board of Social Work (phone: 612-617-2100) and the Minnesota Board of Psychology (phone: 612-617-2230), which are the state licensure boards that regulate my practice.

Right Not to Be Subjected to Harassment

You have the right to not be subjected to harassment—sexual, physical, or verbal.

Rights of Adults Judged Not Able to Give Informed Consent

For adults judged not able to give informed consent, the same policy as that for minors (see above) applies regarding permission for services and requests that records be withheld.

Referral Rights

You have the right not to be referred or terminated without explanation and notice. You have the right to active assistance from me in referring you to other appropriate services.

Your Responsibilities

As a client, you have responsibilities as well as rights. You can help yourself by being responsible in the following ways:

To Be Honest

You are responsible for being honest and direct about everything that relates to you as a client. Please tell me exactly how you feel about the things that are happening to you in your life.

To Understand Your Plan

You are responsible for understanding your counseling plan to your own satisfaction. If you do not understand, ask me. Be sure you do understand because this is important for the success of the treatment plan.

To Follow the Treatment Plan

It is your responsibility to discuss with me whether or not you think you can and/or want to follow a certain counseling plan.

To Keep Appointments

You are responsible for keeping appointments. If you cannot keep an appointment, notify me as soon as possible so that another client can be seen. In any case, you will be charged for appointments when canceled with less than 24 hours notice.

To Know Your Fee

I am willing to discuss my fees with you and to provide a clear understanding for you of the costs of all associated services.

To Keep Me Informed

So that I may contact you whenever necessary, I will rely upon you to notify me of any changes in your name, address, and home or work phone numbers.

Your Therapist's Rights and Responsibilities

I have the responsibility to provide care appropriate to your situation, as determined by prevailing community standards. To accomplish this goal, I also have certain rights, including:

1. The right to information needed to provide appropriate care
2. The right to be reimbursed, as agreed, for services provided
3. The right to provide services in an atmosphere free of verbal, physical, or sexual harassment
4. The right and ethical obligation to refuse to provide services that are not indicated
5. The right to change the terms of this notice at any time, with the understanding I will inform my clients of any changes

Emergency Procedures

Should you feel that your situation requires immediate attention, I am available to return your phone calls from 9:00 a.m. to 5:00 p.m., Monday through Friday.

You may leave a message on my voice messaging service. I check my messages throughout the day, but not in the evenings or on weekends.

If you feel that you are in a crisis and need to talk to me immediately at night, during the weekend, or over a holiday, and I am not immediately available, you may call your local crisis intervention center. If you do speak with me, you may be billed at my current hourly rate for individual therapy for the time I spend with you on the phone. You should be advised that your insurance company might not reimburse you for the telephone consultation charge.

Fee Information

My fee for 1 hour of psychotherapy or counseling, supervision, and consultation services is $145. I will inform you whenever I must raise my fees to keep up with cost of living increases. My fee for any time utilized in a forensic situation is $220 per 1-hour unit. Please note however, under most circumstances, even with client consent, it is usually inappropriate for a therapist to become involved in a client's legal case. This is because engaging in dual roles, as therapist/witness, may be potentially harmful to clients.

Every client receiving services shall be responsible for the full payment of those services. I expect clients to make a payment at each session, or upon receipt of a bill, which is mailed on a monthly basis. Payment for your session should be made directly to me. If at any time you find there are any problems regarding fee payment, or you need to make arrangements for a payment plan, I will be glad to speak to you regarding your concern.

I impose a finance charge of one and one-half percent (1.5%) per month (annual percentage rate of 18%) on all past due accounts. I apply payments to the oldest balance first. No finance charge will be assessed against any billing for services until the charge for such services remains unpaid for 60 days.

There may be circumstances under which I may bill you for my time outside your actual therapy sessions, such as: consultation time between me and other health care professionals, telephone consultations to you, special reports and court evaluation, or communication with your insurance company for prior authorizations for further therapy sessions.

Thank You

I appreciate your decision to work with me. If you have any questions at any time during the course of your therapy, please feel free to speak to me.

Effective April 2003
Revised June 2011

Appendix B

SAMPLE TREATMENT PLAN FORM

Client/patient name _____ Diagnosis _____
Reasons (specific diagnostic criteria)
Date of birth _____
Date of initial evaluation _____

Problems	Goals	Procedures	Estimated Time	Progress

Date _____

Practitioner Signature: _____
Client/Patient, Parent, or Guardian Signature: _____

Appendix C

SAMPLE REVISED TREATMENT PLAN FORM

Client/patient name _____ Current diagnosis _____
Reasons (specific diagnostic criteria)
Date of birth _____ Date of change (if any) _____
Date of initial evaluation   _____
Date of current evaluation _____

Problems	Goals	Procedures	Estimated Time	Progress

Date _____

Practitioner Signature: _____
Client/Patient, Parent, or Guardian Signature: _____

Appendix D

SAMPLE CLOSING SUMMARY FORM

Client/patient name _____ Diagnosis _____
Reasons (specific assessment criteria)
Date of birth _____ At initial evaluation _____
Date of services _____ to _____
Frequency of sessions _____

Problems and Goals	Description of Services	Progress	Outcome and Status at Termination

Date _____

Practitioner Signature: _____
Client/Patient, Parent, or Guardian Signature: _____

Appendix E

SAMPLE CONSENT FOR TREATMENT OF MINOR CHILD FORM

Consent to Provide Treatment to Minor Children

Consent for Treatment of My Minor Child

I agree to therapeutic services provided to my minor child at this office.

Client's Name _____

Address: _____

Parent/Guardian Signature: _____

Address (if different than client's address): _____

_____

Date: _____

As a parent, I understand that I have the right to information concerning my minor child in therapy, except where otherwise stated by law. I also understand that this therapist believes in providing a minor child with a private environment in which to disclose himself/herself to facilitate therapy. I therefore give permission to this therapist to use his/her discretion, in accordance with professional ethics and state and federal laws and rules, in deciding what information revealed by my child is to be shared with me.

Parent/Guardian Signature: _____

Date: _____

Appendix F

SAMPLE AUTHORIZATION FOR RELEASE OF INFORMATION FORM

Sample Authorization/Consent for Release of Information

Client/Patient's Name _____

Parent/Guardian Name (if personal representative, state how authorized to act for client/patient): _____

Address: _____

Client/Patient's Birth Date: ____/____/____

This will authorize: _____to release to _____ the following:

Information from the medical/case record at any time during the next 1 year, or until such time as I revoke such consent, including the following:

_____ Discharge Summary

_____ Social/Court Service Summary(ies)

_____ Consultations

_____ Psychological Testing

_____ Intake Interview

_____ Other

This information is needed, and will be used, only for the following purpose(s):

_____
_____

This information may not be re-disclosed to anyone else, except for the above intended purpose(s).

I understand that I may revoke this consent at any time, except to the extent action has been taken in reliance upon it. I understand that this consent will automatically expire without my express revocation upon fulfillment of the above-stated purpose, or 1 year from this date, whichever is sooner.

Signature of Client: _____ Date: _____

Signature of Guardian/Representative (if representative, state how authorized to act for patient): _____ Date: _____

Signature of Witness _____ Date: _____

Appendix G

SAMPLE CLINICAL SUPERVISION CONTRACT

Face Sheet for Internal Psychotherapy Supervision

Supervisee Name:	
Supervisee Place of Employment:	
Supervisee Employment Address:	
Supervisee Home Address:	
Supervisee Phone Numbers:	Work: After Hours:
Supervisee E-mail Address:	
Supervisor Name:	
Supervisor Place of Employment:	
Supervisor Employment Address:	
Supervisor Phone Numbers:	Work: After Hours:
Supervisor E-mail Address:	
Emergency Contact Name:	
Emergency Contact Phone Numbers:	Work: After Hours:

Face Sheet for External Psychotherapy Supervision

Supervisee Name:	
Supervisee Place of Employment:	
Supervisee Employment Address:	
Supervisee Home Address:	
Supervisee Phone Numbers:	Work: After Hours:
Supervisee E-mail Address:	
Supervisee Employment Supervisor:	
Clinical Supervisor Name:	
Clinical Supervisor Place of Employment:	
Clinical Supervisor Employment Address:	
Clinical Supervisor Phone Numbers:	Work: After Hours:
Clinical Supervisor E-mail Address:	
Clinical Emergency Contact Name:	
Clinical Emergency Contact Phone Numbers:	Work: After Hours:

General Information

Name, degree, qualifications, credentials of psychotherapy supervisor: _____

_____

Name of supervisee: _____

Name of graduate school supervisee has attended/is attending: _____

_____

Supervisee's professional degree/status of current professional training:_____

_____

Name of regulatory board, if supervisee is meeting licensure requirements: ____

Name of place of employment/employer: _____

Purpose of psychotherapy supervision (e.g., level of licensure pursuing, etc.): ___

Type of supervision requested (individual or group): _____

Number of supervision hours required: _____
Frequency of supervision sessions necessary to meet requirements: _____

Description of supervisee's client population: _____

Treatment methods and modalities supervisee will use with clients: _____

Types of cases required to meet supervision requirements: _____

Date formal supervision evaluation(s) must be conducted: _____

Criteria that will be used in formal evaluations: _____

Names and addresses of individuals to whom supervisory evaluations will be sent: _____

Policy/method supervisee will use to contact the clinical supervisor: _____

Procedures supervisee will use to respond to client emergencies: _____

Psychotherapy Learning Needs Assessment

Transcripts of supervisee's academic courses (attached).
Current job description (attached).

Résumé or list of prior professional experiences, responsibilities, and duties (attached). Prior professional experience that is relevant to the supervisee's current patient population: _____

Knowledge and skills supervisee acquired from previous professional training and experience, such as diagnostic assessment and treatment; ethical standards of practice; state and federal laws and rules; record keeping; cultural competence, for example, knowledge and experience with cultural norms of behavior for clients served by the supervisee (e.g., ethnicity, race, age, class, gender, sexual orientation, religion, immigration status, literacy, and mental or physical disability); commitment to maintaining cultural competence as an ongoing process; methods for establishing treatment relationship with clients and patients; methods for including family members in clients' treatment when appropriate; communication with other professionals in developing diagnosis and treatment plans and assuring continuity of care:

_____

_____

_____

Professional strengths supervisee has that supervisee, teachers, and former supervisors have identified:

_____

_____

_____

Professional weaknesses or concerns about supervisee's practice that the supervisee, teachers, and former supervisors have identified:

_____

_____

_____

Supervisee's greatest sources of professional concerns and anxiety:

_____

_____

_____

Supervisee's specific learning needs, including skills supervisee needs to develop:

_____

_____

_____

How supervisee learns best:

_____

_____

_____

Learning barriers and accommodations, if any, needed:

_____

_____

_____

Supervisee's Rights

- The right to have weekly (or other predictable frequency) supervisory sessions that will focus on my learning needs and my clients' treatment needs
- The right to understand and to participate in the development of my learning objectives, activities to meet learning objectives, and standards for mastery of learning objectives
- The right to know my supervisor's professional qualifications (training, licensure, competencies, experience, education, treatment approach, biases, etc.)
- The right to have regularly scheduled performance evaluations and to have my performance evaluations sent in a timely manner to the appropriate institution (e.g., graduate school, regulatory board, employer)
- The right not to be discriminated against in the provision of supervisory services on the basis of my race, gender, ethnic origin, disability, creed, or sexual orientation
- The right not to be harassed or exploited to meet my supervisor's personal needs

Supervisee's Responsibilities

- To collaborate with my psychotherapy supervisor in developing a learning needs assessment and supervision plan
- To bring my psychotherapy cases, including records, to my clinical supervisor for honest and direct discussion and review
- To provide my psychotherapy supervisor with access at any time to my patients' records for review
- To thoroughly present each of my clients' cases verbally and in writing, including all factors relevant to diagnosis and treatment, including but not limited to: presenting problems; history of problems; significant childhood, family relationship, work, and other life history; medical treatment; medications; past treatment; mental status observations; diagnoses and treatment plans; my process of providing informed consent; my clinical interventions, including attention to high-risk or safety concerns; preventive action taken; referrals; means of evaluating my clients' progress, record keeping, and other professional issues, including transference and countertransference.
- To inform my patients of exceptions to confidentiality, including that my psychotherapy supervisor will be discussing my sessions, reviewing case notes and electronic recordings of patient sessions
- To obtain my patients' informed consent in writing for any electronic recording of sessions for purpose of supervision

- To read, understand, and adhere to my office's and psychotherapy supervisor's security and privacy policies and procedures
- To follow state and federal laws and rules and professional ethical standards and to discuss ethical and legal questions or other problems as they arise in each of my cases

Psychotherapy Supervisor's Responsibilities

- To provide supervision appropriate to my supervisee's professional needs and that meets the requirements of professional ethics and state and federal laws and rules
- To schedule regular supervisory meetings with my supervisee and be available for emergencies (or specify another supervisor available for emergencies)
- To develop a learning needs assessment with my supervisee and establish clear learning objectives and criteria for mastery of learning objectives
- To teach practical clinical skills, including the characteristics and contents of good clinical records, and help my supervisee integrate theoretical knowledge with clinical skills in order to develop professional competence
- To help my supervisee appropriately manage transference, counter-transference, and professional boundary issues
- To help my supervisee understand cultural norms
- To help my supervisee understand ethical standards
- To help my supervisee identify when a patient may have special problems that require another professional's consultation
- To regularly assess and provide feedback on my supervisee's progress, including identification of strengths, weaknesses, and errors, and to work with my supervisee to develop plans for improvement
- To conduct formal performance evaluations at 6-month intervals (or other predetermined interval)
- To honestly communicate my supervisee's performance evaluation results, including professional strengths as well as any unresolved practice errors or clinical and ethical concerns, to those persons who require supervisee's performance evaluation
- To meet and adhere to supervisor requirements of the (licensure board that regulates my practice)

Psychotherapy Supervisor's Rights

- The right to information needed to provide appropriate supervision
- The right to be compensated promptly for supervision services as agreed upon and when payment arrangement is applicable

- The right to provide supervision in an atmosphere free of verbal, physical, or sexual harassment
- The right to terminate supervision when in my professional opinion it is not effective
- The right to determine terms and conditions of termination of supervision contract, which are that this supervision contract may be terminated with 2 weeks written notice by either party

By signing, we agree that the above information is accurate and that we agree to follow the terms, rights, and responsibilities as outlined in the psychotherapy supervision contract.

Supervisee Signature: _____

      Date: _____

Supervisor Signature: _____

      Date: _____

Other Signature(s): _____

      Role: _____

      Date: _____

Addendum for External Psychotherapy Supervision (Occurring outside of training program or employment)

When the supervisor who is providing clinical supervision is not employed by the supervisee's place of employment or training program, there are additional considerations that the external clinical supervisor needs to discuss with the supervisee and the professional staff within the supervisee's training program or place of employment. These may include the need to define the external psychotherapy supervisor's competence to supervise the cases from the training program, agency, or clinic, and so forth; the need to define respective supervisory responsibility and limits of responsibility for the supervisee's practice; methods for handling discrepant direction from training supervisor or employer versus the external psychotherapy supervisor; confidentiality and privacy; mandated reporting; performance issues.

The following can be discussed and agreement reached before beginning the supervisory relationship:

Describe treatment modalities utilized/required by the training program, clinic, agency, and so forth:

_____

_____

_____

Describe treatment modality competencies held by the external psychotherapy supervisor:

_____

_____

_____

Reason for referral to external psychotherapy supervisor:

_____

_____

_____

Describe who has responsibility for the supervisee's performance:

_____

_____

_____

Describe what information from supervisory communications will be shared with the training program, agency, or clinic:

_____

_____

_____

Describe how conflict between agency and supervisor expectations will be negotiated:

_____

_____

_____

Describe how patients' therapy records will be handled to protect patients' privacy and confidentiality:

_____

_____

_____

Describe exceptions to supervisee's privacy and confidentiality:

_____

_____

_____

Identify the supervisor responsible for the supervisee at the place of training or employment and his or her contact information:

Name: _____

Address: _____

Phone: _____

E-mail: _____

By signing this addendum, I give permission for my supervisor and employer or training program to communicate on any issues that may create ethical or legal issues or practice problems.

Supervisee's signature: _____ Date: _____

Supervisor's signature: _____ Date: _____

Name/title of staff member administratively responsible for supervisee at place of employment:

Signature: _____ Date: _____

Patient's or Patient's Guardian's Informed Consent to Therapist's Training or Licensure Status and Psychotherapy Supervision

I, (patient name _____) have been informed by my therapist (therapist name and degree _____) that my therapist is (check applicable status below)

- Currently in _____ training program _____
- Currently fulfilling requirements for _____ licensure requirements _____

I understand my therapist is therefore required to obtain psychotherapy supervision on a regular basis (state frequency, e.g., weekly or other _____).

I understand the purpose of my therapist's psychotherapy supervision is to help my therapist in the following ways: to understand me, to establish and revise as needed appropriate diagnoses and treatment plans; to work collaboratively with me toward meeting my goals in therapy; and, should problems arise in my therapy, to make recommendations that are likely to be beneficial to me and unlikely to be harmful, including to communicate as needed with supervisors in the training program or place of employment who are responsible for my therapist's practice.

I understand that methods of supervision my therapist and his/her psychotherapy supervisor will be using include (check all that are applicable):

- Discussion of my therapy sessions _____
- Review of my treatment records _____
- Review of electronic recordings of my therapy sessions _____

By signing, I am stating that my therapist has discussed the above information about his/her training status and psychotherapy supervision with me and that I have agreed to the above.

Patient's Name _____ Date of Birth _____

Patient's signature _____ Date _____

Therapist's signature _____ Date _____

Psychotherapy Supervision Case Log

Supervisee Name: _____

Supervisor Name: _____

Date:	Time:	Duration:	Location:

Patient(s) Reviewed (de-identify as necessary):

_____

_____

_____

Date:	Time:	Duration:	Location:

Patient(s) Reviewed (de-identify as necessary):

_____

_____

_____

Date:	Time:	Duration:	Location:

Patient(s) Reviewed (de-identify as necessary):

_____

_____

_____

Psychotherapy Supervision Progress Note

Supervisee Name: _____

Supervisor Name: _____

Date:	Time:	Duration:	Location:

Type of Supervision Provided: _____

_____

_____

Patient Reviewed (de-identify as necessary): _____

_____

_____

Issues, Topics, and Themes Discussed and How Presented (verbal report, audio or video recording, etc.): _____

_____

_____

Impressions, Comments on Supervisory Discussion: _____

_____

_____

Supervisory Recommendations and Plan for Follow-up: _____

_____

_____

Issues/Topics for Next Supervision Meeting: _____

_____

_____

Supervisor Signature: _____

Supervisee Signature: _____

Appendix H

SAMPLE INFORMED CONSENT STATEMENT FOR MENTAL HEALTH EVALUATION IN A PERSONAL INJURY CASE

I, _____, ____/____/____, plaintiff in a civil suit, agree to undergo
    (Name)   (Birth Date)

an evaluation by _____, for the
                  (Name, Degree, and Licensure of Evaluator)

purpose of evaluating me for possible psychological damages. I understand this is an evaluation requested by my attorney, _____

_____, and that _____
(Name of Attorney and Law Firm)   (Name of Evaluator)

may, or may not, arrive at findings adverse to my litigation. I also understand that my evaluation report is likely to be made available to both plaintiff and defense attorneys, and other legitimate parties to this legal action.

I understand and willingly agree to the above, and agree to hold _____

_____
(Name of Evaluator)

harmless in the proper exercise of this evaluation. I give permission for _____

_____
(Name of Evaluator and Evaluator's Consulting Colleagues)

to exchange information as necessary for _____
                      (Name of Evaluator)

to arrive at his/her professional opinions and to develop his/her report.

_____
Name of Evaluee   Date

_____
Name of Evaluator   Date

Appendix I

(Date)
The Honorable (insert name of judge)
Family Court (insert name of court)
Re: Name of case (e.g., *Jones v Jones*)

Dear Judge (name):

I am a (cite title, e.g., clinical psychologist or marriage and family therapist) in (cite practice setting, e.g., private practice or community mental health center), providing psychotherapy to (name of child and age) whose parents are disputing custody and visitation rights in your courtroom. I received a subpoena from the attorney representing (name of child)'s mother/father, asking me to appear in your courtroom next week (date and time). I am writing to respectfully request that the court dismiss me from the obligation of appearing for the following ethical and clinical reasons:

First, (name of parents) hired me to provide psychotherapy to their son/daughter (name of child). They and their child understood from the beginning of his treatment that what he disclosed to me in his therapy was to be held in confidence. They understood that I am professionally obligated to maintain the confidentiality of all parties involved in the therapy.

Second, I am professionally obligated to "do no harm." The cornerstone of the therapy relationship is trust. In my professional opinion, it would be detrimental to my therapeutic relationship with my patient (name of child) and (his/her) family were I to engage in a dual role. If I were to testify in your courtroom, I would be departing from my primary role of assisting my patient with (his/her) psychological and family problems. I would be assuming a different role of judging and evaluating. It is important that I remain in my neutral, supportive professional role with my patient and his parents in order to prevent harm to the child.

Third, in my role as therapist, I have not evaluated either parent regarding their "fitness to parent," because that is not my professional role. Such an evaluation would be most appropriately conducted by an independent, neutral examiner who is not, nor will be, in the role of therapist to the family and/or child.

Finally, I have informed both parents of my position in this matter and they have agreed with me that it is not in their (son's/daughter's) best interest for me to testify.

My intention is to be cooperative with the court. I therefore wish to inform the court of potential problems that will arise should I be required to testify in this case. I hope the court will understand the ethical problems I would face should I be called to testify in this legal situation. If the court requires mental health information regarding this child and (his/her) parents, I respectfully request that the court appoint an independent examiner to conduct an evaluation.
Thank you for your time and consideration.

Respectfully submitted,

(Name, degree, and license of therapist)

Appendix J

LIST OF SELECTED PROFESSIONAL
ORGANIZATIONS AND THEIR WEB SITES

American Academy of Forensic Psychology (http//www.aafp.ws)

American Academy of Psychiatry and the Law (http://www.aapl.org)

American Association for Marriage and Family Therapy (http://www.aamft.org/iMIS15/AAMFT)

American Association for Psychoanalysis in Clinical Social Work (http://www.aapcsw.org)

American Association of Christian Counselors (http://www.aacc.net)

American Association of Pastoral Counselors (http://aapc.org)

American Association of Sexuality Educators, Counselors and Therapists (http://www.aasect.org)

American Board of Examiners in Clinical Social Work (http://www.abecsw.org)

American College Personnel Association (http://www2.myacpa.org)

American Counseling Association (http://www.counseling.org)

American Group Psychotherapy Association (http://www.agpa.org)

American Health Information Management Association (http://www.ahima.org)

American Hospital Association (http://www.aha.org)

American Medical Association (http://www.ama-assn.org)

American Medical Informatics Association (https://www.amia.org)

American Mental Health Counselors Association (http://www.amhca.org)

American Music Therapy Association, Inc. (http://www.musictherapy.org)

American Nurses Association (http://www.nursingworld.org)

American Psychiatric Association (http://www.psych.org)

American Psychoanalytic Association (http://www.apsa.org)

American Psychological Association (http://www.apa.org)

American School Counselor Association (http://www.schoolcounselor.org)

American Telemedicine Association (http://www.americantelemed.org)

Association for Specialists in Group Work (http://www.asgw.org)

Association of Professional Chaplains (http://www.professionalchaplains.org)

Association of State and Provincial Psychology Boards (http://www.asppb.net)

Australian Association of Social Workers (http://www.aasw.asn.au)

British Association for Counselling & Psychotherapy (http://www.bacp.co.uk)

British Association of Social Workers (http://www.basw.co.uk)

British Columbia Association of Clinical Counsellors (http://bc-counsellors.org)

California Association of Marriage and Family Therapists (http://www.camft.org)

California Board of Behavioral Sciences (http://www.bbs.ca.gov)

California Society for Clinical Social Work (http://www.clinicalsocialworksociety.org)

Canadian Association of Social Workers (http://www.casw-acts.ca)

Canadian Counselling and Psychotherapy Association (http://www.ccpa-accp.ca)

Canadian Medical Association (http://www.cma.ca)

Canadian Psychiatric Association (http://www.cpa-apc.org/index.php)

Canadian Psychoanalytic Society (http://www.psychoanalysis.ca)

Canadian Psychological Association (http://www.cpa.ca)

Christian Association for Psychological Studies (http://caps.net)

Clinical Social Work Association (http://www.clinicalsocialworkassociation.org)

Commission on Rehabilitation Counselor Certification (http://www.crc-certification.com)

Employee Assistance Professionals Association (http://www.eapassn.org)

European Association for Body Psychotherapy (http://www.eabp.org)

European Federation of Psychologists' Associations (http://www.efpa.eu)

Federation of State Medical Boards (http://www.fsmb.org)

International Association for Correctional and Forensic Psychology (formerly American Association for Correctional Psychology) (http://www.ia4cfp.org)

International Association of Applied Psychology (http://www.iaapsy.org)

International Federation of Social Workers (http://www.ifsw.org)

International Society for Mental Health Online (https://www.ismho.org/home.asp)

International Society for the Study of Trauma and Dissociation (http://www.isst-d.org)

International Union of Psychological Science (http://www.iupsys.net)

Irish Association for Counselling and Psychotherapy (http://www.irish-counselling.ie)

Multi-Health Systems, Inc. (MHS) (http://www.mhs.com)

National Academies of Practice (http://www.napractice.org)

National Association of School Psychologists (http://www.nasponline.org)

National Association of Social Workers (http://www.socialworkers.org)

National Board for Certified Counselors (http://www.nbcc.org)

National Career Development Association (http://associationdatabase. com/aws/NCDA/pt/sp/home_page)

National Council for Hypnotherapy (http://www.hypnotherapists.org.uk)

National Student Nurses Association: Code of Professional Conduct (http://www.nsna.org)

New Zealand Association of Counsellors (http://www.nzac.org.nz)

The Association for Clinical Pastoral Education, Inc. (http://www.acpe.edu)

The Association for the Treatment of Sexual Abusers (http://www.atsa.com)

The Australian Psychological Society Ltd. (http://www.psychology.org.au)

The British Psychological Society (http://www.bps.org.uk)

The New Zealand Psychological Society (http://www.psychology.org.nz/ cms_display.php)

The Psychological Society of Ireland (http://www.psihq.ie)

The Royal Australian and New Zealand College of Psychiatrists (http:// www.ranzcp.org)

World Medical Association: Ethics Policies (http://www.wma.net/ en/10home/index.html)

World Professional Association for Transgender Health (http://www.wpath.org)

Appendix K

CONTENTS OF ACCOMPANYING CD

The CD that accompanies this book contains forms referenced within each chapter. Readers have permission to use the forms and alter them for their practice, for example, inserting letterhead and changing terminology as necessary.

If you find you need a form not included on this CD, please contact your professional organization for assistance.

Sample Client/Patient Information Form (includes notice of privacy practices)
Sample Face Sheet, Acknowledgement of Receipt of Client/Patient
    Information Form, and Statement of Understanding and Consent for
    Treatment and Billing
Sample Client/Patient Questionnaire
Sample Treatment Plan Form
Sample Revised Treatment Plan Form
Sample Closing Summary Form
Sample Consent for Treatment of Minor Child Form
Sample Authorization for Release of Information Form
Sample Clinical Supervision Contract (forms listed below are included as
    separate files)
    Face Sheet for Internal Supervision
    Face Sheet for External Supervision
    Supervision Contract
    Addendum of Contract for External Supervision
    Patient's or Patient's Guardian's or Representative's Informed Consent (re
    Therapist's Training or Licensure Status and Purpose of Supervision)
    Supervision Case Log
    Supervision Progress Note
Sample Informed Consent Statement for Mental Health Evaluation in a
    Personal Injury Case
Sample Letter from a Therapist to a Judge in a Child Custody Case
Sample Record of Disclosures Form
Sample Letter or Advance Directive for Designated Agent
Sample Checklist for Letter or Advance Directive for Designated Agent

Sample Informed Consent Statement for Mental Health Evaluation in a Personal Injury Case

Sample Consent for Treatment of Minor Child

Sample Authorization for Release of Information

List of Selected Professional Organizations and Their Web Sites

Index